Music Education
on the Verge

Music Education on the Verge

Stories of Pandemic Teaching and Transformative Change

Edited by
Judy Lewis and Andrea Maas

Foreword by Randall Everett Allsup

LEXINGTON BOOKS
Lanham • Boulder • New York • London

Published by Lexington Books
An imprint of The Rowman & Littlefield Publishing Group, Inc.
4501 Forbes Boulevard, Suite 200, Lanham, Maryland 20706
www.rowman.com

86-90 Paul Street, London EC2A 4NE

Copyright © 2022 by The Rowman & Littlefield Publishing Group, Inc.

All rights reserved. No part of this book may be reproduced in any form or by any electronic or mechanical means, including information storage and retrieval systems, without written permission from the publisher, except by a reviewer who may quote passages in a review.

British Library Cataloguing in Publication Information Available

Library of Congress Cataloging-in-Publication Data

Names: Lewis, Judy, 1958- editor. | Maas, Andrea, editor. | Allsup, Randall Everett, writer of foreword.
Title: Music education on the verge : stories of pandemic teaching and transformative change / edited by Judy Lewis and Andrea Maas ; foreword by Randall Everett Allsup.
Description: Lanham : Lexington Books, 2022. | Includes bibliographical references and index.
Identifiers: LCCN 2022024571 (print) | LCCN 2022024572 (ebook) | ISBN 9781793654137 (cloth) | ISBN 9781793654151 (paperback) | ISBN 9781793654144 (ebook)
Subjects: LCSH: Music—Instruction and study. | COVID-19 Pandemic, 2020—Social aspects.
Classification: LCC MT1 .M982417 2022 (print) | LCC MT1 (ebook) | DDC 781.71—dc23/eng/20220525
LC record available at https://lccn.loc.gov/2022024571
LC ebook record available at https://lccn.loc.gov/2022024572

Contents

List of Figures — vii

Foreword — ix
Randall Everett Allsup

Prologue — xi
Judy Lewis and Andrea Maas

Acknowledgments — xvii

PART I: FLINT STONES AND FOUNDATIONAL FRAMEWORKS — 1

1. Reflecting on Pandemic Teaching and Technology — 3
   Emmett James O'Leary

2. A Thriving Form of Communication: Understanding *Chat* within an Online Discussion-Based Course — 19
   Sheelagh Chadwick

3. Discovering Potential in a Pandemic: Performing, Responding, Connecting, and Creating in Instrumental Music Teaching — 37
   Jonathan G. Schaller

4. The Digital Audio Workstation in the Aural Skills Classroom: Using *Reason* as a Tool for Dictation Practice — 53
   Jerod Sommerfeldt

5. Sound Learning: The Pedagogical Pivots of Teaching Artists — 67
   Michelle Amosu Thomas, Michelle Mercier-De Shon, Patrick K. Freer, and Luiz Barcellos

In Dialogue: Letters Across the Pond — 87

PART II: CULTURE, CARE, AND COMMUNITY HEARTHS — 95

6 Reclaiming the Musical Kauhale: Kanikapila and Mo'Olelo
as Choral Curriculum — 97
Jace Kaholokula Saplan

7 The Playlist Project: Exploring Culturally Responsive Practices
through Online Learning — 109
Tamara T. Thies

8 Learning to Be Human: The Art of Care, Compassion,
and Empathy in Music Education — 127
Nicholas Ryan McBride

9 From Wide Roots to Connected Branches: Perspectives on Early
Childhood Music Education across Brazil during the Pandemic — 143
*Tiago Madalozzo, Vivian Agnolo Madalozzo,
Angelita Vander Broock, and Regiana Blank Wille*

In Dialogue: The Courage to Change—A Dialogue of Experience — 161

PART III: DEMOCRACY AND DUMPSTER FIRES — 167

10 Remodeling Choral Experiences: Historic Preservation
or Gut-Job Renovation? — 169
Andrea Maas

11 Curating Open Spaces: Digital Learning and
Democratic Pedagogy — 187
Judy Lewis

12 Choir Disrupted — 205
Nils Klykken

Epilogue: Transformative Change and Music Teacher Education — 219
Andrea Maas and Judy Lewis

Appendix — 225

Index — 229

About the Contributors — 233

List of Figures

Figure P.1	Lucio Fontana, *Concetto Spaziale (Spatial Concept)*	xiv
Figure 4.1	Rhythmic Dictation Example	56
Figure 4.2	Rhythmic Dictation Example Written in Reason's MIDI Editor	56
Figure 4.3	Notation Example from Our Introduction to Drum Set Notation	57
Figure 4.4	Notation Example Written in Reason's MIDI Editor	57
Figure 4.5	Melody in Western Notation	58
Figure 4.6	Melody in MIDI Piano Roll	59
Figure 4.7	Adding Articulations to a Melodic Dictation	59
Figure 4.8	Melodic Dictation Articulations in MIDI Piano Roll	59
Figure 4.9	Adding Reverb to Organ Sample in Reason	61
Figure 4.10	"Herzliebster Jesu, vas hast du verbrochen" by J. S. Bach	62
Figure 7.1	PowerPoint Slide Outlining Playlist Project Reflection Expectations	114
Figure 7.2	Screenshot of Morgan Paddock's Video Project—iPhone	120
Figure 7.3	Screenshot of Morgan Paddock's Video Project—Conversation	121
Figure 7.4	Screenshot of Evan Wicks's Video Game—Level 1	122
Figure 7.5	Screenshot of Evan Wicks's Video Game—Level 2 Reflection	122
Figure 9.1	Pictures of the Musical Drive-Thrus at Alecrim Dourado	147
Figure 9.2	Screenshot of a CMI/UFMG Project's Online Class	150
Figure 9.3	Two Pictures and a Screenshot of UFPel Project's Classes	153

Foreword

Randall Everett Allsup

> Dr. Rieux resolved to compile this chronicle, so that he should not be one of those who hold their peace but should be a witness in favor of those plague-stricken people; so that some memorial of the injustice and outrage done to them might endure; and to state quite simply what we learn in a time of pestilence: that there are more things to admire in men than to despise.
>
> Albert Camus (1913–1960), The Plague[1]

How do you introduce a volume about music teaching during an ongoing global pandemic? This being my second plague—I first heard about a virus killing gay men during my senior year of high school, 1982—I have come to understand that during dark times, as did Dr. Rieux in Camus's *The Plague* or as did the late gay activist Larry Kramer throughout his adult life, *we must do more than merely endure*: we must bear witness and chronicle, and if we can, we try to reflect upon how the events of our day changed us, and repair. In this way, the essays and dialogues found in this book are necessarily stories, though ones without heroism or platitude. Contained are stories of individuals who began to think more carefully about music, education, and well-being; about schools as communities; and about communication and concern. "Public welfare," Camus's Dr. Rieux chronicled, "is merely the sum total of the private welfares of each of us."[2] We did what we had to do, simply put, and this book is a public testament to these efforts.

Let's not talk about silver linings with so much grief left unattended. We can, like this book does however, address the existential nature, *qua* Camus, of life and work—the fact that plagues stand for the challenges of being rational in the face of irrationality, and that living together means taking care of one another. Don't forget that in addition to the pandemic spread of a novel corona virus, the year 2020 witnessed a global reckoning with race, forged by anger of the killing of George Floyd and other Black men at the hands of American police. In 2021, we thought more closely about the fragility of democracy. And throughout the pandemic we saw, *really saw*, maybe for the first time, the faces of delivery workers and kitchen cooks. Masks and unmasking became metaphor and state of being.

I recall Maxine Greene, who at the age of 80 wrote, "I still wonder at how unaware I was of so many frequencies."[3] I still wonder at the masks that fell from my eyes. Like the authors in this book, I began to connect my music teaching to issues of health, meditation, and well-being. I renewed my focus on race and gender. In classes, I admitted to trauma, and attended to voices of pain. My pedagogy became more quiet, more attuned to witnessing than dialectic. Assessment made sense only through portfolios: collections of stories and chronicles of truths. And I was never more student-centered.

Editors Judy Lewis and Andrea Maas are right to assert that we can't go back. Imagine living through the pain of a pandemic and then restarting our (teaching) lives as if nothing ever happened. Existentialists like Greene and Camus would warn us that it is not so easy to stay vigilant. It won't be easy to stay wide-awake when today's plague is gone, and when all we want to do is to forget our stories of pain, rather than retell or refashion them anew. This book's value is its public commitment to both unforgetting and relearning. Indeed, its point is this: it's not a question of whether we will experience another plague (my third, or your second), but what we do with what we have learned, and how we have cared.

Randall Everett Allsup
March 29, 2022
New York City

NOTES

1. Albert Camus, *The Plague* (New York: Vintage International Random House), 308.
2. Ibid., 88.
3. Maxine Greene, *Variations on a Blue Guitar* (New York: Teachers College Press, 2001), 192.

Prologue

Judy Lewis and Andrea Maas

How does one begin to tell the story of *life, interrupted*?

One moment we were all going about the motions of a "normal" life—working too much, complaining about working too much, hugging our kids, fighting with our kids, saving for a dream vacation or to pay the bills. In the next moment, we were hunkering down in terror in our homes not knowing what terrible news tomorrow would bring. Work became home and home became work. Our children were now schooled in our living rooms; our grocery stores became radioactive war zones from some apocalyptic movie we were afraid to enter. On further thought, *interrupted* does not adequately describe what we experienced. This was a shattering—of the surface that was our taken-for-granted reality. An abyss opened and our lives fell in.

DISRUPTION

The *Cambridge Dictionary* (accessed December 2021) defines *disruption* as "the action of preventing something, especially a system, process, or event, from continuing as usual or as expected." We all experience disruption to larger or smaller degrees in the span of a lifetime—moments when our old ways of doing things are no longer viable. We learn to manage those moments, to change course (or resist) and get on with the business of living. This moment is different. We are discovering that our conventional frameworks do little to help us understand and navigate a major disruption of the proportions we are experiencing.

Yet, it is out of this absence of existing frameworks that the discoveries and innovations presented in this book grow. The COVID-19 pandemic offered us an *opportunity to transgress* (hooks 1994), to "look at things as if they could be otherwise" (Greene 1988, 3) outside of accepted paradigms of who we are and what we do when we teach music. It catalyzed an unbalancing of power by positioning individual teachers as "policy crafters" in their uniquely situated contexts (Shieh 2022, 9) and at the same time as part of a grassroots movement to reimagine our classroom spaces and ourselves.

This collection of narratives is concerned with the ways that music teacher-educators responded to our communal *life, interrupted* in their work with their students. It is a *stepping back* and reflecting on the events, challenges, triumphs, and innovations experienced by these authors in this time of crisis.

WHY STORY?

> Telling stories is an astonishing thing. We are a species whose main purpose is to tell each other about the expected and the surprises that upset the expected, and we do that through the stories we tell.
>
> −Bruner 2002, 8.

We are all hopelessly addicted to stories.

We continually construct stories of who we are and what our place is in the world. Through stories, we interpret the past and imagine the future, make meaning of our lived experiences, and shape our lives. Our stories creep out in chats with friends. They play incessantly, like movie scripts, in our heads. Sometimes, the story told to us by another resonates so powerfully that we add bits of it to our own story, blurring the authorial boundaries of the narrative at hand.

We are drawn to stories from an early age.

Children's imaginary play is the embodiment of our need to construct stories (Ahn and Filipenko 2007). Jonathan Gottschall (2013) suggests that "story is so central to the lives of young children that it comes close to defining their existence" (7). Story-based video games are wildly popular today because, among other things, they allow the player to become a character in the unfolding drama of the game. Social media allows us (no, encourages us) to "serialize our autobiographies" (18), to mass market our stories for a global audience.

Our communal identities are also rooted in story. From patriotic and religious myths and legends to conspiracy theories from hundreds of years ago to present day, stories are ultimately an expression of our human hunger to construct meaning, our "need to make sense of the world" (Gottschall 2013, 17).

Given the ubiquity of stories in our everyday lives, Patrick Lewis (2011) asks: "If story is so central to human existence and understanding why, in the research world, is there not more storytelling?" (506). That is where narrative inquiry—and the stories of this volume—finds relevance to our discourse. Narrative inquiry as "the everyday practice of storytelling" (Lewis and Adeney 2014, 161) spotlights the personal and the local as rich ways of knowing (Lewis and Christophersen 2021) and in so doing offers something other than what normative research can provide. It reveals and lays bare the "tensions, surprises, the disappointments and reversals and achievements" (Crites 1971, 306) of "people as people and actions as actions—instead of reducing them to examples of something else" (Bowman 2006, 9).

We've all been taught to be careful, when doing research, not to let our own voice skew the data or the results. We are instructed to write about such intrusions of personal voice as a *limitation* to the studies we conduct. In narrative inquiry, whether we are telling our own story or re-telling the stories of others, the personal voice is amplified. And, like all good stories, we have a protagonist facing the predicaments of the human condition, searching for answers, for meaning, for sense.

Thomas King (2003) suggests: "We live by stories. We also live *in* them. . . . If we change the stories we live by, quite possibly we change our lives" (153). Along a similar line, Peter Moss (2014) proposes the power of alternative narratives born out of crises:

> It starts by telling a new story or put another way, adopting a new mode of thought, thinking differently, which, in Foucault's terms, occurs when "one can no longer think things as one formerly thought ." With this new story, we weave a new reality, viewing the world in a different light from a different perspective—the familiar is made strange, what was formerly self-evident no longer seems so. Then, once we can no longer think things as we formerly thought them, "transformation becomes both very urgent, very difficult and quite possible." (8)

That is the purpose of this volume and each of the authors presented in it—to *tell a new story* and, through those stories, to uncover the *urgent*, the *difficult*, and the *possible*.

In each of the chapters of this book, the authors offer us alternative narratives of what, why and how we teach and learn music born out of their personal struggles, challenges, and discoveries in the midst of the pandemic that has disrupted us. Given the situated and personal nature of storytelling, no two chapters are alike. Each author's voice is distinct. Part I, "Flint Stones and Foundational Frameworks," highlights the stories of teacher-educators who revisited foundational ways of teaching and learning and discovered new pedagogical insights and possibilities. Part II, "Care, Culture, and Community Hearths," shares the stories of teacher-educators who created rich experiences for their students and themselves by focusing on humanizing pedagogy through the lived experiences of their students. The final part, "Democracy and Dumpster Fires," presents the stories of three teacher-educators who used the challenges and opportunities of the pandemic to open up their classroom spaces in search of democratic practices. Interspersed between the sections are two "In Dialogue" interludes in which pairs of colleagues in distant settings share experiences, insights, and hopes for the future.

Hendry (2007) reminds us that "Stories are spaces of resistance" (23). As such, the stories presented here are also stories of resistance: to taken-for-granted narratives of who we are and what we do as music educators and music teacher-educators; to disciplinary discourse both before and during the pandemic; and to the temptation to merely replicate old methods online. In a second entry, *Cambridge Dictionary* defines *disruption* as "the action of completely changing the traditional way that an industry or market operates by using new methods or technology." Fueled by a sense of resistance, the authors of these chapters confronted our common crisis, took action, and through their search for new openings *became a disruption* that will hopefully push our discipline forward anew.

RE-STORYING THROUGH DISRUPTION

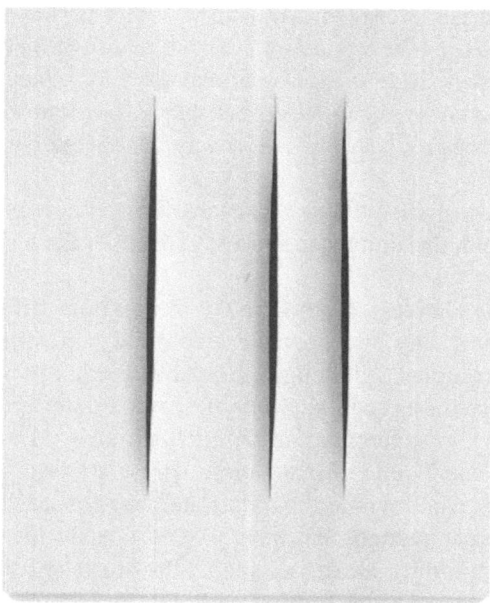

Figure P.1 Lucio Fontana, *Concetto Spaziale (Spatial Concept)*. Credit Bit Nr. 5. Milan. 1967.

Regarding Concetto Spaziale shown above (Bit Nr. 5 Milan), Lucio Fontana writes,

> Making a hole was a radical gesture which broke the space of the canvas as if to say: after this we are free to do what we like. . . . The cuts, or rather the holes, did not signify the destruction of the canvas. . . . it introduced a dimension beyond the painting itself. (In conversation with Daniela Palazzoli. In: Bit Nr. 5. Milan 1967)

We find Fontana's canvas a fitting metaphor for our experiences of the past two years as music teacher-educators. Like the cuts in Fontana's canvas, the pandemic revealed new dimensions; new spaces to imagine and to step into, beyond the canvas of our accepted disciplinary constructs. Seen this way, the pandemic was an invitation—to embrace the unknown; to take risks; to cull our adventurous spirit of discovery and innovation; to seek out openings (Allsup 2016).

In his powerful book *The Ignorant Schoolmaster: Five Lessons in Intellectual Emancipation* (1991), Jacques Rancière offers the following advice to teachers in search of emancipatory pedagogies: "Let them begin teaching what they don't know, and maybe they will discover unsuspected intellectual powers that will put them on the road to new discoveries" (107). The pandemic forced all of us into a position of "teaching what [we] don't know." The authors in this book represent those who embraced that *not knowing* and, by "reordering and remaking (and rereading) past and present realities" (Allsup 2016, 32), reveal new visions of who we are as music educators and music teacher-educators.

Dwayne Huebner (1999) writes: "It takes us by surprise when we are at the edge and end of our knowing . . . when known resources fail and somehow, we go beyond what we were and are and become something different, somehow new (403). We have all become "something different, somehow new" as a result of the pandemic. We have been broken and we have thrived; we have stumbled backward and pushed forward; we have locked our doors while at the same time reaching for new openings in our work as educators.

Lewis (2011) reminds us that in the face of crisis "we must act, even if it means stumbling along the way and in that act we engender story and through story's recursiveness we may make small discoveries and see anew the wonder in the quotidian" (510). We invite you to step into these stories of disruption and discovery, to listen to the voices of the authors, and through them to imagine and reflect on your own "small discoveries" and *see the wonder anew*.

REFERENCES

Ahn, Jiryung, and Margot Filipenko. 2007. "Narrative, Imaginary Play, Art, and Self: Intersecting Worlds." *Early Childhood Education Journal* 34, no. 4: 279–289.

Allsup, Randall Everett. 2016. *Remixing the Classroom: Toward an Open Philosophy of Music Education*. Bloomington, IN: Indiana University Press.

Bowman, Wayne D. 2006. "Why Narrative? Why Now?." *Research Studies in Music Education* 27, no. 1: 5–20. https://doi.org/10.1177/1321103X060270010101.

Bruner, Jerome. 1991. "The Narrative Construction of Reality." *Critical inquiry* 18, no. 1: 1–21.

Cambridge Dictionary, s.v. "disruption." Accessed February 19, 2022. https://dictionary.cambridge.org/us/dictionary/english/disruption.

Crites, Stephen. 1971. "The Narrative Quality of Experience." *Journal of the American Academy of Religion* 39, no. 3: 291–311. https://www.jstor.org/stable/1461066.

Gottschall, Jonathan. 2012. *The Storytelling Animal: How Stories Make Us Human*. Boston, MA: Houghton Mifflin Harcourt.

Greene, Maxine. 1998. *The Dialectic of Freedom*. New York: Teachers College Press.

Hendry, Petra Munro. 2007. "The Future of Narrative." *Qualitative Inquiry* 13, no. 4: 487–498. https://doi.org/10.1177/1077800406297673.

hooks, bell. 2014. *Teaching to Transgress*. New York: Routledge.

Huebner, Dwayne. 1999. "Education and Spirituality." In *The Lure of the Transcendent, Collected Essays by Dwayne Huebner*, edited by Dwayne Huebner, Vikki Hillis, and William F. Pinar, 401–416. Mahwah, NJ: Lawrence Erlbaum.

King, Thomas. 2003. *The Truth about Stories*. Toronto, ON: Anansi Press.

Lewis, Judy, and Catharina Christophersen. 2021. "Frontiers of Difference: A Duo-Ethnographic Study of Social Justice in Music Education." *Music Education Research* 23, no. 1: 90–104. https://doi.org/10.1080/14613808.2021.1887114.

Lewis, Patrick J. 2011. "Storytelling as Research/Research as Storytelling." *Qualitative Inquiry* 17, no. 6: 505–510. https://doi.org/10.1177/1077800411409883.

Lewis, Patrick John, and Robin Adeney. 2014. "Narrative Research." In *Qualitative Methodology: A Practical Guide*, edited by Janet Mills, and Melanie Birks, 161–180. London: Sage Publications.

Moss, Peter. 2014. *Transformative Change and Real Utopias in Early Childhood Education: A Story of Democracy, Experimentation and Potentiality*. New York: Routledge.

Rancière, Jacques. 1991. *The Ignorant Schoolmaster: Five Lessons in Intellectual Emancipation*. Stanford, CA: Stanford University Press.

Shieh, Eric. 2022. "How Teachers See Policy: School Context, Teacher Inquiry, and Policy Visibility." *Journal of Education Policy*, Jan 23: 1–23. https://doi.org/10.1080/02680939.2021.1959650.

Acknowledgments

The idea for this book started over coffee in June of 2020. Both of us had just finished two months of teaching that we could never, in our wildest dreams, have imagined. As we compared experiences that day, six feet apart on Andrea's porch, we came to a thought—*This moment is too critical to ignore.* As we shared stories of our own radical revisioning of the courses we teach and discoveries we had started to uncover, we began to wonder—*How are others rethinking their ways of teaching and learning music in the face of this crisis?* At that moment, we decided that those stories needed to be documented. The rest is, as they say, history.

We want to thank all of the authors who have shared their stories in this volume. Their investment of significant time spent in revisions and Zoom conference calls and their unwavering dedication to this project inspire us. We acknowledge their willingness to be vulnerable and share these intimate stories which unfolded as they continued to confront the numerous challenges of this pandemic. We feel privileged to have collaborated with each of them and have learned so much from their experiences and perspectives.

The chapters in this book underwent a multiple review process, from abstract proposals to final drafts. We are forever grateful to the external editors who generously invested their time and thoughtfulness, offering comments and suggestions to the authors throughout the process—Marsha Baxter, Cara Bernard, Claudia Cali, Jim Frankel, Maxwell Grube, Ailbhe Kenny, Nils Klykken, Peter McCoy, Emmett O'Leary, Sarah Perry, Clint Randles, Eric Shieh, Ann Marie Stanley, and Peter Webster. Your work with us and the contributors made this book possible.

We would also like to thank Holly Buchanan at Lexington Books/Rowman & Littlefield, who held our newbie hands throughout this process, answering questions and offering advice and encouragement.

Finally—and perhaps most importantly—we must thank our students who went on this wild ride with us. It is because of your generous and adventurous spirit, your determination to meet this crisis head-on, and your willingness to imagine possibilities that the stories presented in each of these chapters came to fruition. You are our greatest teachers, always.

PERSONAL THANKS

I am forever grateful to have found a philosophical soulmate and partner-in-crime in Andrea Maas. Your dedication to this project, your open thinking, and your tireless work to move our discipline forward are inspiring. Thank you for saying *yes* to this idea two years ago. I look forward to a future filled with many collaborations.

As always, to my kids Yitzhak, Aviva, Moishie, and Nonnie who are, and will always be, my inspiration to do meaningful things in this world. And to my eternal mentor, Randall Allsup—you sit on my shoulder every time I enter a classroom or put pen to paper.

I would like to dedicate this book to my dad, Burton H. Levine (1927–2022), who taught me to never stop questioning.

Judy Lewis

I will be forever grateful for my students who were willing to be vulnerable and courageous throughout the past two years.

It has been a tremendous privilege to work with Judy Lewis, who I am so lucky to call my friend and colleague, on this book. I'm humbled by your trust, inspired by your perseverance, and have learned so much from you as a writer and educator.

Bryson, who went from diapers at three-years-old, to breakdancing at five during the course of writing this book. You are an inspiration for energy, creativity, and silliness.

Finally, I could not have done this without Andy Elrick, who so coolly helped to navigate the challenges of working, parenting, and cohabitation during a pandemic. Thank you for never giving up on me.

Andrea Maas

Part I

FLINT STONES AND FOUNDATIONAL FRAMEWORKS

Chapter 1

Reflecting on Pandemic Teaching and Technology

Emmett James O'Leary

As I shifted to online learning in March 2020, I felt a sense of ease and almost hubris with the challenge of adapting my work. I was well-prepared for pandemic teaching. I am a technology enthusiast and often an early adopter of new educational technologies. Before the pandemic, colleagues and students frequently turned to me for tech support. I am an avid consumer of tutorials and articles about new technologies. I research educational technology, technology integration, distance learning, and asynchronous musical ensembles (Bannerman and O'Leary 2021; O'Leary 2017). I have led courses about best practices for technology integration. If anyone could handle the transition to online learning well, it should have been me. Yet, I made pedagogical and technological changes urgently and without the typical diligence, reflection, and planning that would typically inform my choices. What could have been a comfortable transition into technology-based teaching became a year filled with challenges and lessons learned.

This chapter is a critical reflection on how my previous experiences with technology and the constraints of a global health crisis shaped my teaching during the COVID-19 pandemic. Using frameworks of technology integration, pedagogy, and curricular inquiry, I reflect on the technological choices I made during pandemic teaching, some areas I offered support to others, and how this year will influence my future praxis. Nothing was easy in pandemic teaching, but I learned a lot and came to appreciate more how technology functions in my work. I hope to make visible some of the nuances of technology in music education and what music educators can gather through a renewed examination of frameworks for technology integration. I have organized my reflection around two central technology frameworks, the TPACK (Technological, Pedagogical, and Content Knowledge) framework of teacher knowledge (Mishra, Punya, and Koehler 2006) and the SAMR model for technology integration (Puentadera 2011). These frameworks were central to the way I made technological choices before the pandemic but were not considered meaningfully as I adapted to pandemic teaching. Each framework offers a valuable lens on the choices I made and how music educators might make informed choices about technology going forward.

My pandemic teaching consisted of three settings. First, in the spring of 2020, I was an associate professor of music education at the Crane School of Music, SUNY Potsdam, where I led courses in teacher education, elementary general music, and secondary general music. My courses began as typical face-to-face courses and transitioned to being fully online and asynchronous roughly halfway through the term. Second, during the summer of 2020, I led two graduate music education courses, one in curriculum development and the other in popular music pedagogy. These courses were offered as fully online intensive asynchronous courses and ran for just three weeks. Finally, in the fall of 2020, I transitioned to a new position at Virginia Tech, where I taught hybrid classes in instrumental music education. Teaching in three different contexts showed how technological challenges change depending on setting and modality.

TPACK AND HOW TECHNOLOGY MEDIATES INTERACTIONS

Zoom mediated much of my teaching, and the nature of the mediation determined much of what was possible in interactions with students. According to Jones and Hafner (2012), "a medium is something that stands in between two things or people and facilitates interaction between them" (2). In this case, our class interactions were limited by the affordances of the Zoom platform and the hardware that my students and I used to engage with it. While I anticipate anyone who used Zoom for teaching has stories of triumph and tragedy while interacting with the platform, there were two instances where I noticed the benefits and limitations of Zoom most: presenting material and facilitating small group discussions. I discuss each context below.

I started a new position in the fall of 2020 as an instrumental music education professor at Virginia Tech. It was a big adjustment. Pandemic restrictions had been in place for just five months when my family and I moved. Moving to a new institution is never easy but doing so amidst the pandemic made the process particularly difficult. I missed the security of knowing my colleagues and working with students with whom I had already built relationships. At Virginia Tech I had to find a way to build rapport with a new community of learners, but without the typical types of interactions we would have in a face-to-face setting.

We were teaching our courses in a hybrid format. We planned to hold instrumental classes outside and in person but were delayed as we awaited the arrival of bell covers and other protective equipment for our instruments. These protective measures were required by public health guidance at the time on our campus. So, in the intervening weeks we met via Zoom. The first classes were particularly challenging. I had never met any of the students beyond exchanging brief e-mails. In a normal environment I would take time to greet each student and introduce myself to them as they arrived in the room, but at the first class they all logged on at the same time and there was no way for me to engage anyone individually. Still, I was eager to begin, and it was great to see a grid of students looking back at me. I had what I thought would be an engaging introductory lesson planned, and after saying hello to the group, I shared my screen, hit *present* on the slides, and entered a void.

I felt oddly alone. I had been looking at more than twenty faces prior, and my screen was now just the slides and a small window overlay including four students. The others were still there, but I could not see them. I had practiced using the slides before with Zoom and knew where all the controls were, but I had never practiced with a large group of people in the meeting. The experience was stressful, and I briefly felt a sense of worry and almost panic. All the skills I had developed in face-to-face teaching were insufficient for the situation. Since most of the students were invisible, I had no way to determine how they reacted to the content. Adding to the feelings of solitude, with students leaving their microphones muted, the only sound I could hear was the hum of the air conditioner, my computer's cooling fan, and my own voice. I am sure being new to the institution made this more difficult, but still that dramatic shift in the teaching environment was jarring. In this scenario what I could see and what I could interact with changed with the push of a button.

After the first class session, I immediately wondered what I could do to become more comfortable. I was confident the second class would be easier than the first and I think more than anything else, I was looking for a way to be more in control of the tools; to know better what would happen in the classroom and what I could influence through the platform that would mediate the work. Looking at the experience through TPACK, I felt a need to develop more technological knowledge. There was more to learn about the Zoom platform and comfort with the software might lead to more comfort in the classroom.

The TPACK framework is an extension of the work of Lee Shulman (1986), who posited that successful teachers bring expertise in the subject matter they teach (content knowledge) and pedagogical skills (pedagogical knowledge) to the classroom. These two types of knowledge combine to form *pedagogical content knowledge*, the knowledge to teach specific content effectively. The TPACK model (Mishra, Punya, and Koehler 2006) adds technological knowledge to the model recognizing that teachers using technology for instruction would not only need to be aware of how to use the tools (technological knowledge) but how to use tools in ways that support students in learning the specific content (technological pedagogical content knowledge). Bauer (2014a) suggested that TPACK could be a valuable framework for understanding musical activities and the knowledge needed for a teacher to facilitate them (Bauer 2014b; Bauer, Hofer, and Harris 2012). Here I use TPACK as a reflective heuristic to discuss the tools and experiences I used through pandemic teaching. While in regular practice, it would be best to choose tools to complement the goals, in essence, applying TPACK to the selection of educational technology. This was not an option. The tools were selected institutionally, and the task became making the content and pedagogy fit the tool.

Having taught for nearly twenty years, I have taken for granted the levels of comfort I feel with most of the tools I use. For example, I can enter a classroom and without any stress connect my computer to a projector, share slides, or play audio through a sound system. Doing so in a new environment generated all types of concerns, such as how to know what is visible to the students, how to share audio or video examples, and to be sure the students hear the same audio that I do. To achieve comfort with Zoom, I needed to know more about how it functioned and to reliably be able to perform basic teaching functions without worry about how to manipulate the software.

Within the TPACK framework, technological knowledge is specific expertise in using technology. There are countless resources available to develop technological knowledge ranging from online tutorials to social media. I began my learning with professionally produced tutorials available through an online learning platform that my institution provides to faculty. I found two courses focused on Zoom, one on the software specifically and one on *leading effective and engaging calls*. The resources helped me address most of the basic technological information I lacked. For example, I learned about the dual-screen mode that allowed me to keep the full view of the students along with my shared content they could view. In addition, I explored the features and benefits of breakout rooms and options to have small group discussions. I learned practices such as playing slides within a window instead of full screen to more carefully manage the content for presentation software. These resources were valuable and music educators engaging with new software might consider how a primer or overview set of tutorials might inform them about the features and benefits of the tool before they use it in a teaching setting. Through my initial research I addressed the significant challenges I experienced in the first class, but I remained unsatisfied and needed to move beyond technological knowledge alone.

The TPACK model is often represented as a Venn diagram showing how the different domains-technology, pedagogy, content-combine to form new types of knowledge. Core to the framework is the concept that discrete skills in one domain of TPACK are of limited value if they do not overlap with other domains. In my case, while my technological knowledge advanced, the pedagogy did not. The comfort and control I felt with the software did not help me engage the students any more deeply during the classes. There was a need to revamp how I presented and more broadly, how I used presentation as an instructional strategy. I was seeking to develop my technological pedagogical knowledge, which as Bauer (2014a) explained, is "the combination and interaction of technology knowledge and pedagogical knowledge and references teachers' understanding of how to use common technologies for teaching and learning across subject matter disciplines." Yet, for this challenge I needed support that went beyond software tutorials.

The professional development I needed came to my attention at precisely the time I needed it most through my personal learning network (PLN). A PLN is a way to leverage professional development through the many resources made available through the Internet (Bauer 2010). For me, this includes blogs and websites that I subscribe to via RSS, a collection of bookmarks I tag and organize using an online folksonomy platform, and several podcasts I subscribe to discussing educational topics. In this case, it was a podcast that crystalized the technological pedagogical knowledge I needed. The Teaching in Higher Ed Podcast, episode 324, featured an interview with Dan Levy (2020), who wrote *Teaching Effectively with Zoom*. While the text was filled with specific tips about the Zoom platform, the more significant revelation was how Levy discussed Zoom in terms of mediating engagement with students. For example, in Zoom, I can share information through presentation or annotation, and students have the opportunity to engage through speaking, voting, writing, working in groups, or sharing their work. As a result, I expanded my thinking beyond being on a Zoom call and more broadly considering what students were doing through the Zoom session.

By thinking in terms of engagement, I felt empowered to transform how I would lead future classes. My presentation skills improved dramatically, but even more importantly, I felt less of a need to rely on presentations and more capability to lead classes through interactive activities. It was a clear illustration of technological pedagogical knowledge at work. Before the pandemic, I used group work as a staple of my classroom teaching. I had the pedagogical knowledge to recognize best practices for group tasks, such as creating rich and challenging tasks, assigning student roles, and providing structure for what is expected of them (Minero 2019). In face-to-face teaching, this might have meant preparing a graphic organizer before class for students to use, dividing students into groups and placing those groups on slides, or organizing the classroom to facilitate group interactions. As students worked, I would be circulating in the room to answer questions and redirect groups as needed. Knowing the means of engagement meant that now I could think through how I could use Zoom's specific affordances to bring that pedagogy to online teaching.

In future classes, I used a combination of Google Slides and Zoom to facilitate engaging small group work. Before class, I would create a template slide with role assignments, directions for completing the task in the presenter notes section, and links to needed media or resources. For example, in an instrumental methods lesson, students explored questioning strategies and best practices for class discussion (Bernard and Abramo 2019), students responded to two contrasting recordings of the same song—in this case, the original version of "You Are My Sunshine" by Jimmy Smith and Ray Charles's subsequent cover. Then, using open, guided, and closed questions (Allsup and Baxter 2004), students listened to embedded YouTube videos of the songs and reflected on the pedagogical use of each questioning strategy. I monitored their progress by joining the breakout rooms as needed and seeing their work progress through the Google Slides document. I have taught this content numerous times prior, but this Zoom-mediated version became one of the most successful. The students were able to interact somewhat independently and had control of how they listened, giving them opportunities to replay sections and discuss specific musical elements. By recognizing my frustrations as more pedagogical than technological, I refined my teaching to be appropriate for the medium and developed a strategy where technology enhanced students' engagement with the material.

TPACK and Zoom taught me how much I should consider the affordances, features, and constraints of the tools that I use and to recognize how teaching is mediated. That much of my frustrations were technology-based is no surprise given the challenges of online teaching, but what I found informative was that I turned first to technological knowledge to solve pedagogical problems. Certainly, the technology was a part of the challenge, but once I considered the pedagogy, technology, and content together I was able to adjust for more meaningful interactions in the class.

MANAGING A LEARNING MANAGEMENT SYSTEM

In the summer of 2020, I led a three-week graduate course in curriculum development. I had taught the course before, and curriculum is one of my favorite topics. The class included twenty-three pre- and in-service teachers. Given the short term, I knew the work was going to be intensive. As I planned the course, the pandemic was just one month old in the United States, and everything felt like an emergency. At SUNY Potsdam, we had just pivoted to online instruction for the spring 2020 courses, and this was the first chance

I had to plan a class knowing it would be delivered online. Where the sudden change in modality of the spring semester was more emergency remote teaching (Calderón-Garrido and Gustems-Carnicer 2021), I felt the need to be better prepared and provide a more polished experience for the summer.

I taught the course asynchronously and offered daily optional discussion sessions on Zoom. This allowed students more flexibility but also created a very different teaching and learning experience than I was used to in prior iterations of the courses. I spent hours preparing videos, organizing and preparing documents, and creating assignment and discussion links for students. The largely solitary work was exhausting, and the process of making materials without the ability to consider how the students interacted with prior lessons forced me to make assumptions about the students' perceptions of the material without any of their feedback or thoughts. While I initially felt comfortable adapting the course content and even enjoyed making the videos, I failed to anticipate the centrality of the learning management system (LMS) to the experience. The LMS would go from being a supplement to the educational environment, to become the educational environment. Rather than a physical classroom where we would interact, students' engagement in this course would be primarily through this software.

LMS have been a substantive part of my teaching for years. In face-to-face settings, I use the LMS as a supplement to the classroom. Students find details on assignments, readings and handouts, slides used in class, and the course grade book on the LMS. In planning to teach asynchronously, I reflected on how I used the LMS before the pandemic. Recognizing that students needed support using most any technology in teaching and learning contexts (Bannerman and O'Leary 2021), I would teach students about the LMS throughout face-to-face courses. For example, if there were an assignment to be turned in through the LMS, I would take time at the beginning or end of class, project my screen for all to see, place the LMS in the student view (where it appears as they would see it without the teacher-related interfaces), and demonstrate where and how to complete the work. The process typically took just one or two minutes and was valuable for many students. I began this practice after my first year teaching an introduction to music education course when I would receive assignment questions between 11:00 p.m. and 2:00 a.m. about the assignment due the next day. I was rarely available to answer their questions at those hours, and the added stress taught me to provide more support. I needed a new approach for asynchronous teaching. Without seeing the students frequently, I could not offer preemptive guidance, plus I now required the LMS to do much more than outline assignments, provide readings, and record grades.

Thinking again through the TPACK framework, I was confronted with the core of TPACK—technological pedagogical content knowledge. My needs went beyond finding tutorials on the software; I needed to consider how this software would be the hub of our community. The first days of any class set the tone for the rest of the semester. In face-to-face settings, I try to get students excited about the course, have them get to know each other, discuss course expectations, and begin some sort of learning activity. Leading a successful first class in which students feel welcome, curious about curriculum, and informed of course expectations (see Lang 2019) requires great pedagogical content knowledge. Doing so through an LMS adds technological knowledge to the challenge. Since students would be engaging with the materials at different times and places, I chose to focus first on familiarizing students with the course and establishing community.

To welcome students to class, I created a guided tour of the course and LMS. While there were excellent tutorial and technical support resources available to students through my institution's distance learning department, I wanted students to hear my voice, see me, and get an orientation to this specific course, offered in this particular term. I then invited students to interact with one another through the Flipgrid video discussion platform. Students made brief video introductions and responded to a prompt that asked them to discuss some of the central driving questions they might have about curriculum development. I benefited from some of the established practices in developing an online community (Bowman 2014; Shackelford and Maxwell 2012), including establishing presence in the classroom, and using media to provide an interpersonal connection between students and instructor. This can be done through introduction videos where students can put a voice and face with the instructor, and through sharing information about my background and what I particularly like about the subject matter. Anything I could do to humanize the experience would potentially help the students feel more of a personal connection to the course. As the course continued it was challenging to sustain the community environment after the initial interactions. With just a couple of weeks of class and more than two dozen students, producing video or media-based feedback was impractical. Similarly, as they were balancing the demands of several classes, students' ability to interact beyond text was limited.

Following introductions, students immediately engaged with the content. There were twelve units, and each included readings, discussion posts, and a series of videos where I discussed and annotated slides with key topics. I offered daily discussion times via Zoom, but less than half of the class would attend on any given day. I began to feel disconnected from some of the students and needed to make some changes as the course progressed. My initial proactive steps to integrate teaching presence were successful, but I failed to continue that process. Ekmekci (2013) explained that online teaching presence is "a critical component of the learning experience that needs to be planned and managed through critical reflection" (36) and I found myself looking to be more present as the class was underway. I made some minor changes to better involve students. For example, I updated discussion prompts to invite students to share more of their reactions to the content and expand my responses to be more detailed, personalized, and, when appropriate, include anecdotes from my teaching experience. Still, my feelings at the conclusion of the class were more of disconnection than I had wanted. I had read pages upon pages of work and reflection from the students, but still felt frustrated that I had not engaged with them more or built the relationships I typically would.

Reflecting now, I wish I had done more. While I was pleased with the students' work, and the course evaluations were positive, I remain challenged by the TPACK needed to lead an effective asynchronous course. My knowledge of the LMS as a supplemental tool to face-to-face instruction made using some of the other features challenging. Again, thinking in terms of TPACK, I have the pedagogical content knowledge to ask effective questions to engage students in the course content. Still, I struggled to make those questions resonate in an online discussion forum. I made some content adjustments to fit the mediated format of the course better, but I could have made more. The course included some challenging readings that benefit from thoughtful class discussion and interaction. However, I failed to consider how to guide students through readings that challenged some of their strongly held beliefs about teaching. I missed the opportunities to discuss and debate the readings with the students, something I feel needs to be done more interpersonally where people can hear each other's tones of voice, inflections, and intentions. Additionally, I had failed to recognize just how much students would respond through text. So much of their work and the responses I provided were written. In text, it is not as easy to determine tone of voice, when a student is unsure of an idea, or where I could add to or challenge their conclusions. I could have added more interest to their work by varying interactions between written, spoken, and video recorded content. Using media more would not have been a cure for every frustration, but it would have generated more connection, but I largely deferred to the most basic functions of the LMS. Instead of the course being a series of thorough written comments, we could have had distributed conversations and engagements with vocal inflection, expressions of understanding, and more engagement.

SAMR

The SAMR model (Puentadera 2011) is a helpful heuristic for understanding technology integration. As Bauer (2014a) explained, "The basic premise of the model is that the use of technology moves along the continuum from substitution to redefinition, its potential impact on student learning increases." SAMR is an acronym for the levels of technology integration within the model that include substitution, augmentation, modification, and redefinition. Substitution takes place when a technology product is used as a direct replacement for a different tool. Augmentation describes when a product still works as a substitute but adds some functionality not present in the original. At the modification level, the technology affords teachers opportunities to redesign the learning tasks. Redefinition is the pinnacle of the SAMR model and represents the creation of tasks that would not be possible without the tool.

The SAMR model helps teachers think beyond the basic features and benefits of a product and more into how those features could transform their curriculum. SAMR does not function alone, as Bauer (2014a) explained, "SAMR can be combined with TPACK by considering the increasingly sophisticated applications of technology when choosing pedagogies and technologies to facilitate the acquisition of curricular outcomes." SAMR also provides a valuable lens to examine some of the technology choices made in pandemic teaching.

SAMR is more than a decade old and was developed when the educational changes forced by the pandemic and the technology available were unimaginable. SAMR began with the premise that technology integration can enhance existing learning contexts. However, in pandemic teaching, music educators found themselves looking to technology for ways to recreate their classrooms in a technologically mediated manner. In the following section, I examine my experiences with virtual ensembles and use SAMR to show how technology might redefine the ensemble experiences both intended and unanticipated.

The Virtual Ensemble

I have been interested in virtual ensembles since Eric Whitacre's first virtual choir project in 2009 (Whitacre n.d.). It seemed like a powerful combination of technology, music-making, and creativity. During my doctoral studies, I explored virtual ensembles through a project called the *Virtual Tuba Quartet* (O'Leary 2017). My thought at the time was that virtual ensembles could be a means for providing performing experiences in higher education distance learning contexts, especially given that options for synchronous collaboration were cost- and resource-prohibitive (Riley, MacLeod, and Libera 2016). The project featured four tuba and euphonium players separated by distance collaborating to produce a recording of two different works. The project was successful, and all participants were pleased with the product. Throughout the process, comparisons to a face-to-face tuba quartet were unavoidable, but we also recognized that the experiences were profoundly different. The product was the same, but the process bore fewer resemblances to a typical ensemble than anticipated.

As American schools shifted to online teaching in March of 2020, I was not surprised when music educators turned *en masse* to virtual ensembles as a possible replacement for their face-to-face groups. I shared my article (O'Leary 2017) in some prominent music education social media groups, and I offered technical support to a few colleagues who reached out for details about the Virtual Tuba Quartet project. Technical concerns were foremost among everyone I spoke with, with good reason. The recording, editing, and production process is daunting but surmountable (Cayari 2021) and led prominent music education technologist Katie Wardrobe (2020) to author the blog post: "Dear Music Teachers: Please stop asking how to create a virtual choir video." In the post, she outlined the technical skills needed to complete a virtual ensemble project and encouraged teachers to consider less technologically intensive alternatives. However, as I watched others grapple with the technology, I became frustrated with the lack of concern for pedagogy and the nature of the students' experience.

In considering virtual ensembles, SAMR becomes a helpful tool to think about how the technology mediated students' and teachers' experiences. While many music educators turned to virtual ensembles to substitute for traditional in-person ensemble experiences, I argue that the virtual ensemble experience is a modification (tech allows for significant task redesign) and even a redefinition (Puentadera 2011) of collaborative performance. Below I offer an example of a clear contrast between face-to-face and virtual ensembles that were often unconsidered during pandemic teaching.

Rehearsals are a process of iteration and refinement. Consider the basic framework for a face-to-face rehearsal. A group of musicians systematically works through a piece of repertoire, stopping as needed to discuss changes or improvements, and then performs again to implement changes. That basic cycle continues multiple times throughout the rehearsal. The iterative process is organic and largely built-in to the rehearsal experience. In a virtual ensemble setting, iteration must be modified. If it is going to take place at all, the process needs to be carefully planned. For example, in the Virtual Tuba Quartet project (O'Leary 2017), the musicians rarely shared their first recordings to be combined with the other parts. Instead, they reported toiling through the recording process, often starting and stopping at the most subtle errors. There was an ethic to the work, one that took place independently, but with an awareness of how their parts would fit with the other musicians. The musicians could not make any changes in real-time and could not react to other musicians as they would in a typical ensemble experience. Their individual recordings were the result of refinement and diligent practice, but they received no immediate feedback.

The Virtual Tuba Quartet committed to submitting and editing materials for three consecutive rounds of edits to facilitate a collaborative process. We modified the process of performing in a face-to-face group to fit the asynchronous environment. For example, editing and combining the tracks had to take place three times, and the feedback could not take place until the edits were complete. If we had been a larger group, the time and work in editing might have prohibited more than one round of recordings. After each round, I compiled and shared the edited track. Then, members of the group offered feedback to one another that informed the next recording. The feedback was modified compared to the typical discussions embedded in face-to-face rehearsals. Comments had to be articulated in text and shared through the group's website. Nuances such as tone of voice, urgency, and other components of communication were missing. The way the group communicated was fundamentally different, and the options available for our interactions were limited to what was afforded by the technology.

A virtual ensemble experience is a transformation of the face-to-face ensemble experience, but the extent of the transformation is debatable. As I reflect on the experiences with the Virtual Tuba Quartet, the overall sentiment from the group was the experience was better than not having a musical outlet, but not as good as being in a face-to-face ensemble. They gained an opportunity to collaborate and make a musical product but lost the feelings of connection and camaraderie that they valued so much in their chamber ensembles. They appreciated the opportunity to refine their parts and think about their contributions in more detail but lamented the lack of control they had over how the parts were combined and balanced. They viewed it as a poor substitution for the typical experience but still enjoyed the process. However, in that process of comparing the experience to a face-to-face ensemble, many unique and beneficial facets of the virtual experience were lost. For example, the performers reported actively practicing their parts, listening carefully to the other musicians, and analyzing the repertoire to greater extents than they had in prior ensemble experiences. Yet, with all that was lost, the modifications brought some gain.

SAMR reminds educators that technology can transform learning tasks, but the transformation is not always for the better. For example, for virtual ensembles, educators looked for the best ensemble experience they could provide given the constraints of the pandemic, but in that process may have missed some of the opportunities to facilitate reflection and iteration in the process, and to consider broadly the experience of performing in an ensemble beyond the product.

MOVING FORWARD

For music educators, the lasting impact of the pandemic is unknown. As I write this chapter in the late spring of 2021, I am preparing for a fall semester that resembles more of a pre-pandemic world. Many educators are evaluating how they go forward after a year of crisis and adaptation. Simply resuming prior practices and casting aside what we did curricularly and technologically is an option. Still, I think embedded in the stress and tragedy of the pandemic were several lessons to take forward.

Now that I can think more intentionally about the choices I make with technology, frameworks such as TPACK and SAMR remain valuable tools. For example, I will apply much of what I learned about LMS to my new courses in the coming year. Even though I will see the students in person each week, I will view the LMS now as an extension of our learning environment and make efforts to welcome students to that space as much as possible. The TPACK I gained through the pandemic will continue to shape my work. Similarly, SAMR reminds me that technology can transform an experience, sometimes in ways we seek out, other times in ways we ignore. I learned from virtual ensembles to think through the entire experience, consider it from both the teacher and student perspective, and recognize if the technology changes it for the better.

Pandemic teaching, perhaps most importantly, was a reminder about how much there is to learn and know about teaching. My PLN (Bauer 2010) expanded to include resources in distance learning and connections through social media with other music educators making online content. I reconnected with pedagogical texts that improved my work (Lang 2016; Levy 2020), and I am looking forward to thinking more deeply about how I teach moving forward. The pandemic fomented professional development and a renewed drive to improve my teaching and that will pay dividends for years to come.

Technology integration requires behavioral change. In pandemic teaching, the behavior change was drastic and a means of professional survival. It was also a reminder that using a new tool requires a rethinking of how we go about our work, and at least for some time, things become more complicated rather than easier. In music teacher education this means that we should expect challenges as we implement new tools into our courses, and that we should prepare our students for the frustration, discomfort, and eventual benefits technology can offer. Technology rarely revolutionizes our lives without us making efforts to learn and adapt to it. With educational technology, we must be patient with and critical of the changes that are made for it. Educators need to make sure the technology adds to the educational experience and that we build the needed TPACK to bring it into the classroom thoughtfully. Again, recalling my experiences of the last year, I am lucky to have had the tools I did, but learning, implementing, and troubleshooting every task was exhausting, especially knowing that much of what I was learning had to be used by students immediately. Continuing to engage students and see their studies continue was worth the efforts, but that came at a cost in hours learning the tools and anxiety over how they would function, not to mention the stress, uncertainty and frustrations the students similarly felt. Future technology integration will be done, I hope, with less urgency, but the work will not necessarily be easier.

I entered pandemic teaching confident, and I leave humbled. Yet I am a better educator for the experiences. Adapting to online teaching revealed gaps in my technological pedagogical knowledge that I had not expected. I developed a renewed interest in frameworks for technology integration and for critically considering the ways technology mediates the experiences I have with students. TPACK offered a way of considering my knowledge and skills and SAMR the transformative potential of the technology for learning. By recognizing the LMS as the hub of a learning community, I began to consider ways that I can make that space more welcoming and engaging. My PLN served me well and I am reminded that the time I spend cultivating that network and managing my resources is often time well spent. Finally, and perhaps most importantly, I am reminded of how joyful teaching music can be and grateful that despite the pandemic, I was still able to share time with students and colleagues that know and seek that joy as well. I am fortunate to have worked with colleagues and students who showed grace and perseverance throughout. Few years of my professional life have taught me more than this one and I look forward to better years to come and how the lessons of this year will shape my work for the better.

REFERENCES

Allsup, Randall, and Marsha Baxter. 2004. "Talking About Music: Better Questions? Better Discussions." *Music Educators Journal* 91, no. 2: 29–34.

Bannerman, Julie, and Emmett O'Leary. 2021. "Digital Natives Unplugged: Challenging Assumptions of Preservice Teachers' Technological Skills." *Journal of Music Teacher Education* 30, no. 2: 10–23. https://doi.org/10.1177/1057083720951462.

Bauer, William. 2010. "Your Personal Learning Network: Professional Development On Demand." *Music Educators Journal* 97, no. 2: 37–42.

Bauer, William. 2013. "The Acquisition of Musical Technological Pedagogical and Content Knowledge." *Journal of Music Teacher Education* 22, no. 2: 51–64. https://doi.org/10.1177/1057083712457881.'

Bauer, William 2014a. "Music Learning and Technology." *New Directions* 1. https://www.newdirectionsmsu.org/issue-1/bauer-music-learning-and-technology/.

Bauer, William. 2014b. *Music Learning Today: Digital Pedagogy for Creating, Performing, and Responding to Music*. New York: Oxford University Press.

Bauer, William, Mark Hofer, and Judi Harris. 2012. "'Grounded' Tech Integration Using K-12 Music Learning Activity Types." *Learning and Leading with Technology* 40, no. 3: 30–32.

Bernard, Cara, and Joseph Abramo. 2019. *Teacher Evaluation in Music*. New York: Oxford University Press.

Bowman, Judith. 2014. *Online Learning in Music: Foundations, Frameworks, and Practices*. New York: Oxford University Press.

Calderón-Garrido, Diego, and Josep Gustems-Carnicer. 2021. "Adaptations of Music Education in Primary and Secondary School Due to COVID-19: The Experience in Spain." *Music Education Research* 23, no. 2: 139–150. https://doi.org/10.1080/14613808.2021.1902488.

Cayari, Christopher. 2021. "Creating Virtual Ensembles: Common Approaches from Research and Practice." *Music Educators Journal* 107, no. 3: 38–46. https://doi.org/10.1177/0027432121995147.

Ekmekci, Ozgur. 2013. "Being There: Establishing Instructor Presence in an Online Learning Environment." *Higher Education Studies* 3, no. 1: 29–38.

Jones, Rodney, and Christoph Hafner. 2012. *Understanding Digital Literacies: A Practical Introduction*. London: Routledge.

Lang, James. 2016. *Small Teaching: Everyday Lessons from the Science of Learning*. New York: Josey-Bass.

Lang, James. January 4, 2019. "How to teach a good first day of class." *The Chronicle of Higher Education*. https://www.chronicle.com/article/how-to-teach-a-good-first-day-of-class/.

Levy, Dan. 2020. *Teaching Effectively with Zoom*. Cambridge, MA: Dan Levy.

Minero, Emelina. January 11, 2019. Group Work that Works. *Edutopia*. https://www.edutopia.org/article/group-work-works.

Mishra, Punya, and Matthew Koehler. 2006. "Technological Pedagogical Content Knowledge: A Framework for Teacher Knowledge." *Teachers College Record* 108, no. 6: 1017–1054.

O'Leary, Emmett. 2017. "The Virtual Tuba Quartet: Facilitating Asynchronous Musical Collaboration in a Chamber Ensemble Setting." *College Music Symposium* 57. https://doi.org/10.18177/sym.2017.57.itm.11351.

Puentadura, Ruben. 2011. "SAMR and TPACK: Intro to Advanced Practice." *Hippasus*. http://hippasus.com/resources/sweden2010/SAMR_TPCK_IntroToAdvancedPractice.pdf.

Riley, Holly, Rebecca MacLeod, and Matthew Libera. 2016. "Low Latency Audio Video: Potentials for Collaborative Music Making Through Distance Learning." *Update: Applications of Research in Music Education* 6: 1–7. https://doi.org/10.1177/87551233145544903.

Shackelford, Jo, and Marge Maxwell. 2012. "Sense of Community in Graduate Online Education: Contribution of Learner to Learner Interaction." *The International Review of Research in Open and Distance Learning* 13, no. 4: 228–249.

Shulman, Lee. 1986. "Those Who Understand: Knowledge Growth in Teaching." *Educational Researcher* 15, no. 2: 4–14. https://doi.org/10.3102/0013189X015002004.

Wardrobe, Katie. March 23, 2020. "Dear Music Teachers… Please Stop Asking How to Create a Virtual Choir Video." *Midnight Music.* https://midnightmusic.com.au/2020/03/dear-music-teachers-please-stop-asking-how-to-create-a-virtual-choir-video/.

Whitacre, Eric. n.d. "About the Virtual Choir." Accessed February 15, 2022. http://ericwhitacre.com/the-virtual-choir/about.

Chapter 2

A Thriving Form of Communication

Understanding Chat *within an Online Discussion-Based Course*

Sheelagh Chadwick

Music teacher educators in North America were forced to rapidly pivot to online teaching as a result of the global COVID-19 pandemic, and for many, the Zoom platform became their teaching environment. The move to online practice was not a choice, and as such, I was resistant to (or even scared of) Zoom as a modality for teaching from the start. Any possible advantages of the platform remained hidden as I wrestled with the basics of meeting my students on screen and trying to recreate course experiences for this unfamiliar online environment. I was used to teaching in a room full of natural light, sitting around a big conference table in comfortable chairs with a large whiteboard and additional space for small discussion groups and few distractions. And so, I struggled to imagine my students trying to connect with each other while building understanding around complex ideas when they could no longer take for granted the social cues for basic conversation, let alone navigate the inconsistencies of technology, or interferences from their now hybrid home-learning environments.

I teach a course called Foundations of Music Education which explores philosophical questions and their practical implications. Students are asked to consider different arguments for the value and use of music education and then imagine what such positions would mean for their own teaching. In the course, students explore education as "a process that seeks to help students find and situate themselves within genuinely conflicting schools of thought, and to choose discerningly among possible modes of engagement or action" (Bowman 2003, 14). They learn to be critical, and to ask who is not included or served when positions and values such as these are considered to be *foundational*. For students to develop such critical and philosophical dispositions, they need to interact, discuss, and construct meaning together. Discussion has always been at the heart of this course, characterized by students posing questions, sharing experiences, and taking positions on what music and music education are and their potential value for young people. Through discussion, students learn to listen carefully to one another, respond in the moment, articulate their thoughts and convictions, and discuss and debate important issues in music education. Centering discussion in Foundations classes encourages students to consider and imagine the kind of teachers they want to become and to articulate why.

On the Zoom screen, the personhood of the speaker is altered, replaced by a two-dimensional, miniature square which may be filled by the student's video stream, a photo, or simply a name over a black box. These student avatars can substantially undermine classroom interactions, leading to an increased sense of isolation, the destabilization of community, and limiting access to and inclusion in the very heart of the course (Munoz, Pellegrini-Lafont, and Cramer 2014). Cesare Schotsko suggests, "Zoom compromises, by its very nature and its technology, the spontaneity of the live encounter" (2020, 277). If that is true, I wondered: How can discussion thrive, or even limp along, in the online Zoom environment? What happens when eye contact, body language, and even seeing the speaker can no longer be taken for granted or used in the creation of an interactive dialogic space? What constitutes participation in this unfamiliar space?

This chapter explores discussion in my Foundations of Music Education course during the winter semester of 2021 and my students' use of the chat function in Zoom as a complement to and extension of class discussions. Students in the course began using chat during the class without any invitation from me to do so; in fact, the chat unfolded in ways that it had not in any of my other Zoom courses and in ways that surprised me.

CYBER VOICES

I did not set out to formally research my online classroom, or to investigate the use of chat in synchronous Zoom discussions. In fact, my assumption at the end of a year of online teaching was that I would have little, if anything, to learn from the Zoom experience. It was the call for chapters in this volume that awakened me to the possibility of reflecting on my teaching through the positive lens of resistance to acceptance. Teaching two Foundations classes during the year, one in each term, prompted me to consider how different the experiences had been and to wonder why. Two differences stood out: first, the level of participation in discussion (an ongoing concern even with in-person teaching) and secondly the social cohesion of the groups, even when several students in the more social group had serious internet limitations. These contrasts led me to look back at the Zoom chats, collected almost by accident when I had to record class for students who were absent. Zoom saves the accompanying chat text so I had five class chats from a total of eighteen, two-hour classes.

The saved chats represent only one dimension of our discussions as other students would be speaking in tandem with the chat. And while it is impossible for me to recreate these discussions, I do give some context below to try to situate the chats in the context of our discussion. My reflections are largely centered on the chats.

In copying from the saved chat files, I have kept the exact wording used by the students and included the time stamps to show the pace of the exchanges. I have left out the chats by students who did not consent to participate through the ethics process and changed students' names to protect their identities. The nine undergraduate students in the course were fourth- and fifth-year Music Education majors, and all but one had taken a previous Foundations course with me in person.

CHAT: MORE THAN A BACKCHANNEL

According to *Merriam-Webster* (n.d.) the meaning of *chat* originates from the chatter of birds, and as such it is often characterized as frivolous conversation or gossip, lacking any substance or importance. Chat has now become synonymous with online communication—epitomized by social media platform Twitter, whose logo is a bird and whose posts are called *tweets*.

Chat in Zoom is a place where students can type written communication during class, akin to texting in its immediacy. I could read the chat during class and see students' participation in a discussion, and even incorporate that into our ongoing verbal discussions. Students' chats used a mixture of formal and informal expression. For some students, the chat was a necessary lifeline which made up for poor internet connections hence their only way to join the discussion, while for others it was a fluidly morphing performance space for creating online identities and forging closer social connections interwoven with discussions on readings and course content. And while Bruff (2020) terms the chat a "backchannel," (online blog post) I could see that for many students, it was more: an equally important space for participating in the course, and a public digital notepad where content ranged from social graffiti to serious engagement with issues of social justice.

Students wove the chat on their own, moving from formal to informal, serious to humorous, personal to public. Their varied uses reflect so many of the suggestions in the literature (Lee et al. 2021; Sweetman 2021) for building community in online learning: performing identity, commenting (or quipping) on the topic at hand, celebrating and upvoting each other's ideas and work, telling stories and joking to lighten the atmosphere.

While the content of students' chats was multipurpose and multifaceted, Garrison et al.'s (2010) concept of *social* and *cognitive presences* in asynchronous online learning provides a useful way to understand the two most prevalent ways students used the chat during my Foundations class. The authors define *social presence* as "the ability of participants to identify with the community (e.g., course of study), communicate purposefully in a trusting environment, and develop interpersonal relationships by way of projecting their individual personalities" (Garrison 2009, cited in Garrison et al. 2010, 32). *Cognitive presence* is understood as "participants [students] in any particular configuration of a community of inquiry [being] able to construct meaning through sustained communication" (Garrison et al. 2000, 89 cited in Szeto 2015, 192). Morueta et al. (2016) further divide cognitive presence into four stages—identification of an issue, exploration through discussion and reflection, construction of meaning, and resolution through the application of meaning—and in what follows, the use of chat for cognitive purposes can be understood as both exploration and meaning construction (stages 2 and 3). These presences—social and cognitive—work together to "support deep and meaningful online inquiry and learning" (Morueta et al. 2016, 123), and although the Zoom environment is synchronous, given the challenges of projecting oneself and one's ideas over this medium, the importance of creating and maintaining these presences remains vital to learning.

The two most prevalent uses of the Zoom space in my Foundations class were for social interaction (creating and maintaining *social presence*) and content interaction, which would parallel Garrison et al.'s (2010) *cognitive presence*. Given the importance of social connections for learning, it is hard to say with confidence that any chat comments could be interpreted as purely social with no connection to learning or class content. The chats seemed to fall on a spectrum with social-forward interactions at one end and content-forward comments at the other. In the middle there was an in-between space where the humor and playfulness of social interaction was integrated with content in a way I label as "riffing" (Merriam-Webster n.d.). To use Garrison's terms, riffing is neither exclusively *social* nor exclusively *cognitive* in nature, but a way for students to play or experiment with content, while also exploring and developing meaning.

SOCIAL-FORWARD CHAT

Students availed themselves of opportunities to create and project an online presence as they might in social media. Some displayed a profile photo which appeared when their video was turned off in Zoom, a *selfie* alone or with other people, such as family members and partners, or even a treasured possession such as a car or musical instrument. Other students used Zoom backgrounds throughout the course to cover up their home setting. Students often commented on these images and the chat was sometimes used to acknowledge and celebrate how students had crafted these visual identities. One day, Macey typed in the chat (referring to a profile photo), "Alana's photo looks real!" and Alana replied, "The prime selfie spot LOL."

Students could be allocated a social presence by their peers, even when they had not served to cultivate it themselves. In an early class, Macey made an out-of-character sarcastic comment, and the chat became a place to joke about it, and to create an exaggerated persona for this often quiet and reserved student:

16:41:11	Alana: We love a sassy queen
16:41:25	Macey: I'm your queen<3. (Author note: This shortcut typed into Facebook would create a red heart, but in Zoom it doesn't work.)
16:41:30	Cris: Duchess of sass
16:41:33	Alana: brassy sassy and always classy

and then later Macey made another sarcastic comment as if she was now living up to her new "sassy" label, which then raised the following:

17:14:34	Ariane: Sarcasm Queen strikes again

The beginning of Zoom classes can sometimes feel awkward as students just appear on screen, whereas for in-person classes they would have walked from one room to another, waited in the hallway together, or come in and set up in the room while talking. Students sometimes used the Zoom chat as a way to ease into the *new* class space and reconnect with the group after suddenly appearing in class through the click of a mouse. I was keen to encourage these interactions as another way to establish community and provide connection in what was often a very disconnected classroom experience. One example was a conversation about our birth order and what that meant for our family lives. We had a little debate about whether it was harder to be the first born or the last, our chat sliding in and out of humor, commenting on the perceived *persecution* of the eldest (or the youngest) child, but there was also a seriousness in terms of expressing how our environments can shape us.

In another class transition the students were sharing memes they made in their ICT course, when one of the students created a meme on the spot based on the Bernie Sanders' mittens image. Sharing the meme, my apparent ignoring of the meme (I had not seen it in the chat), and the subsequent meme generated as a comment on this, took only a few minutes but provided a much-needed moment of levity. I still have the meme on my bulletin board as a reminder.

Students imported their social media language and habits to the chat space. From simple shorthand such as "RT" (Twitter language meaning this comment is worthy of a *retweet*), to overt expression of support and enthusiasm, chat became a place to indicate the equivalent of *likes* on social media. Here is one exchange that took place following a student's presentation:

16:10:56	Kay: You killed it, H!! Great presentation
16:11:20	Macey: Yes H! Great presentation!!
16:11:33	Alana: Much Love @H<3
16:11:37	Cris: Ayeee that was dope H!!!!

As Brookfield and Preskill argue, "democratic classrooms stress respect, mutuality, and civility," and therefore "a logical extension of these notions is finding space and time to express our appreciation to one another" (2005, 49). Students found the chat a very immediate way of showing their appreciation without disrupting the flow of the class.

CONTENT-FORWARD CHAT

While humor was often present in the chat, sometimes the chat was a more serious forum for content-focused comments, or projecting cognitive presence, providing an extension of our voiced conversations. In addition, for a few in the class with internet problems, the chat was often their only means to contribute to the ongoing discussion.

In one class, students presented chapters of their choice from the *Social Justice in Music Education* handbook (Benedict, Schmidt, Spruce, and Woodford 2015). Eli chose to talk about Deborah Bradley's chapter *Hidden in Plain Sight* (see Benedict et al. 2015). His conclusion posed some provocative questions which, in turn, generated good verbal in-person discussion, and one student acknowledged in the chat, "That's a damn good question." Here the chat was not only a space to comment on the topic of racism in music education, but it may have made it easier for students to comment on more sensitive issues. Students in the class are white and persons of color, so race and multiculturalism are not abstract, but very real concerns. Here is a section of that *chatalogue*:

17:10:36	Macey: Different
17:10:47	Cris: difficult
17:10:48	Kay: There's a difference
17:10:51	Alana: I think that we can use multiculturalism in education to help us teach Social justice?
17:11:11	Kay: Social justice covers multiculturalism
17:11:25	Alana: I feel like they go hand in hand
17:11:26	SC: We could be multicultural in our approach but with no view to SJ at all
17:11:55	Ariane: I think they lead to one another but maybe directly the same
17:12:00	Kay: Pushback from guardians, educators do not care to educate themselves on topics, admin pushback
17:12:21	Alana: I think it relates to what Eli said about how teachers may be hesitant to teach multiculturalism due to authenticity
17:12:32	Macey: It's not high on the priority list

Students previously commented in my course evaluations that sometimes discussion goes by too quickly making it hard to contribute or interject without disrupting the conversation. Zoom chat affords students the opportunity to make a comment the moment they think of it without having to wait. And while this could be distracting for them and for others it also seemed to create an opportunity that would otherwise be missing.

One purpose of the course is for students to get comfortable with talking about their own ideas; specifically, the value of music education and how it may or may not be serving all students and what is to be done about that. The chat opened up opportunities to make those statements or pose additional (better) questions; here students unpack the notion of mastery to decide on a meaning that makes sense in the context of music education. Alongside the chat in real time, we were discussing Silverman and Elliott's (2016) *Arts Education as/for Artistic Citizenship* where the authors unpack the Greek concept *paideia* and associated notions of mastery and excellence. I note how many students used the chat in this discussion, and I wonder if it was an easier or safer way to explore these ideas than speaking out loud:

16:10:13	Cris: mastery
16:10:18	Eli: academic excellence
16:10:38	Eli: can we have more greek philosophy readings
[student comment deleted]	
16:11:57	Ariane: reputation
16:13:01	Macey: Experience
16:13:12	Peter: It could be the mastery of teaching
16:13:36	Alana: I feel like it is always changing
[student comment deleted]	
16:13:51	Peter: Well no, but being good at it. just using the same words we used for "master of instrument"
16:14:02	Alana : So even if you "master" it, the methods and strategies are changing
16:14:17	Kay: I admire those who make a positive impact to their students (can send a message)
16:14:18	Eli: What do we consider really great teachers then? I've seen really great clinicians that can constantly adapt to different situations and bands
16:14:27	Alana: Maybe mastering it is the ability to adapt
16:14:56	Ariane: yes and for different students
16:16:00	Eli: Can you associate musical potential with getting a music degree

RIFFING

Riffing seems an appropriate term to describe a particular kind of interchange I witnessed in the chat almost every class. The definition, "a rapid energetic often improvised verbal outpouring *especially* one that is part of a comic performance" (Merriam-Webster, n.d.) seems very apt for the way students would comment on a new term from our readings. The exchanges were a form of play, like passing a ball from one person to the next, or wordplay where students tried to build a meaning from an unfamiliar idea by connecting it to their own knowledge and experience. This playfulness is something Brookfield and Preskill (2005) illuminate as a serious form of engagement where "the best conversations maintain a tension between seriousness and playfulness" (39). It can also be seen as part of constructing meaning (cognitive presence) through exploration.

One discussion centered on Freire's (1970/2000) *Pedagogy of the Oppressed,* and students used the chat to explore the word *conscientization*:

16:16:02	Kay: humanization?
16:16:08	Ariane: autonomous thinking
16:16:11	SC: fully human
16:18:00	SC: conscientization
16:18:16	Ariane: Is that like metacognition?
16:18:34	Ariane: Thinking about your thinking
16:18:42	Alana: I don't even know what I don't know
16:19:03	Cris: Existential crisis

While humor creeps in, the students are still riffing on the term *conscientization* providing possible synonyms in quick succession, playing on the connection between knowing and being. Similarly, in another class, the unfamiliar term *eudaimonia* morphed through "pandemonium" to "eucalyptus," and the Greek term arête (also the French word for stop—hence what followed) was the source of this exchange:

16:08:24	Peter: Stop
16:08:28	Alana: stop
[student comment deleted]	
16:08:33	Alana: Just stop
16:08:36	Kay: excellence
16:08:41	Kay: also stop
16:08:47	Macey: arête
16:08:58	Ariane: oo fancy (Author note: commenting on Macey's use of the accent above the letter e)
16:09:02	Kay: eeeeeeeeeeeeeeeeeee3'
16:09:09	Peter: you also have to have the options on your keyboard
16:09:30	Kay: I would just copy and paste accents from Wikipedia
16:09:52	Alana: I think it only works on mac
16:09:57	Macey: Yeah

This kind of rapid-fire wordplay would be unlikely to happen in a face-to-face classroom because students would not be able to contribute one after the other in quick succession in quite this way. And while chat moves fast, its visual texting-like nature records what is typed, creating space to read, to pause and think, and to add alongside spoken words. And as with a game, speed and wit are prized skills.

WHITHER DISCUSSION IN ZOOM?

> . . . conversation is one of the most important ways for human beings to make meaning, to construct a worldview, and to provide a "meetingplace of various modes of imagining."
>
> (Oakeshott 1962, 206, cited in Brookfield and Preskill 2005, 38)

While I still fully concur with the preceding quotation, my previous understandings of what constitutes conversation and participation were called into question through the move to online teaching. I previously equated active participation in discussion with actual speech, believing that to be inclusive and democratic, and to meet Brookfield and Preskill's (2005) ideal of *engaged pluralism*, the actual voices of students needed to be heard and acknowledged by others. The chat space expands these ideas, opening up the conversation to anyone in the space at any time, alongside spoken discussion. Through their instinctive, creative use of the accompanying chat, students found new ways to work toward understanding in combination with spoken words. And while all teachers must learn to think on their feet and respond verbally in the moment to students in their classes, the often-continuous line of spoken discussion in class may be more readily available to those who are confident in their ideas, verbally adept, and respond quickly, perhaps voices from dominant groups.

Somewhat ironically, my course syllabus lists helping "students think about creative alternatives to routine instructional and curricular arrangements" as a key learning outcome. And this year of *alternative* online teaching certainly reminded me about what I am asking of my students and just how hard such re-imaginings might be. I have always embraced constructivism as a foundation for learning. And while I understand and have witnessed the value of interaction for student learning and meaning making, the move to Zoom helped me appreciate that such interactions need to be guided and nurtured and that the social fabric of a group cannot be taken for granted.

Chat became the students' space; they shaped its character and determined its purpose. The blank slate of chat encouraged playful interactions as well as exploration of content, formal and informal expressions, teacher and student roles; it was taken up as a "meeting place of various modes of imagining" (Oakeshott 1962, 206, cited in Brookfield and Preskill 2005, 38). This space seemed to be something the students found useful for generating and incubating their ideas, even for a second, while also continuing to connect, entertain, and support each other, particularly in the absence of in-person contact. What could that mean for in-person discussions moving forward? Students sometimes hesitate to add their thoughts to an ongoing spoken discussion because they feel their ideas are not yet fully formed. Class discussion creates an expectation of formality and linearity akin to performing rather than improvising. Students may need to dwell on the more fundamental aspects of reading such as new words, or to have an additional layer of reflection prior to engaging in spoken discussion. It could mean that a few opportunities for levity are necessary even when, or maybe particularly when, discussing important or difficult questions and issues. Maybe my expectations for students to take these questions seriously, to fully engage, and to share their thinking as it evolves are unreasonable or blinkered, particularly alongside the disruptions to learning and life caused by a global pandemic. Maybe I appear to center readings even in my attempts to make students' ideas the focus. Maybe the voices of those music education philosophers and researchers loom too large, and students somehow think they have to match the complexity and fully formed clarity in their own thinking. Is the chat safer because it does not come with such weighty expectations? Or any expectations at all? And if so, can I create that same safety when we resume in-person classes while still addressing these questions?

One of the biggest challenges in developing a safe space for discussion to thrive is encouraging students to listen and speak to one another rather than to me. The habit of speaking and then looking toward me quizzically, or even asking, "Right?", is a well-entrenched habit from years in school classrooms. Far too often it is also something to which I respond, thus breaking the flow of discussion. Worse, this can encourage students to keep looking to me for encouragement or reinforcement rather than engaging with their peers. However, in the chat my voice was rarely present and when it was, I was usually clarifying, posting questions, or joining in idle banter before class began. Chat is where students can speak and respond to their peers without the expectation of teacher intervention or even control. Given their comfort with texting and social media, carrying on conversations in this kind of format and keeping track of the thread, albeit halting at times, is perhaps more second nature than doing so with the ongoing spoken conversation.

Both the riffing and the visible notes in chat were different forms of interaction and collaboration among students that would not have appeared in a face-to-face classroom. The canvas of the chat provided a space where students could comment one after another in quick succession and build on each other's contributions without worrying about talking over each other or interrupting the flow. Even those students who did not physically type into the chat could read and see the ideas come to life. And although the chat took place during class, it somehow had its own time frame slightly away from the ongoing discussion, creating a pause, or time to reflect, even an alternate path, that would be less likely to occur during a face-to-face class.

The outcomes of this course cannot be guaranteed. Part of the motivation to build discussion in every class is to encourage other approaches to teaching and learning that center student perspectives and understanding in a setting where speaking and listening are equally valued. I also aim toward creating a more socially just space where students genuinely consider Cathy Benedict's (2021) probing question: "How do my actions with others encourage or prohibit engagements of inclusivity" (10)? Gary Spruce (2015) expresses concern for the often "monological" (296-297) character of music education in many schools. Rather than supporting students in the construction of their own understanding and framing of their own questions, the teacher's authority as knower of Western classical music is often the dominant lens. A course grounded in discussion may help future music teachers consider the importance of student voice, and dialogue as a means to centering that voice. Making room for multiple experiences and interpretations and creating a classroom community where students feel their contributions are valued may in some small way open students' minds to the possibilities for their own future classrooms.

ENDURING HESITATIONS

Following this experience, I am left with several questions.

What if chat is distracting? I have traditionally discouraged laptops in class because of their potential to distract and therefore to undermine student engagement. Might chat present a similar obstacle? It is hard to be in two places at once. No matter how quick the response or how few words are typed, students have to disengage from the discussion in order to post in the chat. Enwezor (2003) calls this movement to-ing and fro-ing, a "restless, ceaseless engagement with the present" (5) and such back and forth from one space, mode, and focus to another could mean students are even less present in the discussion than if they remain silent. From my vantage point the chat seemed to fluidly intertwine with and extend the discussion, but it may have been more distracting than I realize. And at times it certainly was for me as I tried to listen and read at the same time. Yet, students of this generation may be more accustomed to such fragmented attention and moving among modalities and conversation strands, and perhaps such movement may even be their preferred form of engagement.

What if the discussion is not inclusive? While a few students relied on the chat to keep connected to class, some rarely chatted. As with spoken discussion, it may be that the chat supported students with rapid typing skills and a preference or facility for written over verbal communication. And while chat could be considered another avenue into discussion, it could function to exclude some students. And could it also create a mini-social media atmosphere where some students are displaying their connectedness and friendships while others feel isolated and alone? Such concerns would need to be considered and discussed with students at the beginning of term when we develop our terms of use policy for similar kinds of technology.

What if they only agree? One area where students can be tentative in face-to-face discussions is presenting opposing viewpoints. They are comfortable critiquing arguments or positions from class readings, but when they get into sharing their own perspectives there is little by way of dissent or even asking for further justifications in support of arguments. Authors who claim discussion or dialogue as a preferred approach for democratic education (Skregelid 2021; Brookfield and Preskill 2005) highlight the importance of questioning and critique as vital aspects of that democracy. Emphasis on social connections could potentially be undermining to such positions, as students work hard to find points of agreement or what is similar or comfortable in what others are saying—to *like* rather than dislike. Perhaps in a year when students are already feeling isolated and anxious, they need to feel connected more than critical. Brookfield and Preskill (2005) suggest that students come to a critical stance over time and that it is important to build community first before expecting critique.

WHAT OF DISCUSSION IN THE FUTURE?

I am looking forward to the end of Zoom classes and the return to in-person teaching. But I am also grateful for this disruption to my discussion-driven courses and the opportunity it provided to reflect on the interwoven nature of community, identity, and growth, the interactions between more formal cognitive and informal social presences and what I can do going forward to enhance student experiences in this course.

Our students regularly use social media to create communities within their degree programs and to connect, share information, compare notes, and to learn. This year, opportunities for students to meet informally in the hallways, the library, or over coffee were largely removed, and creating a social environment seemed to become even more crucial than in other years where such connections would be made more "naturally." My students seemed to need to create a presence online and use that presence to connect, support, question and play, to reach through physical and technological divides and build community. These connections possibly provide a platform—a foundation—for better discussions. Social presence is not all there is to learning but without it learning is potentially diminished. Who students are to themselves and to each other is an important part of being in a learning community focused on interaction.

The relationship between technology and community is still one I want to explore. Seeing how students used chat in class has led me to investigate the social annotation platform *Perusall*. Readings can be uploaded and chat-like commentary can take place alongside pdf documents as a way to get discussion going before the class starts. Students can comment, pose questions, respond to comments of others, and it gives me the opportunity to see where confusion or interest might be before class begins—a kind of enhanced flipped classroom.

Face-to-face teaching may remove some of the urgency to connect through technology during class, but it would be interesting to explore how a digital outlet could enhance discussion and community as we navigate social distancing and mask wearing as our *new normal*. Students' use of Zoom chat seems to suggest that they appreciate multiple modes of contributing to discussion. Is there a role for technology in expanding access to and participation in spoken discussions? Platforms such as *Slack* are used to connect groups in working environments, but also have real educational potential to parallel the way chat was used in our Zoom class. *Slack* could create that space for participation, a way to include multiple learning styles and mitigate student anxiety which could enhance and promote involvement in discussion while building community (de Peralta, Kohl, and Robey 2018). Having an online chat open alongside spoken word would allow students to contribute their thoughts in the moment or make note of an idea so that the class can return to it at the end of a phase of discussion. The ideas are seen and saved, allowing students to contribute in their own time. One student in this Foundations course commented on liking chat for this very reason. Bruff (2020) recommends inserting "voice of the chat" (see "Backchannel" section) moments during class to respond to questions and read comments from the online discussion thread. Incorporating chat as part of the class would reflect how it was used by students in this Foundations course and may be useful as distancing and mask wearing become a possible new norm.

As I re-read these chats, I noticed where students had contributed ideas connected to class topics that had gone unnoticed by me at the time. Using a more permanent platform would be valuable to archive, review and revisit some aspects of discussion, sharing them online or coming back to them in a future class. That kind of re-treading or looping back to an idea could be beneficial for everyone in the room.

Technology, specifically the affordances of Zoom chat, would seem to point toward a future where discussion was supported, enhanced and prepared for using a range of platforms and apps. But my most important learning in this backward look at the Zoom chats was about student participation in face-to-face discussion. A question I return to every year is whether to stop assessing class participation. I am concerned that showing value through grading is creating a performative environment but perhaps students would be more relaxed and willing to join in discussion when marks were not at stake or when there was no sense that their thinking was being judged. Perhaps this creates competition for my attention in ways that compromise the creation of cooperation and community.

Chat was a space for student vernacular, where the language of texting and social media came into the classroom. It was a space where most students seemed to be at ease with communication, where informality reigned, and identity crept out. It seems that students were showing me that when they are learning and trying to come to grips with developing an understanding of new ideas, they need more opportunities to play, experiment, try ideas on for size, test the field, spar with others before or while also speaking those ideas out loud.

I am reconsidering my initial nostalgia for our comfortable, sunlit seminar room as the ideal setting for the lively challenging discussions so vital to teacher preparation. Perhaps meeting students where they are and honoring their facility with technology in general, and social media and texting in particular, is another way to make them more comfortable in this class, whether in person or online, and to add another dimension to our discussions. And with more effort and intention put toward creating and sustaining a positive inclusive community of inquirers who are serious and humorous, formal and informal, and open to play as well as to new ideas, maybe student resistance to sharing and discussing, questioning and critiquing will also diminish. As for my own resistance to Zoom discussions, this opportunity to reconsider this course and my students' use of chat has helped me better understand the significance of social fabric in discussion and to consider how technology might enhance and sustain social connections alongside more traditional classroom practices in the future.

REFERENCES

Benedict, Cathy. 2021. *Music and Social Justice: A Guide for Elementary Educators*. New York: Oxford University Press.

Benedict, Cathy, Patrick Schmidt, Gary Spruce, and Paul Woodford, eds. 2015. *The Oxford Handbook of Social Justice in Music Education*. New York: Oxford University Press.

Bowman, Wayne. 2003. "Re-Tooling 'Foundations' to Address 21st Century Realities: Music Education Amidst Diversity, Plurality, and Change." *Action, Criticism, and Theory for Music Education* 2, no. 2. http://act.maydaygroup.org/articles/Bowman2_2.pdf.

Bradley, Deborah. 2015. "Hidden in Plain Sight: Race and Racism in Music Education." In *The Oxford Handbook of Social Justice in Music Education*, edited by Cathy Benedict, Patrick Schmidt, Gary Spruce, and Paul Woodford, 190–203. New York: Oxford University Press.

Brookfield, Stephen, and Stephen Preskill. 2005. *Discussion as a Way of Teaching: Tools and Techniques for Democratic Classrooms*. 2nd ed. San Francisco, CA: Jossey-Bass. Kindle.

Bruff, Derek. 2020. "Active Learning in Hybrid and Socially Distanced Classrooms." *Center for Teaching, Vanderbilt University*, June 11, 2020. https://cft.vanderbilt.edu/2020/06/active-learning-in-hybrid-and-socially-distanced-classrooms/.

Cesare Schotzko, T. Nikki. 2020. "A Year (in Five Months) of Living Dangerously: Hidden Intimacies in Zoom Exigencies." *International Journal of Performance Arts and Digital Media* 16, no. 3: 269–289. https://doi.org/10.1080/14794713.2020.1827206.

Enwezor, Okwui. 2003. "To-ing and Fro-ing: Interview with Karen Raney." *Engage* 13: 1–10.

Freire, Paulo. 1970 [2000]. *Pedagogy of the Oppressed*. 30th anniversary edition. London: Continuum.

Garrison, D. Randy. 2009. "Communities of Inquiry in Online Learning." In *Encyclopedia of Distance Learning*, edited by Patricia Rogers, 352–355. Hershey, PA: IGI Global.

Garrison, D. Randy, Martha Cleveland-Innes, and Tak Shing Fung. 2010. "Exploring Causal Relationships Among Teaching, Cognitive and Social Presence: Student Perceptions of the Community of Inquiry Framework." *The Internet and Higher Education* 13, no. 1–2: 31–36.

Garrison, D. Randy, Terry Anderson, and Walter Archer. 2000. "Critical Inquiry in a Text-Based Environment: Computer Conferencing in Higher Education." *The Internet and Higher Education* 2, no. 2–3: 87–105.

Lee, Angela, Y., Gloria Moskowitz-Sweet, Erica Pelavin, Omar Rivera, and Jeffrey T. Hancock. 2021. "Bringing you into the Zoom": The Power of Authentic Engagement in a Time of Crisis in the U.S. *Journal of Children and Media* 15, no. 1: 91–95. https://doi.org/10.1080/17482798.2020.1858437.

Merriam-Webster. n.d. "Chat." In *Merriam-Webster.com dictionary*. Accessed July 1, 2021. https://www.merriam-webster.com/dictionary/chat.

Merriam-Webster. n.d. "Riff." In *Merriam-Webster.com dictionary*. Accessed July 1, 2021. https://www.merriam-webster.com/dictionary/riff.

Morueta, Ramon Tirado, Pablo Maraver López, Angel Hernando Gómez, and Victor W. Harris. 2016. "Exploring Social and Cognitive Presences in Communities of Inquiry to Perform Higher Cognitive Tasks." *The Internet and Higher Education* 31: 122–131.

Munoz, Lorena R., Cynthia Pellegrini-Lafont, and Elizabeth Cramer. 2014. "Using Social Media in Teacher Preparation Programs: Twitter as a Means to Create Social Presence." *Perspectives in Urban Education* 11, no. 2: 57–69.

de Peralta, Kathleen Kole, and Sarah Robey. 2018. "Four Reasons Slack Will Change How You Teach." *Inside Higher Ed*, September 19, 2018. https://www

.insidehighered.com/digital-learning/views/2018/09/19/four-reasons-slack-will-change-how-you-teach-opinion.

Silverman, Marissa, and David J. Elliott. 2016. "Arts Education as/for Artistic Citizenship." In *Artistic Citizenship: Artistry, Social Responsibility, and Ethical Practice*, edited by David J. Elliott, Marissa Silverman, and Wayne D. Bowman, 81–103. New York: Oxford University Press.

Skregelid, Lisbet. 2021. "Zoom in on *Dry Joy*—Dissensus, Agonism and Democracy in Art Education." *Education Sciences* 11, no. 28. https://doi.org/10.3390/educsci11010028.

Spruce, Gary. 2015. "Music Education, Social Justice, and the 'Student Voice': Addressing Student Alienation Through a Dialogical Conception of Music Education." In *The Oxford Handbook of Social Justice in Music Education*, edited by Cathy Benedict, Patrick Schmidt, Gary Spruce, and Paul Woodford, 287–301. New York: Oxford University Press.

Sweetman, David S. 2021. "Making Virtual Learning Engaging and Interactive. *FASEB BioAdvances* 3: 11–19. https://doi.org/10.1096/fba.2020-00084.

Szeto, Elson. 2015. "Community of Inquiry as an Instructional Approach: What Effects of Teaching, Social and Cognitive Presences Are There in Blended Synchronous Learning and Teaching?" *Computers & Education* 81: 191–201. https://doi.org/10.1016/j.compedu.2014.10.015.

Chapter 3

Discovering Potential in a Pandemic

Performing, Responding, Connecting, and Creating in Instrumental Music Teaching

Jonathan G. Schaller

How am I supposed to teach a beginning band practicum experience virtually and during a pandemic? This question echoed through my head after I received my schedule for the upcoming year. I needed to trust my preparation as a music teacher educator. During my doctoral studies in music education, my mentors encouraged me to develop an open and flexible teaching disposition that could allow me to adapt to various teaching contexts and grant me longevity in music teacher education. As a former instrumental music ensemble teacher, I realized that traditional approaches to instrumental music that rely solely on conductors' authoritarian instruction and ignore student voices and knowledge limited the development of creative musicians. Intrigued by the incorporation of active student participation in music education, I desired to move away from a master/apprentice relationship between teacher and student that was so ever-present in my classroom as a band director. I began to question one-size-fits all teaching methods I encountered in so many professional development sessions and as a result became interested in the assets that exist within diverse teaching contexts. Most of all, I craved to participate in a future of instrumental music education that expanded our collective imagination of what could be possible rather than only replicating what has been done.

While my teaching philosophies appeared captivating on paper, I never put many of them into practice as an ensemble music teacher. I am myself the product of a teacher preparation program that encouraged their teacher candidates to work toward *excellence* in the performance of *quality* repertoire without questioning the meaning of either adjective. Repertoire lists, *best* practices, handbooks, and emulating master teachers proliferated my thinking about being a good band teacher. My shift in thinking did not occur until after I exited my ensemble classroom and found an opportunity to critically reflect on what I experienced and observed. How could I convince others, especially future instrumental music teachers, to consider curricular transformation if I could not teach from experience? How could I convince myself that I needed to try to do so anyway? As I transitioned from a graduate student to that of a full-time university professor during the height of the quarantine from the COVID-19 pandemic, I discovered the opportunity to uncover answers to these questions. I needed to explore my own potentialities as an educator as well as aid my students in finding theirs.

In this chapter, I reflect on my experiences facilitating a virtual beginning band practicum for undergraduate preservice music teachers and uncovering my own capabilities as a teacher educator during the COVID-19 pandemic. I juxtapose my reflections with vignettes constructed from conversation and interactions with my students, referred to by pseudonyms. I harmonize the successes and challenges I experienced with a re-envisioning of instrumental music teacher education.

AN OPPORTUNITY

During the COVID-19 pandemic, I taught a methods course in elementary wind band practices and supervised a teaching practicum for teaching beginning instruments. I taught both courses virtually. The *practices* course concentrated on the development of pedagogical content knowledge and theory while the practicum focused on the application of teacher knowledge into teaching practice. Historically, the *practicum* existed as an opportunity for teacher candidates to teach individual and small group band instrument lessons to elementary and middle school children in the community, either with the large local population of homeschooled students or in conjunction with nearby schools.

Now tasked to teach and supervise virtually because of COVID-19, I formulated a plan of action for my courses. In collaboration with my colleagues, we recruited approximately fifty elementary and middle school students from across the United States. I divided these students by age and placed them into homogeneous instrument groupings that ranged from one to five students. I assigned the preservice teachers enrolled in the practicum to student groups based on their major applied instrument. In a handful of situations, some taught on a secondary instrument. The preservice teachers oversaw the scheduling of weekly 30-minute lessons through Zoom with their student group. I maintained an ongoing dialogue with each preservice teacher as they submitted to me detailed lesson plans, lesson recordings, and reflections each week. Once a month, we met together as a large group to discuss their teaching.

At first, we approached the practicum as though it was a virtual community music conservatory. I originally chose a traditional pathway for several reasons. First, I was new to my position and was unfamiliar with my teaching context. Second, I originally taught this practicum with another colleague with more experience teaching the course and followed his lead in designing the course. Finally, I started the semester unfamiliar with the preservice teachers' knowledge and past experiences, and yet I needed to make pedagogical decisions immediately. In conclusion, I wanted to *play it safe*. I did not want to make major changes in this course without meeting my students and getting to know my teaching context better.

As a result, most preservice teachers, with my approval, used a beginning instrument method book as the foundational repertoire of their lessons, assigning and checking off exercises each week. However, problems arose as my students found it difficult to sustain this method of instruction through the virtual medium. They quickly discovered that their students logged into their lessons from an array of devices with varying differences in audio and video quality. These preservice teachers often attempted to address executive skills such as posture, breathing, and hand position with their students but discovered that camera angles and slow Internet connection speeds distorted their ability to observe their students accurately. Many of the preservice teachers planned to discuss tone quality with their students, but often became frustrated by the audio distortion created by their available microphones and devices. They tried to experiment with device placement and application settings, but some were never able to overcome this challenge.

In a similar manner to my students, I discovered I was approaching the facilitation of their field experience in a traditional manner. I asked them to submit lesson plans, teaching recordings, and reflections for each lesson. Then I gave them feedback and provided suggestions. I checked off my students' work as *completed* rather than giving them substantive feedback which could propel them into self-discovery. This routine felt *safe* as I became accustomed to my new teaching position, but I soon became impatient. Just as the status quo became unsustainable for the preservice teachers in the practicum course, it was becoming unsustainable for me. Both my students and I were conforming to traditional approaches, but we were ignoring the particularities and possibilities of our new digital teaching contexts. We agreed that things needed to change.

I saw an opportunity to experiment with my own pedagogy and put into practice my own teaching philosophies that I had set aside. I first asked the preservice teachers to regard their practicum experience as a laboratory class in which they could experiment with their pedagogy and curriculum (Allsup 2016). I encouraged them to try new things and to share their successes and failures, to approach their lessons as an opportunity for their students' individual musical enrichment rather than reaching a specific page or benchmark in a lesson book. I had designed my teaching *practices* course around the four artistic processes of performing, responding, connecting, and creating, and began to encourage the practicum teachers to integrate activities that addressed these processes in their instruction. These four artistic processes are delineated by National Core Arts Standards for dance, media arts, music, theater, and visual arts in the United States (NCCAS 2014). In music, performing is the interpretation and presentation of musical works. Responding is the perception, analysis, and evaluation of music. Connecting is relating musical ideas to personal meaning and external contexts. Creating is the conception and development of new musical ideas and works.

In the past, responding, connecting, and creating were often missing in my own instruction as an instrumental educator, especially as I felt pressure to present public concerts or help students achieve honor band placements. After reflecting on my own teaching, I developed conclusions about how I would like to encourage future teachers to develop their approaches to instrumental music. I recognized opportunities for musical growth in children who engage with music in multiple ways and not only performance. Perhaps the additional pathways that the other artistic process provided could be a way to engage more students in instrumental music in our new digital setting. In the practicum experience, my students expressed their own vulnerability as they reached out for guidance to navigate the technological challenges of teaching online and the unfamiliarity of their virtual teaching contexts. As such, my students welcomed this reorientation of our approach.

PERFORMING IN A NEW ERA

Alex

Alex met me through Zoom to discuss her lessons with her percussion student. "Professor Schaller, I don't know what to do. I've never done lessons this way." A strong student in the practices course the previous semester, Alex displayed knowledge of technique and musicianship in percussion. Her planned instruction emphasized drilling percussion rudiments. The only assessment she included in her lesson plans was a checklist for stick and mallet grip. Alex admitted, "I understand that you want us to break away from drilling skills, but that's all I know to do because that's the only way I've been taught percussion."

I reminded her of our class discussions about placing instrumental skills into a musical context. I asked her, "Alex, there are times that we need to learn skills and to practice those skills, but does it need to be every minute of every lesson? What can you do to spark vibrancy when you are teaching rudiments? How can you introduce them in an imaginative way? How can you make them musical?"

Alex began to brainstorm ideas of how she could make this happen in her lessons. We discussed musical literature that uses specific rudiments as well as looking for examples from popular music examples. I also asked her to connect with Dave to find out what he was doing in his percussion lessons.

Dave

Early in the semester, Dave asked to meet. "I just wanted to make sure I was on track with my lessons since this is a secondary instrument for me." Dave regularly dove further into resources I introduced in both the practices and practicum courses. As a result, he would frequently anticipate points I wanted to make in class before I said them. He was a low brass specialist but volunteered to teach percussion lessons. I was curious to see how he would approach teaching a secondary instrument, especially percussion, in a virtual environment.

He continued, "I decided to focus on rudiments since that's what the method book introduces, but I don't want to do just what the method book presents. I want to incorporate music that my students listen to. I'm thinking about having students name their favorite songs at the beginning of our next lesson and practice the rudiments along to the song using it as a type of metronome."

These two vignettes present two contrasting approaches to teaching the instrument, specifically percussion, lessons online. At the start of the practicum experience, many of the preservice teachers I supervised seemed to share Alex's apprehension to break free from skills-based approaches to teaching instrumental lessons. To many, this practicum seemed no different than any instrumental lesson they themselves experienced. While the lesson was virtual, the *grammars* of the experience were remarkably like the instrumental lessons they received as beginning instrumentalists and continued to receive as music majors (Tyack and Cuban 1995). Each lesson group was small and met a short period of time together each week just like their elementary and middle school instrumental music lessons. I recommended a band method book for the practicum experience. To the preservice teachers, the method book appeared to present skills and technical drills logically and sequentially. The preservice teachers identified the assignment of exercises in this method book for students to practice and then play back each week. Many of the preservice teachers attempted to cling to these familiar hallmarks in their lesson plans and ignored the virtual nature of their classrooms, the availability of technological tools, and their students' needs.

The initial lesson plans I received from teachers focused primarily on instrumental technique development, such as executive skills, tone development, and scale memorization, without a musical context. I commented on many of these lesson plans, "Where is the imagination? Where is the generativity, vibrance, or residue? Where is the music?" These were concepts I discussed in our practices course as well as in our initial meetings in our practicum course. I asked the preservice teachers to include in their instruction activities that allowed students to create new understandings, to uncover personal meaning, and to be residual or significant beyond their 30-minute lesson (Campbell, Thompson, and Barrett 2021). Most of all, I asked the preservice teachers to facilitate musical experiences and not just technique. In their initial lessons, I did not see the attributes of a musical experience.

Therefore, I tasked the preservice teachers to discover ways musical performance could be included in their lessons beyond the demonstration of skills on an instrument. Dave and several other preservice teachers asked their students about their favorite songs. They began to center their students' music choices as the core repertoire rather than the exercises in the method book. Many noted familiar pop songs for their students to practice and perform using these songs to reinforce the skills that were introduced in the method book. One preservice teacher assigned her saxophone student well-known saxophone licks from different popular songs each week. Some preservice teachers incorporated sound-before-sign approaches to instrument teaching such as teaching melodies from their students' favorite songs by rote and then introduced the written notation later (Millican 2012). Some even asked their students to dictate these melodies into written notation to develop their aural skills.

RESPONDING TO OUR CIRCUMSTANCES

Katie and Mike

During a large group meeting with my practicum students, I asked Katie how she felt her lessons with her oboe students were progressing. Katie shared, "I asked each of my students to find a recording of an oboist on YouTube and then show these recordings in our lesson. I asked them to explain why they liked that particular recording and asked them to describe what they liked about the oboist's tone." She continued, "Every oboist has a unique tone specific to them, and I want my students to discover theirs for themselves through their oboe journey and not just become a carbon-copy of what I like." Katie, a dedicated and competent oboist, could have easily and directly told her students how to improve their technique. Instead, she incorporated the artistic process of responding in her lessons. Katie shared that she was teaching her students how to use the application Soundtrap (2022) to record their playing, so they could respond to and critique each other's playing in future lessons, especially as they developed their tone.

I asked the other preservice teachers if anyone else was incorporating any responding in their lessons. Mike raised his hand. He was a clarinetist and saxophonist and an accomplished jazz performer. He taught a group of young clarinet students who loved coming to lessons to not just play music but to socialize with each other. Mike took advantage of their willingness to talk by asking them to discuss recordings of clarinetists each week. "This past week I asked them to listen to a recording of the jazz clarinetist Anat Cohen and then come to our lesson with three interesting findings about her and two questions about her playing. This week I assigned them to watch a video on YouTube of a Balkan music group called BGKO. They are to listen specifically to the clarinet solo, and I will ask them to describe the style of playing."

In the vignette above, both Katie and Mike were not only facilitating opportunities for their students to respond to musical performances, but they were also responding to their students' musical curiosities. Katie's students asked to work on their oboe tone in lessons. Katie could have assigned long tone scales and asked her students to sit with a tuner as they played. Instead, she took advantage of the technological tools that were available through the Internet and incorporated them into the virtual format of her lessons. Mike's students, much to his delight, expressed interest in jazz and improvisation. Mike immediately began to assign weekly listening activities that students could access through YouTube to stimulate discussions about style and improvisation.

As their practicum experience continued, many preservice teachers realized the power of showing their students musical performances and then leading them through conversations about what they saw and heard rather than telling students how to do something. In our wind practices course, we read a chapter in J. Si Millican's (2012) book *Starting Out Right: Beginning Band Pedagogy* that began with a vignette of a teacher who is concerned that her students are only "button pushers" and cannot communicate musically (20). "Button pushers" became a trigger word for many of the discussions in our practices and practicum courses when we recognized lessons in instructional situations focused too much on the nuts and bolts of technique and not enough on the development of students' musical understandings.

YouTube became a resource that many preservice teachers used to enliven their lessons and help their students become excited about their instruments. In-depth musical discussions between preservice teachers and students arose from the sharing of novelty pieces such as a trombone piece that showcased the various sizes of trombones and demonstrations of historical performance practices such as a video showcasing the natural horn. Preservice teachers also shared avant-garde pieces as well as staples from their respective instrument's repertoire with their students. A few preservice teachers even discovered intriguing new repertoire from the recordings their students shared. Each time a teacher facilitated discussion about a performance, they invited students to express their subjective feelings and helped their students develop an aural and technical vocabulary to communicate their musical understandings.

CONNECTING TO OPPORTUNITIES

Catherine

Catherine is a thoughtful student who plays horn. She wrote in an e-mail to me that due to health reasons her student could not always play their horn in lessons. As a result, she wondered how to adapt her instruction to meet her student's needs. During the semester that she took teaching practices, she often remarked about finding ways to meet the needs of students rather than the needs of the teacher.

When we met through Zoom, Catherine explained, "My student experiences breathing issues that are triggered by weather patterns, so I'm adapting lessons so my student can always participate. Sometimes she isn't able to play. I'm trying to find other ways for us to develop musicianship."

I asked, "What did you discover about your student's interests?"

Catherine excitedly responded, "I discovered that she loves to go to Renaissance fairs with her family, and she's fascinated by the Middle Ages. Right now, I'm working on finding music from that time period for us to listen to and potentially play."

A few weeks later, I checked in with Catherine about the progress she was having with her student. Catherine shared, "Things are going great! We worked some on a solo that was inspired from the Medieval period. We looked at some dances from then too. What she's really become interested in is neumes. We're doing this whole thing with learning amount neumes, how they were used as notation, and how to read them. We definitely found ways to be musical without having to always be playing our horn."

Catherine recognized the power that finding and leaning into her student's fascinating interests created in her lessons. When my practicum students met as a group next, I asked Catherine to share about her lessons to demonstrate the possibilities of incorporating student interests and knowledge beyond that of music. Catherine not only helped her student learn about music, but she also helped her learn more about history and ancient cultures, which brought her instruction to a relevant place for her student.

In our teaching practices course, my students often discussed student interests and relevance to student cultures (Lind and McKoy 2016). They expressed a desire to design curricula that would not be a one-size-fits-all for every teaching situation, but instead were tailored to the students' cultures that were in their classrooms and schools. Often, they relied on popular and vernacular music to include students' cultures. I encouraged the preservice teachers to take the development of their lessons further and tailor them to their students' knowledge and interests. I asked them to look for interdisciplinary connections, especially their students' interests outside of music. Using the facets model, a heuristic for examining works of art, I asked teachers to look at the repertoire they were using in their lessons and draw connections to as many disciplines, fields, and subjects as they could (Barrett, in preparation; Barrett, McCoy, and Veblen 1997). Likewise, I asked them to canvass their students for their interests and then find ways to connect those specific interests back to music. Catherine's deep dive into medieval notation was the result of this exercise, but other preservice teachers experienced similar results. The preservice teachers began to incorporate activities such as sound exploration and composition related to animals, arranging of familiar video game and movie melodies, and soundscapes inspired by visual art. Some used narrative storytelling by asking students to create original stories from the music they were performing. During these lessons students learned more about music, but also applied and discovered new dimensions of their prior knowledge and experiences outside of music. Students experienced repertoire in their lessons that held the potential to become more integrated into their personal vantage point of the world.

CREATING OUR FUTURES

Chris

As the practicum teachers continued to discuss the interests of their students and the musical possibilities that were created, Chris chimed in, "My student is really into animals." Chris is a trombonist and advocated in our classes for low brass students to learn more melodic material during instrument lessons since they mostly perform harmonic backing in ensemble settings. He therefore began to look for opportunities to include the artistic processes of performing, responding, connecting, and especially creating in his trombone lessons. He continued, "Since my student is into animals, I thought that we'd create a series of compositions that are inspired by different animals and make a collection of them."

"That sounds like a great idea, Chris. Sort of Carnival of the Animals redone," I responded.

Chris added, "I think we could use these compositions to reinforce skills that are being introduced in the lesson book and also help put them into a musical context that she created."

Jason

Jason stayed on the Zoom call after our large group meeting ended. "Professor Schaller, can I ask you about how to incorporate creation activities into my lessons?" Jason is an enthusiastic preservice teacher who plays trumpet but volunteered to teach beginning saxophone for his practicum experience. He is from a family of instrumental music teachers and loves all things band related. He wrote to me in excitement when I assigned him to write his first lesson plan for an imagined band class because he couldn't wait to teach band. His excitement included teaching band in new and different ways, not just the way he experienced it as a student. "Professor Schaller, I want to do things on Soundtrap and get him composing. I showed him the application and he wasn't interested." Jason continued, "He showed no interest in using it or making his own music. He just wanted to go back to practicing out of the book."

Jason did not want to force his student to do something in which he was not interested. I advised him to revisit composing another time to see if he could pique his student's interest.

At the end of the semester, my students and I reconvened together as a group to reflect on our teaching experiences. Jason smiled, "Guess what Professor Schaller. My student a couple weeks ago asked, 'What was that Soundtrap thing you showed me?' I guess he just needed to think about it for a few weeks. I showed him some things he could do, and he started to make some music using it on his own outside of our lessons!"

Chris and Jason viewed the virtual format of their lessons and the technology available to them as an opportunity for students to find ways to focus on creating their own music. Some preservice teachers, like Chris, asked students to create new music which was used to develop executive skills, technique, and musicianship. Some teachers though, like Jason, experienced resistance from their students when introducing these creative endeavors. However, it appeared that a gentle and unforced introduction helped each preservice teacher eventually find success with their students.

Music is often grouped with creative arts. However, most students in my courses respond in the negative when I ask them if they experienced any creation activities such as composition or improvisation as students in their band classes. Each semester several reply that they improvised, but only in a jazz band context. Instead, they recount participating in ensemble activities that centered around published repertoire. In our teaching practices course, I attempt to show these future teachers the value of improvisation and composition in instrumental ensemble situations. I admit that, as a band director, I too struggled to find ways to incorporate composition into my ensembles' curricula, and I was guilty of relegating improvisation to my jazz bands. When I did attempt arranging or composition activities, I felt as though I was in unfamiliar and uncomfortable territory. Like many other teachers, I did not experience many models of how to teach composition and improvisation in my instrumental ensembles (Kaschub and Smith 2013). Encouraging the preservice teachers in this practicum experience to incorporate creation activities into their lessons allowed them the opportunity to experiment, share, and reflect with others and perhaps gave them the courage to continue similar activities in their future classrooms.

I encouraged the preservice teachers to use the repertoire that was presented in their lessons as a foundation for improvisation and composition activities if they were unsure where to start (Randles and Stringham 2013; Stringham and Bernhard 2019). They created lessons that asked students to compose variations on melodies that were presented in the method book. Some asked students to create new musical material that built upon the short exercises that they were playing. Others used the web-based application Hookpad (2022) to recreate harmonic progressions of familiar songs over which students improvised.

Many of the preservice teachers in this practicum experience found themselves improvising and composing for the first time on their instruments as they introduced activities to their students. They began to arrange and compose repertoire for their students that better suited their students' needs compared to already published materials. Some teachers discovered how fun it was to create on their instruments and, as a result, sought ways to incorporate more creation activities into their lessons.

REFLECTIONS OF EXPERIENCE

As the teachers in this practicum experience reflected on the semester through our in-class discussions and in one-on-one exit interviews with me, they could not help but compare their virtual teaching experiences alongside their imagined experiences of in-person teaching. At the forefront of their reflections was the incorporation of instructional technology into their pedagogy. Many admitted that they were forced into unfamiliar territory with online applications and software but found them to be essential to their teaching of music. They shared that they would not have originally considered many of these tools if teaching in person. I was surprised to discover that until we reoriented our approach to instruction, many ignored these tools, including YouTube. The traditional approach of skill and drill presented in method books dominated their teaching. Simple and even ubiquitous technological resources, such as YouTube and sound recording, seemed irrelevant to their skill-driven approaches.

The preservice teachers also shared about the connections they made with their students, and how they tailored instruction directly to them. As the preservice teachers leaned into these connections, they began to relinquish their dependence on published curricula such as the method book. They created custom arrangements specifically written for their students. They found ways to integrate their students' interests into lessons and allowed their students to guide their lessons. One preservice teacher remarked, "I discovered that a student could function as the teacher!"

As the practicum supervisor, I was excited to discover the freedom this experience provided to both the preservice teachers and their students. Because the children in this program were not affiliated with one particular music program or community, the preservice teachers and students enjoyed the independence to find musical pathways forward each week. They did not need to maneuver through the expectations of a school administration or community influencing their progress. Each group enjoyed the flexibility to pursue their own interests and needs. Without this freedom, I am not sure that these preservice teachers could have developed the connections they were able to with their students. They would likely have placed more emphasis on a final product or destination such as preparing a piece for a concert or recital in their lessons rather than embrace the complex journey that developing musicianship truly is. Engaging in this journey together allowed the preservice teachers and their students to develop a musical bond.

At the end of the practicum experience, I noticed I experienced similar feelings about my own teaching. We all recognized a developing confidence in our teaching, but we still held apprehension for future teaching experiences. We all found ways to make our instruction and facilitation work for this virtual context. We developed positive relationships and successfully navigated challenges. I recognized my own agency as a teacher educator. Even as a new professor in a new teaching context, I possessed the ability to put into motion positive change as opposed to continuing to abide in the safety of the status quo. I saw the potential in the preservice teachers I worked with and their teaching contexts, as opposed to allowing them to feel victimized by their circumstances, and I recognized the potential in my own teaching to do the same. While the messaging heard by media outlets, school administration, and colleagues was to *get through* the challenges of the COVID-19 pandemic, I found that I was able to thrive in my teaching by reorienting my focus to what I believed to be important about music education. I put into practice my beliefs of experimentation and creativity in instrumental music education and music teacher education. The structures of this virtual practicum and my teaching context did not discourage their implementation but instead, demanded it.

THE IMAGINED PATH FORWARD

I cannot predict what the path forward will be for the preservice teachers of this practicum. I am warned by other music teacher education scholars that they may revert to the way they were taught once they are given the opportunity to teach instrumental lessons in person (Dobbs 2014; Powell and Parker 2017). This practicum experience may be only a charming teaching anomaly for them; one they will reminisce about in the future as they ask their students to play exercise number 14 out of the method book and check it off in their grade book. I hope not though. I hope they will continue along a different path. Hopefully, a path that includes musical and pedagogical experimentation, vibrancy, and imagination.

While I cannot control the pathways of these teachers, I can control my pathway forward. John Dewey (1934, 281) wrote about the power of consciousness against the "inertia of habit." I cannot imagine a duller descriptor than the inertia of habit for my remaining teaching career. By being conscious of my capabilities, practice, surroundings, place, and students I may avoid teaching instrumental music education as something that seeks to replicate past pedagogical traditions or *habits* unthinkingly, but rather as the *living tradition* that it should be (Allsup 2016; Hansen 2001). I envision my future in teacher education to be one that embraces change rather than fights it. I will continue to seek conversations with colleagues and students that invigorate my own pedagogical innovation and evolution. I will engage in continual reflection on my course activities and experiences to see how my pedagogy can develop to benefit the preservice teachers that exist in my classroom at that moment. Now as my courses change from virtual to in-person formats, I can see my teaching from new and different angles. I recognize the need to embrace imagination, experimentation, and creativity more than ever as the world appears to *revert to normal*. If I expect to continue to thrive as a teacher educator, I will need to remind myself that there no longer is a *normal* and that I am now part of that long sought-after transformation in music education.

Prior to this virtual teaching experience, the continuing evolution of instrumental music education traditions to meet the needs of time and place and those who participate in it was something I only imagined in the abstract as I read others' experiences. Now, I have experienced a movement of *habit* and witnessed multiple preservice teachers in this practicum lead their students down creative pathways. Instrumental music education does not need to only rely on the demonstration of technique and skill in teaching and learning settings. There is a diversity of potential when it is approached as a creative art interweaving the processes of performing, connecting, responding, and creating for the betterment of individual students. I imagine a future where music educators and music teacher educators appreciate their power and agency which can allow their classrooms to be sites of musical creativity and evolving perspective and artistry. This virtual teaching experience has shown me that instrumental music education does not need to be fixed but can continue to be expanded and imagined into multiple futures. I will continue to courageously imagine its futures and possibilities. Hopefully, my students, these preservice music teachers, will join me and others in our field to expand the future of instrumental music education as they transition into their careers as in-service instrumental music educators.

REFERENCES

Allsup, Randall Everett. 2016. *Remixing the Classroom: Toward an Open Philosophy of Music Education.* Bloomington, IN: Indiana University Press.

Barrett, Janet Revell. (in preparation). *Seeking Connections: An Interdisciplinary Perspective on Music Teaching and Learning.* New York: Oxford University Press, in preparation.

Barrett, Janet Revell, Clare W. McCoy and Kari K. Veblen. 1997. *Sound Ways of Knowing: Music in the Interdisciplinary Curriculum.* New York: Schirmer Books.

Campbell, Mark Robin, Linda K. Thompson, and Janet Revell Barrett. 2021. *Constructing a Personal Orientation to Music Teaching: Growth, Inquiry, and Agency.* 2nd ed. New York: Routledge.

Dewey, John. 1934. *Art as Experience.* New York: Perigee.

Dobbs, Teryl L. 2014. "'No Actual Teaching': Expanding Preservice Music Teachers' Imaginaries of Teaching." In *The Musical Experience: Rethinking Music Teaching and Learning,* edited by Janet Revell Barrett, and Peter R. Webster, 294–308. New York: Oxford University Press.

Hansen, David T. 2001. *Exploring the Moral Heart of Teaching.* New York: Teachers College Press.

Hookpad (version 2.21.4). 2022. "Hooktheory." https://hookpad.hooktheory.com.

Kaschub, Michele, and Janice P. Smith. 2013. *Composing Our Future: Preparing Music Educators to Teach Composition.* New York: Oxford University Press.

Lind, Vicki R., and Constance L. McKoy. 2016. *Culturally Responsive Teaching in Music Education.* New York: Routledge.

Millican, J. Si. 2012. *Starting Out Right: Beginning Band Pedagogy.* Lanham, MD: Scarecrow Press.

National Coalition for Core Arts Standards (NCCAS). 2014. "National Core Arts Standards: A Conceptual Framework for Arts Learning." Accessed February 15, 2022. https://www.nationalartsstandards.org/content/national-core-arts-standards.

Powell, Sean R., and Elizabeth C. Parker. 2017. "Preservice Music Teachers' Descriptions of Successful and Unsuccessful Teachers." *Journal of Music Teacher Education,* 26, no. 3: 27–37.

Randles, Clint, and David Stringham. 2013. *Musicianship: Composing in Band and Orchestra.* Chicago, IL: GIA Publications.

Soundtrap. Spotify USA, 2022. https://www.soundtrap.com.

Stringham, David A., and Christian H. Bernhard. 2019. *Musicianship: Improvising in Band and Orchestra.* Chicago, IL: GIA Publications.

Tyack, David, and Larry Cuban. 1995. *Tinkering Toward Utopia: A Century of Public School Reform.* Cambridge, MA: Harvard University Press.

Chapter 4

The Digital Audio Workstation in the Aural Skills Classroom

Using Reason *as a Tool for Dictation Practice*

Jerod Sommerfeldt

In March 2020, the Crane School of Music at SUNY Potsdam—like many other institutions—quickly transitioned to a distance-learning format in response to the increased spread of and threats posed by COVID-19. Following a two-week spring break, our classes resumed entirely online. Each instructor was provided training and support on our learning management system and given freedom regarding method of instruction. Some opted for fully synchronous online learning at a regularly scheduled class time, while others mixed in some asynchronous work.

Many of my colleagues and I prepared our courses in earnest for a mix of synchronous/asynchronous online work or hybrid learning with some in-person elements when it was determined that the fall 2020 semester—and eventually the entire academic year—would again be offered virtually. Special care was given to maintain proper social distancing protocols for those who opted for in-person teaching. Out of an abundance of caution for myself, my family, and my students, I decided to stay home and teach my classes remotely. My fall 2020 semester teaching load included a section of first semester music theory and aural skills and I found unique challenges awaited us as I prepared for a year of remote learning.

BACKGROUND

I am in my eighth-year teaching at the Crane School of Music and eleventh in higher education. I teach electronic music, composition, music theory, and aural skills to a cohort of primarily music education students. My background and training in electronic music forms the crux of my work as a composer and musician and is my main mode of creative expression. Electronic music is my passion and while it is the main focus of my Electronic Music Composition, Computer Music Composition, Computer Music Programming, and Laptop Orchestra electives, I also introduce my music theory students to its practitioners by playing compositions and discussing them as a group throughout the year. Through these listening sessions and discussions, I invite students to respond to the music, informally, using descriptive language to expand their experience with electronic music and its sounds, timbres, and tools.

My music theory classes are informed by analysis, counterpoint, harmonic practice, and opportunities for students to explore writing compositions. Aural skills work is centered around rhythmic, melodic, and harmonic dictation, as well as singing collectively as a group. I aim to blend theory and aural skills into a unified experience. Many class meetings will include, for example, singing music that we then analyze harmonically as a group, or collectively composing a chorale-style harmonic dictation of a top and bottom line that we then activate with contrapuntal inner voices. Above all, I seek to create a welcoming classroom where students are invited to work together to explore concepts and share in the experience of learning and making music.

The shift to distance learning fundamentally altered these approaches in the classroom and invited me to discover new ways of delivering content to my students. Faced with the prospect of not being able to meet collectively, I sought ways to retain a focus on the aural skills work so central to the course—rhythmic, melodic, and harmonic dictation, and singing—using the digital tools available to us. Along the way, we unlocked new methodologies for teaching and learning music theory that I'll share in this chapter.

USING REASON FOR RHYTHMIC DICTATION

Many of our classrooms are outfitted with a piano that, when in-person, facilitates the bulk of our dictation practice. I'm up in front of the class almost daily playing tone clusters, intervals, chords, chord progressions, and melodies. I'll even try my best to read through some of our theory examples on the piano, but my tempos are impossibly slow and the sustain pedal is generously applied.

I've always complemented in-class work with online tools in my aural skills classes, which provides an opportunity for students to engage in individual practice outside of our class meetings and helps them build skills daily. I emphasize small amounts of daily work as a critical component of gaining confidence throughout the semester or year. I assign dictation work in chord quality identifications, interval recognitions, rhythmic dictations, and chord progression ear training exercises, all while providing a platform for students to share their experiences using mobile apps for individual practice. The site *musictheory.net* is a tool that we use early and often in the first semester. The site *trainedear.net* hosts a wealth of dictation examples and has a powerful search filter. It's possible to quickly find something akin to a stepwise melody with leaps of a P5 in a minor key in 4/4 without a pickup, which is not only great for solo practice, but finding examples to play in-class for group work (Mount 2021).

As COVID restrictions took hold, I soon realized that a new connection needed to be made between facilitating aural skills practice and the digital world we were all thrust into. I decided to utilize Digital Audio Workstations (DAWs) and software instruments. These tools provided a platform for our class to explore sampling real-world instruments, adding effects, editing audio, and helped me prepare dictation exercises that I could deliver remotely. I am an avid user of the Reason DAW in my own composing work, and I found its wealth of instruments, sounds, samples, and streamlined workflow sparked my creativity, helping me quickly create high quality content to deliver to my students in our online aural skills class.

Without a piano at home, I used Reason's NN-19 sampler instrument, which was an invaluable tool throughout the year. In the early weeks of the semester, I tried to play dictation examples in real-time for the students over Zoom, however issues with latency became increasingly problematic. Despite a clearly established tempo from a click track, my playing would inevitably fall behind and become difficult to follow. And as much as I wanted it to, the push/pull of tempo couldn't be explained away by claiming liberal use of *rubato*.

To mitigate latency issues, I wrote the melodies, harmonies, and rhythms directly into Reason and played them back within the session itself, circumventing the need to play the examples myself in real-time. By pre-composing the music into the DAW session, I gave myself plenty of flexibility with tempo, timbre, and expression. I could easily change the instrument I was sampling, adjust the tempo, increase/decrease the volume, and be confident in garnering consistent results. Moreover, the more I started composing dictation examples into Reason, the more eager I was to introduce DAWs to my first-year students, so that they could be introduced to this important tool in electronic music and work on their dictation skills within the prism of digital technology.

In my aural skills classes, rhythmic dictation examples are either ones that I compose or are culled from our textbook and read on a single-line percussion staff. I usually sound them on a single piano note for the students as part of our in-class dictation practice. These single line, simple meter examples—especially those in 4/4—are great to clap out collectively as a group for general rhythm practice and provide endless enjoyment when breaking the class into smaller groups and clapping them in canon (generally four parts, although five or more produce deliriously fun results). Played several times, students dictate the example while we go over them together on the whiteboard, noting and rectifying any issues that arise. I also provide space to share tips/tricks for successfully navigating dictations in real time. Figure 4.1 is typical of something I would compose and utilize early in the first semester.

Figure 4.1 Rhythmic Dictation Example. Credit Jerod Sommerfeldt. 2021.

While some DAWs support western notation, many use the MIDI editor, a ubiquitous tool that facilitates the creation of melodic/harmonic/rhythmic ideas and the looping/sequencing of musical events in a grid-like format. Figure 4.2 rewrites the preceding example using Reason's MIDI editor, sampling a closed hi hat sound.

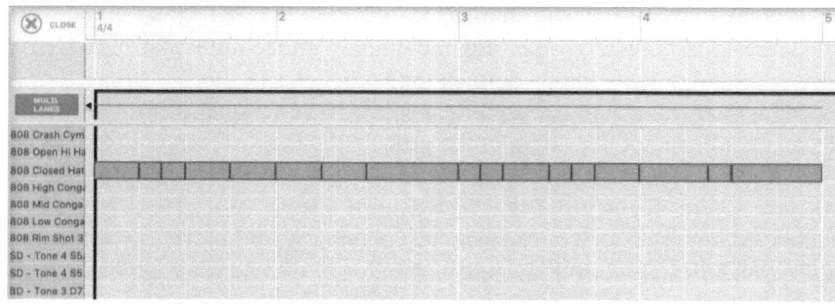

Figure 4.2 Rhythmic Dictation Example Written in Reason's MIDI Editor. Credit Jerod Sommerfeldt. 2021.

The sequencer grid in figure 4.2 is divided into quarter notes, although this can be augmented/diminished at will, depending on the level of detail needed. The numbers 1, 2, 3, and 4 on the x-axis of the sequencer window denote measures of music and smaller marks between the numbers show quarter and eight notes, respectively. The orange boxes represent musical events: the longer the width of each event, the longer the duration of the note in the music. Thus, durations in a DAW are viewed as actual measurements, whereas in western music notation, they are represented by changes in noteheads or flags.

Using the Reason DAW, I unlocked a new world of possibilities for our dictation practice. Rhythmic values could be discussed, heard, and seen in a new way. Reason's massive library of sampled sounds broke the monotony of exclusively using piano. For example, the short attack time and sharp sound of the Roland TR-808 drum machine's closed hi hat sample was effective for clearly hearing simple rhythmic lines and provided an opportunity to discuss the importance of drum machines and their use in music. This led to the idea to use an entire drum set (bass drum, snare, and hi hats) as the basis of our dictation examples, rather than a single, monophonic line sounded on the piano. Not only could we practice three lines of rhythmic dictation at once, but we explored a wealth of examples that expanded genres and styles along the way.

Following a brief lesson on drum sounds and how they are written in western notation, we spent time each week dictating a variety of examples. Figure 4.3 shows one of our earlier rhythmic dictation examples, which I used to introduce our class to conventions in drum set notation on the percussion staff.

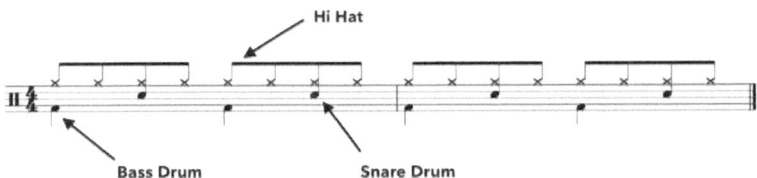

Figure 4.3 Notation Example from Our Introduction to Drum Set Notation. Credit Jerod Sommerfeldt. 2021.

As the semester progressed, we slowly increased the complexity of the examples, using sampled bass drum, snare drum, and hi hat sounds in Reason. Each pattern was easy to notate in western music notation and even easier to input into the MIDI editor. While I demonstrated how these patterns are written in the DAW, all dictations were completed by students on the five-line staff.

Figure 4.4 shows the same example as notated in the MIDI editor. As a future dictation assignment, I anticipate handing out a blank MIDI editor window made on graph paper and having our students write the notation for the dictation example using markers or colored pencils, then comparing the results with notation on the five-line staff.

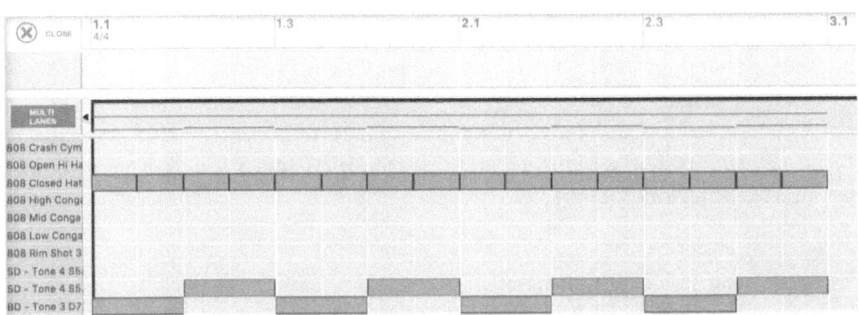

Figure 4.4 Notation Example Written in Reason's MIDI Editor. Credit Jerod Sommerfeldt. 2021.

Further inspired by our use of drum set dictations and the widening exploration of genres and styles that it generated, I introduced "meter detection" exercises. Preparing several examples that sampled 60″ of a given song culled from pop, rock, hip hop, electronic music, and many other genres, I invited the students to respond with the time signature (ex. 4/4) and type of meter (ex. simple quadruple). The success of this exercise inspired the students to request that we start a forum on our online course site where they could upload their favorite examples for everyone to hear. We began each class by playing one of these examples and I invited the student who made the post to share why they chose the particular song and what they liked so much about it. Our sense of community grew tremendously and even early in the morning, the day's musical example elicited lip synching and yes, some dancing over Zoom. In my course evaluations, one student wrote, "I love how you brought popular music into the forefront and showed us another side of theory."

USING REASON FOR MELODIC DICTATION

Encouraged by the students' positive response to these rhythmic dictation exercises, I began creating examples for our melodic dictation practice. These are traditionally played in-class on the piano, but I relied on my DAW to construct remote examples that could be played back over Zoom. This, in the end, offered several advantages that I'll explain further. Culled from *trainedear.net*, it was easy to download an example's MIDI file and further sculpt it using sampled sounds in Reason. The examples on the website use an orienting click track to establish tempo—which is customizable—and so I set up my sequencer to do the same using a clave sample in the Kong Drum Designer's "Modelled Acoustic" set of drum sounds. For the piano sounds, I found the clearest results over Zoom by using Reason's *BRIGHTPIANO* sample in the NN-19 Sampler instrument.

Reason notates melodies in the MIDI editor using its piano roll, which displays a keyboard layout on the y-axis toward the left of the window, with markers for the note C in various octaves. The x-axis displays rhythmic divisions above the notation. Figure 4.5 shows a melodic dictation example that I composed for our class in western music notation, which uses mostly stepwise motion, has a blend of simpler rhythms, spans a narrow range, and has smaller intervallic leaps.

Figure 4.5 **Melody in Western Notation.** Credit Jerod Sommerfeldt. 2021.

Figure 4.6 is the same melody, shown in Reason's piano roll.

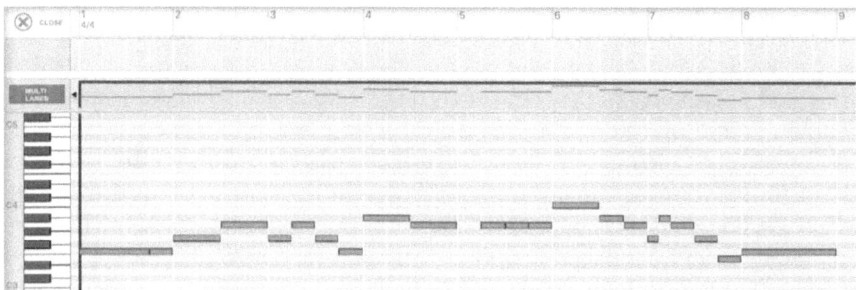

Figure 4.6 Melody in MIDI Piano Roll. Credit Jerod Sommerfeldt. 2021.

Figures 4.5 and 4.6 lack articulations, but this is easy to implement in Reason's piano roll and adds quite a bit of musicality to the playback of each example, allowing the user to shape the phrases. As I entered these melodies into the piano roll and adjusted durations to match articulations, I found it interesting that the MIDI piano roll literally shows the separation of two notes in a *staccato* and the overlapping of them in a *tenuto*. Figure 4.7 adds articulations to the phrase in western notation.

Figure 4.7 Adding Articulations to a Melodic Dictation. Credit Jerod Sommerfeldt. 2021.

Figure 4.8 shows these additions and the visual feedback of overlapped notes on the piano roll.

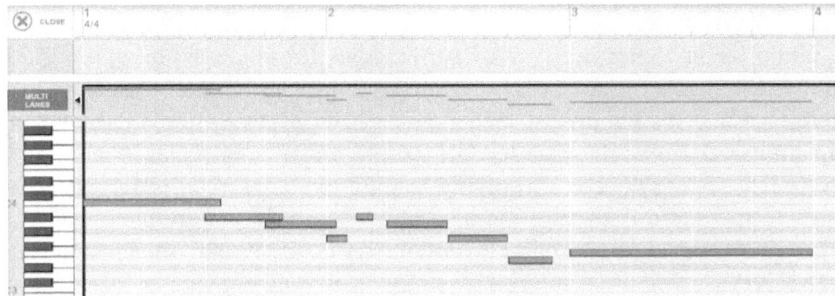

Figure 4.8 Melodic Dictation Articulations in MIDI Piano Roll. Credit Jerod Sommerfeldt. 2021.

USING REASON FOR HARMONIC DICTATION

The piano roll also aided in the composition of harmonic dictation and four-part, chorale-style counterpoint exercises. Reason's pencil tool is used to click and draw notes in the sequencer, much like a music notation software's "simple entry" option for placing notes. Using Reason's pencil tool is useful for editing articulations, but a more facile system exists for composition. By enabling your instrument track to record in real-time, connecting a USB MIDI keyboard and setting a click track, it is possible to simply play the melody along to an established tempo directly into the DAW. If you get slightly ahead or behind the beat, Reason will allow you to *quantize* those notes, thus putting them in line with the tempo of the music and snapping them to each respective beat based on the level of detail you'd like to use. For example, if I'm just slightly ahead or behind a measure's downbeat, quantization will move that note to align properly. Moreover, the user can record several times into an individual track, so it is possible to record each individual line in a four-part chorale separately.

When playing four-part chorales in class as dictation practice, students receive a starting pitch for the top and bottom voices and transcribe those lines, while providing a Roman numeral analysis with chord symbols for each chord in succession. Some students opt to dictate the inner voices as well, but it isn't mandatory. Prior to distance learning, these exercises were always completed with me at the piano and the blank exercise on the whiteboard, which we worked through collectively as a class.

Playback in the DAW was far simpler—but not something that I'll rely on exclusively, as I still enjoy playing piano in class—and afforded me the ability to make quick changes to the individual notes or harmonies. For example, if the last two chords of an example in D major form a V to I cadence, and the V chord (A major) doubles the fifth (E) instead of the root (A), I can quickly make changes in the piano roll to demonstrate an alternative doubling option before resolving to tonic. This is of course possible to do in-real time at the piano, albeit without sampling a synthesizer instrument or other sound.

While we do cover the various conventions for voice doublings in a texture, I don't adhere strictly to one method. Instead, I demonstrate various doublings and resolutions of tendency tones to explore how small changes can impact the overall shape/texture of the chord itself. This is especially useful if I wish to double a resolving leading tone in a V—I progression and listen to the sonic impact of parallel fifths. Moreover, if an example is too low/high for the class to sing or hear, copying the notes and transposing them is also very easy in the piano roll by simply using the copy/paste function and moving the notes up or down.

Reason includes a large library of sampled sounds, which makes it a powerful tool for generating dictation examples that don't rely exclusively on the piano. For example, I was able to sample an organ and add reverb to ponder what our chorale examples might sound like in a church setting. This added depth and context to our work and demonstrated interesting ways that we can sonically craft the notes in the DAW. Figure 4.9 shows a Reason session with the NN-XT sampler, loaded with the *FULL BARS* organ sample chained to the RV7000 reverb instrument.

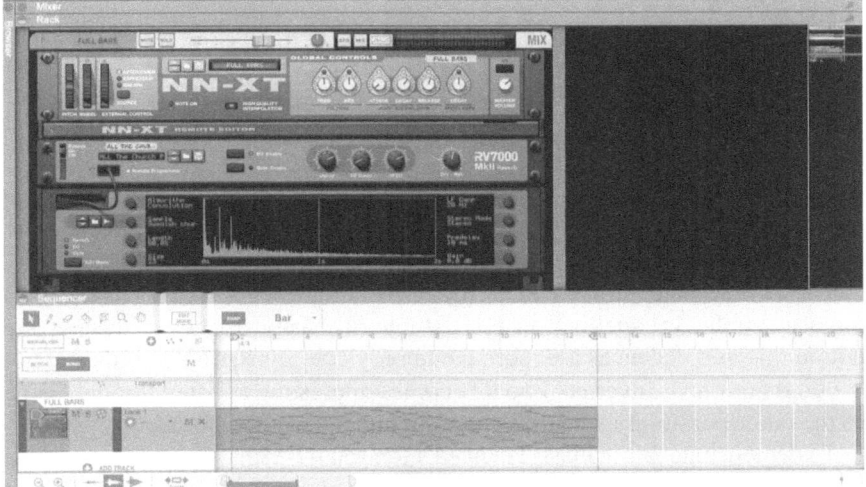

Figure 4.9 Adding Reverb to Organ Sample in Reason. Credit Jerod Sommerfeldt. 2021.

The use of Reason as a playback tool enhanced our educational experience when engaging with voice-leading conventions and discussing issues related to counterpoint. While I have sought out recordings of chorales to play in conjunction with our lessons on voice leading, audio recordings don't support the ability to make changes to the music itself. However, in Reason I was able to quickly switch notes around, move some voices into a parallel octave, or change doublings to demonstrate voice-leading conventions in a more reverberant sound world. This can also be done in-person on piano, however, by changing notes in the Reason piano roll students were able to both hear changes in the music and see changes in the notation in real-time.

Figure 4.10 shows a chorale composed by Johann Sebastian Bach that I used in class as an example of how small alterations to the notes can impact the overall sonic effect of the music. This engendered plenty of conversation regarding voice leading conventions and harmonic progressions.

Figure 4.10 "Herzliebster Jesu, vas hast du verbrochen" by J. S. Bach. Credit Jerod Sommerfeldt. 2021.

The penultimate fermata in figure 4.10 completes a half cadence in B minor, specifically spelling an F#7/A# chord. Many textbooks discuss the notion that half cadences are more commonly comprised of V chords and not V7 (and this one is inverted!), so it becomes interesting to listen through some of the other possibilities heard by the dominant seventh chord.

To demonstrate this in class, I created a Reason file using a pipe organ sample with three different versions of the cadence. One landed on an F# chord in root position, another with an F#7 chord in root position, and lastly an F#7/A# chord. After we listened to each version, we discussed our favorites and speculated on why the composer might've chosen the inverted V7 chord as the outcome. Moreover, the A# in the lowest voice is approached from an E, which is something that when in person we've tried singing together and amending to different versions that avoid the tritone interval. In distance-learning, we changed the bass line in the MIDI file and listened to the results. There are other examples in this chorale that go against common conventions of the style and time and we enjoyed amending the composition, exploring these musical "what ifs" and coming to our own conclusions about why, in the face of so many possibilities, the composer chose their specific harmonic, melodic, or contrapuntal path.

USING REASON FOR SINGING WORK

Singing together in-class has always been a critical component of my approach to teaching aural skills. It creates an indelible sense of community and fosters collective music making in the class. We sing musical examples from our textbook, attempt new music compositions, and sing our own group part-writing exercises that we compose as a class. I'm hopelessly fond of the sonic experience of composer Johann Sebastian Bach's chorales, which are great to sing in-person. I vividly remember a colleague whose office was next door to our classroom chiding me that our 8:00 am class always sounded like a Lutheran church service. I'm not completely kidding when I say that by the time I retire, approximately 1/8 of New York state music teachers will be able to sing *O Ewigkeit du Donnerwort* from memory, in solfège. In the spring semester of this course, we go on a sight singing "tour" around campus whereby we polish our best work and end the year by singing SUNY Potsdam's Alma Mater in front of Satterlee Hall, a beautiful building adorned with ivy and topped by a clock tower that is evoked in the college's logo.

I have always blended traditional choral work, contemporary music, creativity, and collective musicianship in my music theory classes. For example, we practice scale patterns using solfège that increase in difficulty throughout the year. We sing them as a full group, in smaller groups, teams, pairs, and will also hear volunteers who would like the opportunity to sing solo. We'll write our own lyrics to them, sing our patterns with a long *crescendo* or *decrescendo*, try singing them as fast or as slow as possible, improvise with them using bitonality or in canons, among other ideas that the students or I might come up with during class.

Group singing was tremendously difficult in our distance-learning format and digital tools again became a commonplace part of our course for completing singing assignments. Due again to the limitations of latency and Zoom audio, we did very little singing together as a group, or even individually. Instead, students were assigned the same examples in our textbook as normally follows the pace of the semester, but instead of singing in person—either in-class or for exams—I collected video files of their exercises. This provided some great opportunities for more enhanced feedback, as I could rewind their videos at will and spend more time supplying them with more detailed notes.

Utilizing videos for assessment of singing work was a very effective strategy in our class. It is common for our students to spend countless hours practicing their repertoire in practice rooms and they've become accustomed to record those sessions and listen back as a means of self-evaluation. Identifying spots for improvement via recordings is an activity many engaged in well before the pandemic. This practice was instilled in me when I was an undergraduate and it occurred to me that the same scrutiny could be applied for singing work.

MOVING FORWARD

Core musicianship skills for all students and future music educators in the twenty-first century require literacy in digital tools for music making, including—but not limited to—DAWs. By including DAWs in aural skills early in the undergraduate curriculum, it is possible to provide our students with a working knowledge of recording, thus expanding their knowledge of twenty-first-century digital tools while improving their musicianship skills.

For example, sight singing duets can be easily recorded by one individual into multiple tracks in the DAW, which poses the challenge of singing to a click track. This not only keeps a consistent tempo for the singer, but also assists with the coordination of their singing and conducting patterns. Moreover, multitrack recording in a DAW while monitoring previously recorded tracks poses the challenge of being aware of pitch and tuning.

Greg McCandless writes that it is important to integrate "theory/composition topics and audio engineering/sequencing techniques into our core curriculum" as a means to promote "digital musicianship" (Mantie et al. 2017, 2). By introducing students to these skills in their freshman year, it is possible to instill a working level of familiarity and comfort with these digital tools early on in their careers. For example, incorporating the DAW piano roll and MIDI editors as a notation unit in the music theory sequences expands on students' working knowledge of notation in a wider variety of contexts. Exploring notation in the Reason DAW invariably leads to sampling from its robust library of sounds and software instruments: future composition projects can invite students to compose their own melodies, add articulations, and sample sounds from Reason's instrument library. Moreover, students could compose their own dictation exercises for practice and compare/contrast western notation and piano roll notation as options for composition.

Familiarity with navigating, reading, and understanding MIDI is a critical skill for all musicians and future teachers: McCandless further advocates for the inclusion of audio theory and MIDI sequencing in the first year of music theory and I completely agree (Mantie et al. 2017, 2). Laptop orchestras, digital music ensembles, and instrumental auditions on electronic digital instruments (EDI) are a curricular reality at several institutions and as they become more ubiquitous, their popularity will continue to grow. Meeting the needs of incoming students who utilize digital tools as their main mode of creative expression—and by extension understand their music world through the prism of MIDI—will be critical for institutions of higher learning. As of this writing, I am anticipating a semester-long sabbatical project to create a new degree program for music students to audition for admittance to our institution on EDI and have a complementary course of study in music theory and aural skills that utilizes DAWs and MIDI.

Music theory textbooks that incorporate DAW work into the curriculum are already in existence. *Music Theory for Computer Musicians* introduces students to the tenets of music theory in an effective, engaging text that covers the physical properties of sound, MIDI, DAW work, and the theoretical concepts of pitch, intonation, scales, modes (including non-western scales), and extended harmony (Hewitt 2008). *Learning Music Theory with Logic, Max, and Finale* is a comprehensive resource for learning music theory in the Logic DAW and introduces students to the graphical programming software Max, which—alongside its closely related open-source software Pure Data—is a popular tool among electronic musicians (Kidde 2020). I introduce Max and Pure Data in my electronic music courses and some students use those programs in our Laptop Orchestra. I also teach an upper-division elective course on computer music programming for musicians; however, introducing students to basic programming skills for music in their first semester theory course is an exciting prospect.

As I envision the incorporation of DAWs into my future classrooms, my mind wanders with exciting new ideas for our future music educators: suddenly it is possible to visually demonstrate the separation of *staccato* notes or slight overlapping of *legato* on the piano roll; simple melodies in western notation could be rewritten in MIDI, perhaps as a written activity on graph paper with colored pencils before moving to software; composition projects can include individually written four-part chorales that are translated to MIDI and performed using powerful software instruments; sight singing exams can include singing along to a click track and reading a top line to a pre-recorded bottom line; the tenets of voice leading can be presented in conjunction with multitracking parts from a MIDI keyboard; basic recording techniques and microphone use can accompany in-class singing practice; dictation exercises can be practiced using electronic instruments, which will engender discussions on timbre and orchestration; students will have a theory/aural skills curriculum that includes an introduction to digital music. This list goes on and I'm eager to experience what the future holds for our students and our classes.

REFERENCES

Cycling '74. Max. V. 8. Cycling '74. MacOS or Windows. 2021. https://www.cycling74.com.

Hewitt, Michael. 2008. *Music Theory for Computer Musicians.* Boston, MA: Cengage.

Kidde, Geoffrey. 2020. *Learning Music Theory with Logic, Max, and Finale.* New York: Routledge.

Mantie, Roger, Sarah Gulish, Greg McCandless, Ted Solis, and David Williams. 2017. "Creating Music Curricula of the Future." *College Music Symposium* 57: 1–9. https://doi.org/10.18177/sym.2017.57.fr.11357.

Mount, Andre. 2021. "Welcome." Accessed December 28, 2021. http://trainedear.net.

musictheory.net LLC. "Exercises." Accessed December 28, 2021. https://www.musictheory.net/exercises.

Puckette, Miller. Pure Data. V. 0-52.1. Miller Puckette. MacOS or Windows. 2021. http://msp.ucsd.edu/software.html.

Reason Studios. Reason. V. 12. Reason Studios. MacOS or Windows. 2021. https://www.reasonstudios.com.

Chapter 5

Sound Learning

The Pedagogical Pivots of Teaching Artists

Michelle Amosu Thomas, Michelle Mercier-De Shon, Patrick K. Freer, and Luiz Barcellos

They were alone. But they were together.

The ball was in play. His vision narrowed, and his focus became clear. The visual and auditory distractions of the crowd in the arena disappeared. He could clearly see his options. He was a single player, but his teammates depended on what he did next. He sensed his next move. He acted.

Music teachers acted much as basketball players when the COVID-19 pandemic focused attention on the young musicians in their care. They were suddenly alone, but they were together through pixelated images in little rows of video boxes on a computer screen. The ability to know how to proceed through uncertainty is akin to moments of heightened *court vision* in basketball, when a player can sense and understand everything within the boundaries of the court (Custodero 2002; Csikszentmihalyi 1991; "Magic Johnson's Court Vision" 2020). In an instant, distractions fade away, players know their purpose, they decide on the optimal action, they execute the needed play, and they advance the ball toward the goal. Music teachers were instantaneously called to do the same with the shift to virtual instruction. Much like NBA star LeBron James's character in the 2021 basketball-themed movie *Space Jam 2*, we replied to the shift with a version of his quote, "Chill out, man, you know I've got full court vision," to which his young protégé asked incredulously, "How does he do that?" This chapter explores how music teachers "did that," first by focusing their vision alone, and then by advancing toward the goal together with their colleagues and students.

The task of advancing music education, an endeavor associated with real-time group interaction, offered unique challenges to educators in a virtual world (Carrillo and Flores 2020). Music education has, at least partially, operated in the digital world for decades. But the COVID-19 pandemic forced music educators to pivot rapidly toward exclusive function in an online domain. As this chapter documents, what was initially perceived as a disruption became an opportunity for the discovery of new and advantageous opportunities in the professional work of music educators (Camlin and Lisboa 2021). We call this *pivoting*, from the basketball technique. The pivoting basketball player keeps one foot on the ground while turning to view new opportunities to advance the ball toward the goal. We found that we could similarly pivot, remaining true to our philosophies, goals, and objectives even as our pedagogy needed to shift directions. We eventually learned that the shift—the pivot—could enable music education to advance anew.

The contributors to this chapter are five Georgia State University music education doctoral students and our two faculty advisors.[1] Each of us is a practicing music educator. We guide the *Sound Learning* program, a collaboration between the Center for Educational Partnerships in Music at Georgia State University, several Atlanta area elementary schools (K–5), and local freelance performers, often referred to as "teaching artists" (Myers 2003). The focus of the *Sound Learning* program is the teaching artist-led integration of general classroom curricular subjects (e.g., social studies, math, science, reading, and music education). The program is an addition to the regular curricular work of the participating schools; it is not a replacement for any subject. However, the unique structure of *Sound Learning* provides students with musical experiences not otherwise available to them.

Working with, observing, and conversing with those charged with continuing *Sound Learning* afforded us a view toward how the pandemic pushed an already established music-focused collaboration to become a truly holistic educational experience. We witnessed the creativity of the visiting artists falter and then thrive anew during the pandemic as they approached the disruption with an optimistic perspective. They pushed themselves to discover innovative ways to create performance experiences for the students and found new ways to engage students through the computer screen and beyond. We observed and assisted as the visiting artists created digital musical content to be utilized from the safety of the students' homes. Classroom teachers told us how they adapted their own instructional styles to utilize the new music education approaches provided by these artists.

Though pandemic-era *Sound Learning* lacked the traditional exuberance of 40 or more students grouped in one room singing, dancing, and clapping, its replacement was 200 students seen individually in Zoom galleries, showcasing excitement and enjoyment as they sang, danced, and clapped in the comfort of their own homes. Students were free to be silly and engage in ways they might not when incurring the gaze of their peers during in-person sessions. We all delighted in the students feeling comfortable enough to share their musical experiences, opinions, talents, and questions in a way never experienced quite as freely in the face-to-face meetings.

Sound Learning's assessment artifacts traditionally included student worksheets and extensive binders filled with teacher-generated program documentation and evaluations of students. The pandemic-era reliance on technology allowed for discovery of how student learning could be evidenced through a variety of digital tools, including recorded archives of the sessions, chat logs, and a range of student work samples. Student work samples included questions asked directly of the teaching artists, reflections offered following the *Sound Learning* sessions, the performance of lyrics in rhythm, and responses to larger questions (the *Driving Questions*) that connected the multiple curricular areas addressed in the *Sound Learning* program.

The tale of how these teaching artists pivoted within the ever-changing circumstances of the pandemic is a powerful one. They experienced the loss of physical togetherness, and the lockdown-related isolation of being alone in their homes. Their *court vision* brought them together, with their students, through the experiences newly afforded by virtual platforms.

PANDEMIC-ERA PORTRAITS OF THREE TEACHING ARTISTS

Omarion: Expanding Possibilities

Omarion is a jazz saxophonist whose trio of musicians collaborated with the *Sound Learning* program for several years prior to the pandemic. Using his focus on jazz integration and his experience with music technology, he was able to easily transition the trio's pandemic-era *Sound Learning* experience to a virtual platform. Omarion saw that the pandemic offered some positive impact, particularly regarding the trio's extensive library of digital recorded content. He noted, "We had a digital library of various recordings ... of example tracks of the blues, the blues form, how to sing over it. We have all these different songs they can go back and listen to. There's other recorded examples from various albums and projects we've been on." Omarion's recorded content was extensive, and he granted teachers and students access to the library at any time. Teachers commented that they were able to bring this content into their lessons, including those outside of the *Sound Learning* program itself.

Omarion obviously did not experience traditional face-to-face interaction with students during his trio's *Sound Learning* lessons. Instead, Omarion reported that it was much easier to simultaneously interact with more students via the Zoom sessions and chats. We watched as students eagerly typed questions in the chat box and a member of the trio quickly responded. This was representative of the changes in engagement techniques exhibited by the

Sound Learning teaching artists. For example, they utilized the chat boxes to address students' questions rather than pausing the whole lesson. They also made use of the mute feature in Zoom to control background noise and disruptions. These changes, sometimes developed in response to an in-the-moment opportunity, highlighted a contrast in *Sound Learning*'s scope pre- and mid-pandemic. Before the pandemic, meeting space capacities limited *Sound Learning* sessions to two classes (groups) of students at a time. During the pandemic, the use of virtual platforms allowed teaching artists to simultaneously work with all students in an entire grade level.

An advantage unique to Omarion and his trio was access to the abundance of instruments and technology they had in their own homes and offices. We and the school children watched on our computer screens as the trio moved about their personal spaces demonstrating and performing with instruments they would not normally have during in-person sessions. "Each of us were in our own personal office recording studios where we have access to our wealth of instruments and technology . . . we just had access to our entire library of content of you know, of instruments. And that really diversified what we could show the students."

Omarion quickly noticed the level of comfort and openness the students exhibited in asking questions through the chat. He said, "they also might feel different, like maybe comfortable enough to just let me shoot a question here through the chat . . . it felt like almost every student was asking questions." Chat boxes exploded with questions and answers, including moments when students noticed someone else asking the same question and replying with "I wondered that too" in the chat.

> You're just cycling through questions . . . you can answer it right there in the chat, you're still moving along, you're still delivering content. And you can either address it to the whole group, you can address a question individually . . . students are so much more comfortable not having to vocalize with the intimidation of being surrounded by other students where they might feel judged or feel, you know, uncomfortable in that way.

By exploiting the affordances of technology to enter each other's home space, Omarion and his trio created uniquely personalized musical experiences. Students occasionally appeared more engaged when alone at home than with their classmates, showing a confidence about dancing and singing aloud in the familiarity of their homes. We watched older children, for whom peer pressure can be much stronger, clap, dance, and sing without obvious care, knowing there were just too many screens in the Zoom gallery to worry about someone focusing on them. Omarion acknowledged that online teaching afforded some surprising benefits through the linking of teaching artists and students in the familiarity of each other's home environment:

There's so much isolation, there's so much negativity associated with the general idea of this online format. But, you know, you're still right here, we're still talking to each other, we're laughing, we're having a good time, we're having this organic conversation together. We're learning from each other. All those things are still there, you're just not in the same room as me and that's okay . . . we can still make music together . . . if you're creative, if you have an open mind . . . you look at it with a positive attitude and a receptive attitude . . . it's all about working through, and realizing that what we get to is going to be greater because of that open communication and willingness to receive each other's ideas in that format.

Serenity: Spotlighting Every Voice

Serenity is one half of a folk duo that has been working with *Sound Learning* for many years. She is a teacher in an area school system and had to navigate the transition to virtual teaching and learning for a wide variety of teaching responsibilities. One of her main concerns was how to interact with larger groups of students on Zoom than would typically be present in a physical classroom. Serenity quickly discovered that the Zoom platform allowed her to spotlight students in new ways during teaching sessions. For example, one *Sound Learning* session focused on introductions to the guitar and violin played by the duo. Students who also had guitars in their homes were eager to share their personal instruments with their Zoom comrades. Serenity opened the scope of the lesson to incorporate and highlight these students' enthusiastic participation. Students appeared excited and eager to musically engage in ways they had not before the *Sound Learning* program moved to a virtual space. Serenity told us, "They're in their own little world. So, they're a little less conscientious of other kids. And that can be a good thing or a bad thing . . . their responses to some of the questions are going to be more authentic. They're not really being influenced by other students around them." Serenity also initially struggled with the idea of having the kids sing with her while muted. The students could hear her and her partner, but not each other. Singing in tandem was impossible on Zoom due to audio latency issues.

Serenity discovered new and innovative ways of collecting, showcasing, and assessing student work. One example emerged from a retooling of the songwriting project at the core of Serenity's pre-*pandemic Sound Learning* program. The project was an interactive student-led set of creative rote-learning activities, such as call & response and folk song practices, that culminated with the writing of a class song. Drawing on knowledge from other disciplines such as math, English, and science, students learned about music's fundamentals of pitch, rhythm, body movement, and different instruments. Serenity strove for "a low-pressure situation where it was really just about the joy and the pleasure of music" that encouraged students' creativity and activist power. One such example was the *Changemaker Song* activity in which students were encouraged to use music to express how they believed the world could be a better place.

Serenity began by exploring what was going to be possible with the songwriting project through the Zoom virtual platform. Students expressed an interest in writing a song about family separations at the geographic and political border between the United States and Mexico, a widely discussed current event at that time. Since students were also learning about folk music, the project took on characteristics of a folk-like protest song. Serenity's musical duo guided the children's initial ideas into the creation of an original song, partly by using student's words as typed into the Zoom chat box. Students seemed largely unafraid to share their opinions, dreams, aspirations, and ideas. The shift to virtual learning technology may have encouraged a freedom of expression not possible in the physical classroom.

The live Zoom sessions were recorded and replayed as guides for students as Serenity's songwriting project continued. The students created a collaborative set of lyrics and melody suggestions through Flipgrid, an education-focused website/app designed to facilitate video discussions. Serenity appreciated—and was a bit surprised at—the ability of technology to afford spaces for individual student participation:

> Every child had the opportunity to make something . . . in the past, you know, they would do it as a class, or . . . they would write their own individual lyrics, but only a few people would maybe get showcased . . . but we got to see everybody's content. I actually thought playing each child and watching their faces light up when we chose their video . . . was really special.

Finally, Serenity and her duo partner discovered new ways of assessing the students' learning. In the face-to-face *Sound Learning* experience, Serenity's songwriting venture was a collective one; that is, the group created one class song. Pandemic-era technology transformed the songwriting elements into a video-focused collage of individual student lyrics, instrumentation, and skill. Internet platforms like Google Slides, Flipgrid, and YouTube allowed for the final performance to spotlight both individual and communal creativity.

Harlem: Reaching beyond the Music Class

Harlem is a percussionist specializing in African drumming and world music. He is a seasoned visiting artist. Harlem, like the rest of our team, was skeptical about the community's ability to achieve a personable musical experience in an online environment. The disruption caused by COVID's emergence rattled Harlem, forcing him to adapt his home studio into one that could facilitate navigation of learning and musical artistry via Zoom and YouTube. As the weeks of Harlem's *Sound Learning* work progressed, we observed his triumph over perceived barriers to digital work and his subsequent discovery of new pedagogical techniques.

Harlem sees his entire life's work as focusing on human interaction. As he tells it, he doesn't just do drum circles, he does "people circles." He uses drums, body percussion, and human embodiment of rhythm to teach a host of related concepts. Harlem initially struggled without the human interaction so central to his teaching approach. His solution was to integrate engagement techniques drawn from African oral culture, where poetry, dance, and song are integrated into performance (Agawu 2003). Harlem reflected:

> It's not the same thing as being in the room together but . . . I have the ability to check in, you know. The Ghanaians do this in their teaching, they'll often go, "are you there?," "I'm here," "Are you with me?," "I'm here" and so I've been incorporating much more of that into the virtual world.

The move to a virtual platform forced Harlem to make focused use of the *checking-in* technique in ways he had not previously during his face-to-face sessions. This afforded Harlem the opportunity to purposefully connect with individual students during each session. He used this technique to both assess the in-the-moment effectiveness of his teaching methods and check for student understanding of the intended concepts.

Harlem's self-proclaimed technological deficiency made him apprehensive during the early days of pandemic-era virtual instruction. Harlem set about to record a collection of digital "small bits," as he called them. Each was a music learning video between three and five minutes in duration. The collection of "small bits" eventually grew into a vast online music lesson repository. Harlem organized them into sets of themed modules, with each module comprising six to eight activities or mini lessons. One module was called the "Rhythm Moment Series," with each video introducing various world percussion instruments through rhythm patterns that the students could use to play along with Harlem's musical examples. Each module was focused on concepts, skills, and elements related to social and emotional learning (e.g., mindfulness). The videos included opportunities for students to create, perform, and respond to music. In other examples, modules included "Pop Zing Boom" (focused on science and sound concepts), "Creativity Corner" (focused on creative processes in music), and "Rhythm-Mind" (focused on mindfulness, focus, perspective, and managing change). Despite longing for the face-to-face interactions, Harlem admitted,

> The pre-recorded stuff is probably a little bit more effective . . . because you can really control in small bits, the information . . . life can sometimes get a little wonky, you lose train of thought . . . *The Rhythm Moment* series encapsulates in three to five-minute videos, everything that I have ever done as a teaching artist in 18 years, more or less, in these small little bits . . . when things go live, I believe these pre-recorded lessons can still be very, very valuable.

Harlem's "small bits" were made freely accessible to students and teachers. As was also the case with Omarion's recorded content, students often referenced the digital content they had watched on their own or with their classroom teachers. Harlem designed a teacher guide for each module that included general curriculum connections, key concepts, vocabulary, discussion activities, and follow-up activities. Harlem reflected, for instance, that "The *Rhythm Moment* series has given teachers flexibility. What it's given the students is repetition. You need to hear that concept again? Let's watch it again. You really like that activity? Let's do it again." Harlem referenced the vocabulary taught in the small bits, repeated the concepts, and called on previously viewed video content when teaching the live Zoom lessons. Harlem gradually became more comfortable with the back-and-forth of building on the video repository he had created, seeing advantages to the incorporation of both asynchronous and synchronous material in his teaching.

If not for the disruption of the pandemic, it is unlikely that Harlem would have had the confidence necessary to attempt substantive musical pedagogy in a virtual medium. With Harlem's work at the center, the *Sound Learning* program has subsequently established a YouTube channel for general classroom and music teachers. The videos can be used in general classrooms anywhere with internet access, delivering authentic music instruction experiences to elementary school students and their school communities. By overcoming his aversion to digital technology, Harlem was able to create musical experiences for young students that "travel with them" far beyond their local classroom experiences.

FROM PERIL TO PIVOT: FOUR MUSICAL AND EDUCATIVE SHIFTS

We witnessed some powerful shifts in the work of our teaching artists during the pandemic's infancy. We watched as these educators wrestled with challenges to discover new ways of being with their students both musically and interactively. We focus here on four of the shifts, or pivots. The pivots afforded opportunities to rethink, resume, and revitalize advancement toward the program's educative and musical goals. Halting forward motion was unthinkable; pivoting had to occur. These pivots related to issues of scope and depth, place and proximity, equity and access, and individuality within communities of practice (Wenger 1998).

Pivot 1: From Ephemeron to Iteration

The work of teaching artists has been recognized as an essential component of music education since the early 1990s (Freer 2007; Kenny and Christophersen 2018; Myers 2003, 2005; Rabkin et al. 2011). The *Teaching Artist Journal* has, since 2003, led the field by generating related research and offering implications for practice. Four years earlier, in 1999, the *Sound Learning* program was established to bring the expertise of teaching artists to Atlanta city schools that lacked access to this type of authentic music education. Teaching artists annually became woven into the fabric of the school communities through countless hours of planning, multiple instructional sessions, and extensive professional development for school personnel. Still, the constraints of school schedules and classroom space occasionally forced the program's artists into parameters that limited both direct artist/student interaction and the possibility that a student's interest could be elaborated upon in meaningful ways.

That changed with the pandemic's onset. The teaching artists took advantage of Zoom's functionality to present for 150–175 students and their classroom teachers in each synchronous session. The three teaching artists created repositories of digital content that were used to extend the work as classroom teachers followed with supporting lessons and activities. Teams of *Sound Learning*'s teaching artists and coordinators worked with classroom teachers during professional development sessions to ensure that the program's concepts and skills were reinforced in ways that took advantage of pedagogy-specific apps, websites, and internet resources. In other words, the pivot toward technology-driven teaching and learning allowed the teaching artists to create and curate digital content that moved *Sound Learning* toward a more fully integrated component of daily school life than was previously imagined.

Commensurate with music education's pandemic-era shift toward reliance on digitally mediated interaction, the resource libraries of teaching artist-developed video, audio, and related content quickly became essential to the real-time classroom work of *Sound Learning* (Hash 2020). Yet, technology also allowed elements of *Sound Learning* to become steady fixtures in students' home environments after synchronous work had concluded. The pivot changed the student experience from a limited number of "*Sound Learning* visits" to an unlimited availability of touchpoints with musical content, with conceptual reinforcements, and with the sights, sounds, and words of the teaching artists themselves.

Pivot 2: From Collectivism to Individualism

Reliance on technology platforms transformed the fundamental mode of student participation in *Sound Learning* activities. Whereas earlier iterations of *Sound Learning* were characterized by teaching artist visits *for* groups of students, the virtual medium fostered the direct interaction of individual students *with* the teaching artists. This was seen through the immediacy of chat-based reflections and interjections during the synchronous lessons with teaching artists (Camlin and Lisboa 2021). Beyond simple reactions, however, we noted that students who had not previously been overt participants seemed to become enthusiastic contributors to the conversations and musical activities within *Sound Learning*. We sensed that students felt comfortable sharing as individuals in ways they were not when part of collective, in-person groups. We found that students eagerly sought digitally mediated connections with their peers. This was evidenced, for instance, as students embraced Zoom's *spotlight* feature to momentarily become the sole presenter, then returning to the group and inviting others to become spotlighted. Students did what they could to be collectively connected and individually honored, within the class group and in their private home spaces.

The shift to virtual instruction occurred approximately halfway through the year's planned schedule of *Sound Learning* programming. Our extensive video documentation allowed us to compare student modes of interaction before and after the shift. We noted that only the same few students actively participated during the pre-pandemic real-time, in-school sessions (i.e., by asking or answering questions, by singing, or by moving). We purposefully aimed to increase this level of participation during the period of virtual work as it unfolded. There were moments during the virtual lessons when we sensed that students might feel reluctant and/or vulnerable, such as when they were asked to sing, dance, move, or play instruments. In those instances, we quickly used Zoom's features to hide students' windows from each other, so that we (and the teaching artists) were the only people who could see the students; the students could not view each other. We glimpsed an authenticity of musical participation that we had previously spotted only on rare occasions. Almost every student participated, much to our surprise and delight. Students seemed free to sing with joy and dance with abandon when their peers could not see them (Mercier-De Shon 2012). Students later commented in written reflections that this was a highlight of their experience during COVID-prompted home lockdowns. They felt as though they were individually connected with their own personal teaching artist. The teaching artists responded in kind, particularly as they were able to review recordings of the sessions—with the full gallery of individual students—in preparation for subsequent sessions.

Pivot 3: From Isolation to Collaboration

Whereas the pandemic afforded us opportunities to newly see students as individuals separate from their classroom cohort, the same circumstances engendered previously unrealized collaborative relationships among and between the teaching artists, classroom teachers, and *Sound Learning* program coordinators. Teaching artists reported that they felt like partners in teaching with the school-based personnel and university-based coordinators. This differed from past years when the teaching artists were visitors and guests to the host classrooms. In this reimagined era of pandemic teaching and learning, *Sound Learning*'s teaching artists found themselves at the center of the classroom, with the schoolteachers and coordinators serving in supporting roles. This was uniquely empowering for the teaching artists, a pivot from working alone to working together.

It has long been recognized that an essential capacity for educators is the ability to develop and maintain facility with technology even as it continually morphs and changes. *Sound Learning*'s teaching artists quickly recognized and acted upon this need. As Bannerman and O'Leary (2021) stated in their prescient pre-pandemic writing, music educators need to "(a) recognize professional uses of technology and build skills that transcend passive consumption to include creative applications of music technology, and (b) view technology as an essential component of effective music learning experiences in K-12 schools (p. 20)."

We witnessed powerful teaching moments and supremely musical aesthetic experiences during the work of these teaching artists. The technology of the pandemic forced a uniquely narrow focus on *this* classroom, with *these* students, at *this* moment. The teaching artists later reported feeling more connected through technology than they imagined was possible when the transition to virtual learning began. The *Sound Learning* teaching artists quickly recognized how technology can bring anyone into a musically educative experience with little but a digital device, a camera, and an internet connection. The pedagogy required of these teaching artists flowed seamlessly forward from that realization.

Pivot 4: From Artifacts to Understandings

The digital platforms of COVID-19 era instruction expanded the options available to collect, assess and share student work. Students used Flipgrid, Google Slides, and YouTube to share their homemade instruments, wellness posters, and song lyrics. These platforms allowed the sharing of final products and enabled peer-to-peer mentorship of ongoing work. Classroom teachers communicated across the school community and with parents as they compiled collage-type videos documenting the development of student work over time. These teachers later commented that their students appreciated the opportunity to share without sensing a high-stakes assessment or risky emotional situation.

Assessment also moved forward in unexpected, formative ways. The ubiquity of digital documentation afforded *Sound Learning*'s *adults* the ability to ascertain the impact and effectiveness of our own work. Technology provided an immediacy of communication, certainly, but it also created possibilities for multiple people to make suggestions or revisit previous decisions without the laborious task of scheduling meetings. Everyone was in the same Zoom room at the same time. We found that the teaching artists not only could more readily join with us for planning and assessment purposes, but that they wanted to be active in those discussions. This was a change. Indeed, we sensed that *Sound Learning*'s leadership team desired the communication with each other perhaps more than did the students. Everyone seemed to be invested in turning a difficult situation into a positive one. This was assessment *for* learning, rather than assessment *of* learning . . . or, perhaps more accurately, assessment of teaching and planning for learning (Brown 2019; Shaw 2018, 40–42).

One of the final projects for Harlem's work was the creation of recycled material constructed musical instruments, showcased in Flipgrid videos highlighting the students' creations and demonstrations. The videos served to archive the children's demonstrations of creative thinking through the design of their home-made instruments. Student musicianship, expressivity, and emotional growth were highlighted in the recordings as they performed on their instrument creations. Instead of the 2D project photographs of large groups captured throughout *Sound Learning*'s first two decades, technology of the pandemic era yielded digitized documentation of individual students and their unique creativities.

For more than twenty years, *Sound Learning*'s leadership teams had collected voluminous amounts of artifacts purposed toward providing assessment data about student learning and programmatic strengths. The pandemic forced us to reconceptualize and prioritize the data we needed, the format in which it was collected, and the analytical lenses we used to make sense of that data. We had shifted our assessment emphasis toward what we had been hoping for all along: a pivot toward understanding what the artifacts were telling us.

LEARNING FROM THE PIVOTS

As we reflect on the four pivots—ephemeron to iteration, collectivism to individualism, isolation to collaboration, and artifacts to understanding —we now turn to our discoveries. What conclusions have we drawn from our navigation through these pivots? Our discussion is anchored in two metaphors. First, we turn to a musical metaphor found in the Sonny and Cher song as they sang "The Beat Goes On," relating this to our focus on maintaining pedagogical and artistic integrity in music teaching and learning. Second, we explore the metaphor of being "alone together" to represent the interpersonal and intrapersonal experiences and understandings gained during the pivots. Finally, we discuss the qualities of flexibility and synergy that emerged as critical to the resiliency of *Sound Learning*'s teaching artists.

Maintaining Pedagogical Integrity

Sonny and Cher's hit song "The Beat Goes On" could have been the ostinato that kept the *Sound Learning* program and the teaching artists moving forward. It quickly became clear that pivoting was necessary: rather than dwelling on what we were giving up, we needed to strategize how we could keep moving forward. The delivery medium changed, but the overarching goals did not. The teaching artists found new ways to *hear student voices* and they seized opportunities to place musicianship and aesthetic experiences at the center of their instruction.

Hearing Student Voices

The shift to virtual instruction resulted in an unusual dichotomy when considering how the teaching artists would hear and interact with students. Fears that the teaching artists would lose interactions with students proved unfounded. Both Omarion and Serenity noted a sense of increased capacity to access student responses, hearing their voices in new and unexpected ways. The chat feature of video conferencing platforms provided instant access to student comments, and other apps provided students with options for recording and sharing reflections asynchronously. The teaching artists sensed they were hearing from more individual students over the course of the residencies than were possible in traditional large, face-to-face sessions.

The resonance of student voices in the musical and educative experiences exceeded our expectations. Technology enabled students to extend their dialogue with the teaching artists beyond the live sessions. Students communicated with extended reflections about the music they'd heard, musical ideas and miniature compositions, and stories about music's role in the home and with their families. We still heard some of the typical questions (e.g., "how long have you been a musician? how much did your instrument cost?"), but we also heard detailed descriptions about how students would apply what they'd learned. We learned about the children through their tales of lived musical experience beyond the confines of school buildings.

We also recognize what we did not hear. We sorely missed students' active musical engagement through singing, body percussion, and instruments. Group music-making was a key component of *Sound Learning* visits before the pandemic. It was impossible to experience the innate joy of moving within a shared physical space with young "makers and takers" of music (Jorgensen 2003, 86). There is little that can substitute for live, face-to-face musical engagement. Indeed, we missed the sounds that young people create when given the opportunity to collaborate with teaching artists in a musically rich environment. Virtual technology allowed us to see students vocalizing, moving and jamming, but it was only on rare occasions that we could ask students to unmute their microphones so that we could hear their musicking.

The implications for music teacher education point to the importance of providing opportunities for individual student responses, acknowledging the numerous ways students can demonstrate their skills and understanding. We learned that providing multiple avenues for hearing student voices results in a rich tapestry, woven of threads representing complex understandings and a multitude of musical meanings. Simple, user-friendly digital tools offer options for students to develop responses when and where they feel comfortable, within the classroom or outside the school edifice. Virtual options may be empowering for students who may be reluctant to respond in large group settings. The use of open-ended assessment prompts in both formative and summative assessments hold potential to generate a range of student learning data, as we captured in process portfolios over the course of the year's *Sound Learning* projects. The value of learning about our students' individualities and their unique musical lives may help us better consider ways to provide spaces and opportunities for learning to flourish.

Quality Teaching in an Engaging Musical Experience

The learning goals for *Sound Learning* are collaborative in nature, based on musical and curricular needs, and negotiated anew each year with the visiting artist, the program coordinators, and classroom teachers. Each of the program's teaching artists approaches their residency work as musicians and performers first, then as artists who teach through music. Neither *Sound Learning*'s model of collaborative planning nor the types of learning goals changed during the pandemic. Rather, the challenges centered on meeting the goals while pivoting toward new, virtual delivery systems.

For instance, digitally mediated issues such as audio latency and sound quality are often detrimental to the presentation of live musical performances in the virtual realm. These types of issues caused the teaching artists to focus on their strengths rather than become consumed by their technological weaknesses. The teaching artists might have simply suggested the use of pre-recorded performances and fully asynchronous formats. However, each teaching artist realized that one of the most important components upon which the *Sound Learning* model is built—the interaction of young learners with outstanding community musicians—would be missing if they defaulted to recorded-only performances. Each of the teaching artists pivoted toward hybrid blending of synchronous (live) and asynchronous (recorded) content as they sought ways to retain musical and educative validity in their work.

Harlem presented perhaps the most vivid example of this pivot. At the onset of the disruption, Harlem was acutely affected by the lack of face-to-face human interaction that had been completely intertwined with his pedagogical practice. Instead, he re-focused on his teaching strengths, crystallizing his years of teaching experience into recording the "small bits" of asynchronous modules and reorganizing his home studio space to make it more compatible with virtual teaching. He realized the advantages of providing these "small bit" resources to teachers and students for continual re-listening and reinforcement of related concepts and skills. Harlem reaffirmed what he knew quality teaching to be: a give-and-take with learners through musical engagement, even if through video screens rather than in person. Harlem's experience became one of revitalized trust in the process and a personal reinvigoration of his teaching philosophy. Harlem also made a conscious decision to forgive himself of the imperfections inherent in teaching music virtually.

We are all—adults and children—limited by what we know and have experienced. Our facility with technology is contextually bounded by our direct experiences, and our ability to use technology will change as the technology itself changes. There is an ever-present learning curve. Like the teaching artists in our program, pre-service teachers may feel limited in their use of technologies even as they may be reluctant to voice those concerns (Dorfman, 2016).

It is also important to realize that technological glitches and snafus during virtual instruction occur, often at the most inopportune or unexpected times. In addition, not every form of musical engagement is possible in the virtual format, particularly that of live group singing. The production of *virtual choir*-style performance videos was not a realistic goal for the *Sound Learning* program. The teaching artists shifted away from product toward process. In songwriting projects, students were encouraged to engage within their individual parameters of comfort as they wrote lyrics, recorded performances at home, and offered ideas for group-created lyrics. Serenity noticed an increase in the number of students who seemed engaged; more students submitted digital work samples than when *Sound Learning* was an in-classroom experience.

We would be remiss were we not to acknowledge that issues of equity pervade the effort toward democratic education in the United States. The

COVID-19 pandemic converged with an outpouring of grief and related protests in response to the killings of George Floyd in Minneapolis, Breonna Taylor in Louisville, and importantly for *Sound Learning*, Ahmaud Arbery in Savannah and Rayshard Brooks in Atlanta. Those protests highlighted an array of societal tensions, including economic disparities evidenced in children's access to technology necessary for virtual learning. The school that hosted *Sound Learning* during this period had funding to provide students with digital devices. We recognize that other children were far less fortunate.

It would have been simple to assume that the processes of musical engagement could not continue in a virtual space. We found the drive to make music is ubiquitous, no matter with or without technological support. It would have been equally naïve to suggest that the process could continue but a culminating musical product would lack aesthetic merit. The implications for music teacher education center on confirmation that the process/product binary is pointless. Both process and product are essential to conceptual and skill-based education in music. The immediate goal for *Sound Learning*'s teaching artists was to maintain quality pedagogy and musicianship within an engaging musical experience. The teaching artists began by envisioning the musical/experiential product and worked backward to find the digital tools to support the learning process. Most teachers will begin with the process of learning and discover the musical product that awaits at the end. Our experience is that neither is more important than the other. They must coexist.

ALONE TOGETHER: FLEXIBILITY, COLLABORATION, RESILIENCE

"Alone Together" is defined in the online Urban Dictionary as "when you have such a strong emotional connection to someone that when you are alone or when you are feeling lonely, you know that the other person is feeling the same way." Though this definition was likely geared toward defining romantic relationships, it certainly resonates with how teachers and students experienced their personal connections when the disruption of the virtual shift became our new reality. The feeling of "alone together" in the virtual realm of teaching and learning was very real, as particularly captured in the teaching artists' pivot from isolation to collaboration. The teaching artists exhibited attributes of flexibility and synergy that allowed for the "alone togetherness" in *Sound Learning*'s pandemic-era work.

Flexibility is fundamental to how teaching artists navigate their careers, whether it be interpersonal adaptability or versatility in blending musicianship skills with teaching abilities. Teaching artists' contact time with teachers and students fluctuates since they are typically not permanent fixtures in the school. They must quickly and continually build relationships with members of the school community in ever-changing settings and with such unexpected disruptions as fire drills, last-minute schedule or room shifts, and snow days. Re-grouping and adjusting to these situations are norms in the careers of teaching artists. Flexibility is a necessity. Each *of Sound Learning*'s teaching artists was a master improviser of music: the jazz saxophonist Omarion, the pop singer/violinist Serenity, and the world percussionist Harlem. It is likely that the skills they developed as improvisers contributed to the flexibility they exhibited in their roles as teaching artists when the pandemic unfolded.

The implications for music teacher education are clear: flexibility is certainly a beneficial quality for any music educator. Rigidity may leave us struggling alone, flexibility may bring us together. Music educators spend a great deal of time and effort planning and preparing music instruction to meet the needs of each student. Even though we may see the same students daily and work to build relationships with them, we cannot always predict how they will "show up" to class. The pandemic-related disruption taught us that strict adherence to plans or rigidity will not always be workable options. Flexibility allowed these teaching artists to be resilient. They are reminders that flexibility can help us navigate within seemingly fixed working environments, curricular restrictions, and disruptions to our most carefully constructed plans.

One of the important features of the *Sound Learning* model is its collaborative planning with classroom teachers, music educators/faculty, and teaching artists. The intent behind this is that each professional has expertise to bring forward: a *synergy* of efforts in which the overall impact is greater than the sum of individual elements. Before the pandemic, the level of commitment from the collaboration's partners was often uneven. The shift to fully virtual instruction necessitated strengthened collaboration: it required a combining of everyone's thoughts and ideas to address the challenges. If one partner was less technologically savvy, for example, the urgency of the pandemic made it easier to lean on another partner to find a solution. Collaboration became an essential function—a working synergy—of *Sound Learning* in deeper and more meaningful ways than had been pre-pandemic.

Music educators tend to be physically isolated in school buildings and may approach their programs in an insular fashion, particularly at the elementary level where the music specialist may be the only music teacher in the building. Though a veteran music educator may thrive in such an environment, a teacher new to the field may instead need to experience being "alone together." This is the responsibility of the greater community of music teachers. School communities, much like music-making, are social and collaborative ventures. When a music teacher is alone, we must sense the aloneness and lift them, cooperatively, toward "together." If we learned nothing else from the pandemic, it was the need to work collaboratively in the face of challenges and in the solving of problems . . . alone, together.

NOTE

1. Research support was provided by Tom FitzStephens, Ira Jenkins, and Larry Robinson.

REFERENCES

Agawu, Kofi. 2003. *Representing African Music: Postcolonial Notes, Queries, Positions.* New York: Routledge.
Bannerman, Julie K., and Emmett J. O'Leary. 2012. "Digital Natives Unplugged: Challenging Assumptions of Preservice Music Educators' Technological Skills." *Journal of Music Teacher Education* 30, no. 2 (February): 10–23. https://doi.org/10.1177/1057083720951462.
Brown, Gavin T. L. 2019. "Is Assessment for Learning Really Assessment?" *Frontiers in Education* 4 (28 June). https://doi.org/10.3389/feduc.2019.00064.
Camlin, David A., and Tania Lisboa. 2021. "The Digital 'Turn' in Music Education." *Music Education Research* 23, no. 2: 129–138. https://doi.org/10.1080/14613808.2021.1908792.
Carrillo, Carmen, and Maria Assunção Flores. 2020. "COVID-19 and Teacher Education: A Literature Review of Online Teaching and Learning Practices." *European Journal of Teacher Education* 43, no. 4: 466–487. https://doi.org/10.1080/02619768.2020.1821184.
Csikszentmihalyi, Mihalyi. 1991. *Flow: The Psychology of Optimal Experience.* New York: Harper Perennial.
Custodero, Lori A. 2002. "Seeking Challenge, Finding Skill: Flow Experience and Music Education." *Arts Education Policy Review* 103, no. 3 (January/February): 3–9. https://doi.org/10.1080/10632910209600288.
Dorfman, Jay. 2016. "Exploring Models of Technology Integration into Music Teacher Preparation Programs." *Visions of Research in Music Education* 28, no. 1: article 6. https://opencommons.uconn.edu/vrme/vol28/iss1/6.
Freer, Patrick K. 2007. "Toward the Purposeful Engagement of Students with Artists." *Teaching Artist Journal* 5, no. 4: 269–278. https://doi.org/10.1080/15411790701577519.
Hash, Phillip M. 2020. "Remote Learning in School Bands during the COVID-19 Shutdown." *Journal of Research in Music Education* 68, no. 4 (January): 381–397. https://doi.org/10.1177/0022429420967008.
Jorgensen, Estelle R. 2003. *Transforming Music Education.* Bloomington, IN: Indiana University Press.
Kenny, Ailbhe, and Catharina Christophersen, eds. 2018. *Musician-Teacher Collaborations: Altering the Chord.* New York: Routledge.

"Magic Johnson's Court Vision Was Crazy," posted December 13, 2020 by Hoops. Accessed February 5, 2022, https://twitter.com/hoopmixonly/status/1338318302301577216.

Mercier-De Shon, Michelle L. 2012. ""Music is Waiting *for* You": The Lived Experience of Children's Musical Identity." PhD diss., Georgia State University.

Myers, David E. 2003. "Quest for Excellence: The Transforming Role of University-Community Collaboration in Music Teaching and Learning." *Arts Education Policy Review* 105, no. 1 (September/October): 5–12. https://doi.org/10.1080/10632910309600747.

Myers, David E. 2005. "Preparing Performers and Composers for Effective Educational Work with Children." *Arts Education Policy Review* 106, no. 6 (July/August): 31–38. https://doi.org/10.3200/AEPR.106.6.31-38.

Rabkin, Nick, Michael Reynolds, Eric Hedberg, and Justin Shelby. 2011. *Teaching Artists and the Future of Education: A Report of the Teaching Artist Research Project*. Chicago, IL: NORC at the University of Chicago.

Shaw, Brian P. 2018. *Music Assessment for Better Ensembles*. New York: Oxford University Press.

Wenger, Etienne. 1998. *Communities of Practice: Learning, Meaning, and Identity*. New York: Cambridge University Press.

In Dialogue

Letters Across the Pond

In this written correspondence, Dr. Marsha Baxter (New York University, United States) and Dr. Marie-Louise Bowe (Dublin City University, Ireland) share their discoveries and challenges while teaching during a pandemic and reflect on how this may impact music education. Both teach undergraduate and graduate music education majors and mentor emerging music teachers in their field placements.

NOVEMBER 5, 2021

Marie-Louise: What were your initial feelings of teaching during the pandemic?

Marsha: Well, I felt a certain degree of anxiety each time I clicked the "Start meeting" link mainly because in our virtual classrooms, I no longer had the subtle—and explicit—cues I rely on in face-to-face instruction. Also, my students were about to finish their degree program and would soon enter the field as music educators. I wondered whether virtual instruction would handicap their readiness to enter the field. They also voiced concerns about being ready for their emerging teacher internships.

Marie-Louise: Do you think, on reflection, that virtual instruction *handicapped* their readiness into the field?

Marsha: Not in the least! The work I'm observing by emerging teachers so far is exemplary.

And for you, Marie-Louise, how did you find the experience overall?

Marie-Louise: It was an emotional rollercoaster—weaving through the various stages associated with grief, for sure. There was the initial denial and despair, which festered in procrastination and overwhelm, followed by the particularly memorable angry/frustration stage due to my (very poor) juggle between domestic life, childcare, and *home-schooling*. During the classes, there were the usual cliché moments associated with zoom teaching—that visceral desperation and frustration—energy-sapping—not only in terms of content preparation but more significantly in relation to the sequencing of activities, requiring a level of visualization and technical flair of alchemic proportions! I recall my first class in September 2020, after an intense Summer of professional development with various fancy platforms and digital tools. I was overly focused on content delivery and presentation and had a blind panic moment, while fumbling to share one of the hundred tabs lined up. I was frazzled and disoriented and was forgetting that actual human beings were on the other side of the screen, probably just aching for a connection or just to be acknowledged. It was a good wake-up call to refocus.

Marsha: . . . and at the end of classes?

Marie-Louise: Some felt euphoric while others seemed anti-climactic. Pressing the *leave meeting* button and sitting in deafening silence felt strangely empty—which also bruised my sense of identity and purpose. The final classes of Spring 2021 were pretty poignant, tinged with teary sadness—more for my students, knowing they couldn't celebrate their final classes in college together, face to face. However, transcending all these feelings were some beautiful moments of pure, spine-tingling magic, beauty, and pride, especially when students shared their work, to the point one or two silent tears from my end.

So, generally speaking, some aspects of teaching online worked better than others, depending on the class size and cohort background, module duration and my level of autonomy in coordinating the module. For example, one particularly positive experience, which I want to share with you over the course of this dialogue, relates to a graduate module titled, *Teaching and Learning Music in Post-Primary School*. I had complete autonomy to (re)design this particular module. It had a small cohort of fourteen graduate students from diverse backgrounds and experiences and was spread across two semesters—fall 2020 and spring 2021.

Speaking of design, how much of your teaching changed?

Marsha: The design of my courses did not really shift in significant ways. However, teaching virtually reaffirmed my commitment to create a laboratory space, to better understand what it means to teach from a stance of critical pedagogy, cultural responsivity, and abolitionist Social Emotional Learning and to design curricula from those vantage points. Also, there's a lot of project-based instruction in my classes, an approach that works so well in both face-to-face and virtual environments.

However, Zoom teaching and learning were playing out in radically different ways here in the city where I was mentoring our university's emerging music teachers. In light of issues of equity and realities of digital poverty, teachers in the upper grades often taught music to screens populated with images of their students' ceilings!

So much of the work you and I do in our classrooms helps to instill community among our students. I often kick off the semester with an arts identity assignment from *You Got to Know Us: A Hopeful Model for Music Education in Urban Schools* (Martignetti et al. 2013). It's a beautiful strategy toward building a sense of connection. There is something so mutually affirming when students share their musical identities and histories through selected artwork that has personal resonance.

Marie-Louise: Yes, I get that. This type of mutual exchange was vital in fostering relationships. It not only gauged the emotional temperature of the class, but it also revealed an unforeseen richness I think, unrivaled in previous face-to-face classes particularly for the quieter, shyer voices. Online, we seemed more courageous and bolder to expose ourselves, veiled and cocooned perhaps, behind the safety of our screens . . . rebellious even, to challenge ideas and speak up. For example, whether it was responding to our *Soundtrack to Our Lives* playlist activity which involved me launching each class with their music, or reminiscing on our "musical river" autobiographical reflections (Burnard 2012), I feel we disclosed parts of ourselves, often unintentionally, with brutal honesty and authenticity.

NOVEMBER 22, 2021

Marsha: I'd like to circle back to your comment that you began each class with a student-created playlist. Did you sense that music became a catalyst to some of the personal sharing taking place?

Marie-Louise: Yes, their music served as a conduit to share associative memories, which helped to build connections and that rapport you speak about. For example, I'm reminded of the impromptu *aha* moments where mutual friends were identified—yes, Ireland is that small of a country! Conversations about overcoming adversity, like that of a student recounting the traumatizing impact of losing a finger spring to mind. Others spontaneously spoke to their anxieties, insecurities, hopes, fears, and sometimes their loneliness with some students often lingering around the zoom room at the end of class . . . just for the chats. I found peppering each class with such personal soundbites, narratives and reflections nurtured a sense of intimacy and trust amongst us making important clearings to truly listen and be heard.

Marsha: The space you created to "truly listen and be heard" so clearly speaks to the care you have for your students, Marie-Louise. Did you find your priorities changed when teaching in this new realm?

Marie-Louise: My priority was to find out who my students were and to make sure they were safe and well. My primary intention, thereafter, was to create a place for empathy, compassion, and belonging. Recently, I've discovered this gorgeous notion of an *affinity space*, (Gee 2005) which acknowledges and mediates *difference* in terms of knowledge and divergent thinking in a non-authoritarian/non-prejudiced way. In ways, this beautiful term crystallizes my ideals and aspirations for this module, which Susan O'Neill (2012) best describes as a place that offers a "variety of pathways to participation, informal mentorship and a shared sense of status in supporting each other's growth, artistry and creativity" (173). This resonates deeply with me, punctuating the humanistic need to confirm/affirm and accept the whole potentiality of the other. But of course, the reality is that often it didn't or couldn't happen for various reasons. I recall one particular student who literally sat in their car through the depths of winter, trying to access a public internet connection in a rural car park. Talk about ironic! Participation was a haphazard, exclusive endeavor, and so many remained disconnected and quite literally *outside* the experience. Can you recall where *dis/connection* was particularly felt?

Marsha: Well, I noticed how my students sought out connection through conversations in the *Chat* feature. Its role in our virtual classroom took me by surprise! Their commentary took on a beautiful spontaneity throughout our class. There were also moments of unfiltered banter, even hilarity. And humor is such great medicine in a pandemic!

There were cool things going on in our *Human Development in the Arts* class, often initiated and led by students. In an activity drawn from *The Expressive Body in Life, Art and Therapy* (Halprin 2018), a student guided us in identifying a *life script* around a wounded part of ourselves, and through creative writing, movement, and sound, bringing our redrafted narrative *onstage*. What a powerful moment!

I was also struck by poignant examples of curricular thinking and writing by my students that speak to the moment and tenor of our times, the emotionality of it all, the struggle for political, social, and personal freedoms taking place. Students chose to author projects around themes of belonging, connection, community, identity, and culture. They were pushing beyond traditional curricular norms.

Marie-Louise: Any other particular *standout* moments for you?

Marsha: I mentioned my dismay to observe so many students' ceilings in a Zoom music classroom, however, I also witnessed imaginative, agile collaborative teaching. One particular observation stands out: An emerging teacher and her elementary mentor teacher, like players in a doubles match on the tennis court, seamlessly *volleyed* instructional cues to their class. There was such a sense of flow—and over Zoom! This particular emerging teacher also created some knock-out instructional videos. So, a platform that I perceived to be somewhat cold and impersonal unleashed beautiful examples of ingenuity and creativity!

You mentioned a shift in course design earlier. Tell me more about that.

Marie-Louise: Absolutely. Here in Ireland, we've had significant curriculum reform in the lower levels of post-primary education (grades 7-9), bringing with it a move from a very prescriptive curriculum toward a broader, open-ended outcomes-based approach, including the use of classroom-based assessments. This means the teacher is now the curriculum maker and assessor with increased autonomy and freedom—a huge philosophical shift. The new music curriculum is particularly focused on creating, exploring, and participating and so, for me, this was a timely cadence to think deeper about what the module should or could be. Essentially, it nudged me to review the basic practices and music learning affordances for my students . . .

DECEMBER 18, 2021

Marsha: Marie-Louise, I have a follow-up question for you. Last time, you described the change in course design. I wonder now, what was the biggest aspect of your teaching that changed the most?

Marie-Louise: The intended purpose of modules fundamentally changed. I wanted students to compose and create their own music while building personal relationships to that music, for purposes of their own artistic expression. Making sense of themselves and their musical ecologies, to help towards identity construction was central. Therefore, experimentation, innovation, creativity, and collaboration were at the heart of the experience through the development of digital musicianship skills—not just within my students but myself. Timely, it seemed, only now I could legitimately embrace what Partti and Westerlund (2012) referred to as the "participatory/democratic revolution" (300) being made possible by digital virtual technologies.

Marsha: So, how did you approach this redesign? What did it look like in terms of assessment?

Marie-Louise: I found myself working backwards, aiming to widen the palette of hopefully more meaningful assessment options and modalities for my students. Being catapulted into this emergency online learning felt like the perfect time to stand away from the traditional summative, individual textual formats and get students experiencing more formative, participatory (paired assignments), multimodal assessment options (audio/text/visual, peer and self-assessment etc.). Yes, while I had tinkered with some of these elements before, now, I really focused on the use of E-portfolio-type submissions, as a way to collate student artifacts.

What struck me the most was the subtle impact that sharing privately (just with me) and publicly (with their peers) had, not only on the purpose of the assignments and on the development of student competencies, but on their motivations and commitment to the various challenges . . .

JANUARY 7, 2022

Marie-Louise: So, now, what aspects of the teaching are you happy to leave behind?

Marsha: As the pandemic rages on, and now with a third virus variant, we are living through a time of momentous political and racial unrest in the United States. So many artists called to action are creating works of such power, works that I'm bringing into our classroom. VIGIL, a video piece dedicated to Breonna Taylor by bass-baritone opera singer Davónes Tines, is one such example, also works by visual artists, like Kambui Olujimi's painting, *The 3rd Precinct Burns in Minneapolis.* Kambui, along with many others, created artworks as protests rose up throughout the United States and around the world in response to the senseless, brutal killing of a black man in Minneapolis. I love the way Toni Morrison reminds us that creativity is unstoppable, that "This is precisely the time when artists go to work" (Morrison 2015). Facilitating a process of healing in our arts classrooms, and in turn, our world seems more important than ever.

I've also been thinking a lot of bell hooks since her passing last week. For a while, I kept a copy of *Teaching to Transgress* on my nightstand. Her writings on education and love as a path to freedom, on what it means to care for another person, and Buddhist precepts of loving-kindness and compassion—she was a practicing Buddhist—inspire. They'll be ideals that I bring with me into the future and my work. What did you discover most from teaching over the course of the pandemic? What did your students teach you and what aspects of the teaching are you happy to leave behind?

Marie-Louise: While there's no denying the transformative discoveries and possibilities afforded by virtual technologies, nothing will replace the face-to-face communion of human connection and synergistic exchange to make and create music together, in real time. I'm more than happy to leave the zoom room behind me. However, I discovered the online teaching realm dismantled the traditional teacher/student hierarchy because we were all neophytes muddling through, learning in a *very* public way. This meant we had to be courageous to name and own our limitations and weaknesses and the mistakes that go along with them, bringing with it a heightened and welcome sense of vulnerability. Digging deep to accommodate the messiness of our (musical) stories too, owning our processes and having the courage to ask for help en route, was also integral. Because my students were so undeniably resilient throughout the experience—so patient, kind, respectful, generous, forgiving, hardworking—they taught me that the risk in making myself vulnerable was worth it. The genuine display of vulnerability was refreshingly symbiotic in nature as we needed each other . . . something I'll keep in mind more moving forwards.

Marsha: Your biggest takeaway from it all?

Marie-Louise: Ultimately, it would be that of *self-acceptance*. I often found myself revisiting Arthur Jersild's (1955) seminal book, *When Teachers Face Themselves*, during those online teaching moments when the sneaky gremlins of *imposter syndrome* lurked. Jersild reminds us that education should help children and adults know themselves and develop healthy attitudes of self-acceptance. Fueled by lingering ideals of perfectionism (often pertinent to classically trained musicians), it was brutally important for me to gently acknowledge yet silence these feelings throughout the process. Striving to model continued self-acceptance with compassion is my biggest takeaway, in the hope of nudging our students to be kind to themselves.

I think the Irish proverb, "You can't change the wind, but you can change the sails" best affirms the cliché that change and uncertainty are inevitable. Because music education seems to play constant catch-up with the unrelenting, tremendously paced music industry, teaching to reflect this reality has never been more crucial; and of course, enormously challenging, due to time limitations and an already overcrowded curriculum within our teacher education programs. Prioritizing the time to develop the necessary adaptive skills within our students, on top of the other gazillion competencies expected of music teachers while also keeping an eye on the integrity of the subject is a tricky balancing act. And that's not forgetting the issues surrounding potential burnout and the unquantifiable, often invisible energy needed to nurture and care for our students, from a humanistic point of view. Then of course, there's the willingness and fearlessness required to embrace change. But, as Miles Davis rightly reminds us in his Netflix documentary that I watched last night; "If anybody wants to keep creating, they have to be about change." Amen to this!

Marsha: For sure, it has been a moment to rediscover what is important to us as teachers, to interrogate the norms and values at the core of our pedagogy. I take inspiration from the conversations stirring within our classrooms. With a nod to Miles Davis, we as teachers and teacher educators need to dare to forge a future that does not replicate our past or present, one of new imaginings and possibilities. Just think what this might unleash!

REFERENCES

Burnard, Pamela. 2012. "Rethinking Creative Teaching and Teaching as Research: Mapping the Critical Phases that Mark Times of Change and Choosing as Learners and Teachers of Music." *Theory Into Practice* 51, no. 3: 167–178. https://doi.org/10.1080/00405841.2012.690312.

Gee, James P. 2005. "Semiotic Social Spaces and Affinity Spaces." In *Beyond Communities of Practice Language Power and Social Context*, edited by D. Barton, and K. Tusting, 214–232. Cambridge: Cambridge University Press.

Halprin, Daria. 2002. *The Expressive Body in Life, Art, and Therapy: Working with Movement, Metaphor and Meaning*. London: Jessica Kingsley Publishers.

Jersild, Arthur T. 1955. *When Teachers Face Themselves*. New York: Teachers College Press.

Martignetti, Frank, Brent C. Talbot, Matthew Clauhs, Timothy Hawkins, and Nasim Niknafs. 2013. "You Got To Know Us: A Hopeful Model for Music Education in Urban Schools." *Visions of Research in Music Education* 23, no. 1 (June). https://opencommons.uconn.edu/vrme/vol23/iss1/5.

Morrison, Toni. 2015. "No Place for Self-Pity, No Room for Fear." *The Nation*, March 23, 2015. https://www.thenation.com/article/archive/no-place-self-pity-no-room-fear.

O'Neill, Susan A. 2012. "Becoming a music learner: Towards a theory of transformative music engagement." *The Oxford Handbook of Music Education* 1, 163–186.

Partti, Heidi, and Heidi Westerlund. 2012. "Democratic Musical Learning: How the Participatory Revolution in New Media Challenges the Culture of Music Education." In *Sound Musicianship: Understanding the Crafts of Music*, edited by A. Brown, 300–312. Newcastle upon Tyne: Cambridge Scholars Publishing. https://www.researchgate.net/profile/Heidi-Partti/publication/262763656_Learning_from_cosmopolitan_digital_musicians_Identity_musicianship_and_changing_values_in_informal_music_communities/links/00b49538c5e9ded6cb000000/Learning-from-cosmopolitan-digital-musicians-Identity-musicianship-and-changing-values-in-informal-music-communities.pdf#page=181.

Part II

CULTURE, CARE, AND COMMUNITY HEARTHS

Chapter 6

Reclaiming the Musical Kauhale

Kanikapila and Mo'Olelo as Choral Curriculum

Jace Kaholokula Saplan

Hawai'i is a series of islands separated by water in the middle of the Pacific Ocean. While this is not earth-shattering information, I share Hawai'i's geographical positionality as a *series of islands* to illustrate a crucial concept that influenced how Hawai'i's choral classrooms approached the pandemic: in disconnected isolation or robust community, depending on how you engage with the concept of water and its place within a colonized or decolonized perspective. In other words, will we regard Hawai'i as islands separated by water, or connected by water? When the Hawai'i Department of Education announced extended school closures in the *Hawai'i DOE: Memos and Announcements* (accessed 2021), starting from March 15, 2020, until the inevitable decision to close schools until the end of the 2019–2020 school year, issues around lack of student access to technology and Wi-Fi and failure to implement culturally responsive virtual curricula for students throughout the state became abundantly clear. For example, in the fall of 2020, the Hawai'i DOE used the online program Acellus to provide distance learning for students. However, many Hawaiian cultural practitioners critiqued the inaccurate pronunciation of Hawaiian language terms and how the instruction of crucial moments of Hawai'i's history lacked representation and insight from the Native Hawaiian community. This program was discontinued due to the immense critique from Hawai'i's DOE parents, schools, and communities in October 2020.

Many of our K–12 learners, regardless of the island or population density, reside in multi-generational homes that can span up to four generations, which is especially true for our Kanaka Maoli (Native Hawaiian) learners (Wilson-Hokowhitu 2020, 117). This structure challenged many choral educators at Hawaiian language and culture-based charter schools at the onset of the pandemic as they sought to engage their Kanaka Maoli learners during times of social distancing and virtual instruction.

My positionality to the community of choral educators serving Hawaiian language and culture-based charter schools is directly tied to my professional and cultural identity. As the director of choral activities and the director of the Hawaiian music program for the University of Hawai'i, supporting our choral educators of Hawaiian language and culture-based charter schools through resource sharing, guided professional development, and community building is crucial to my role. As a kanaka 'ōiwi, or a Native Hawaiian whose lineage is tied to Hawai'i, I hold the Hawaiian value of kuleana or ancestral responsibility in high regard. My tūtū, my grandmother, spent her life as a music educator, a mentor, and as a performing musician in my hometown of Hilo. Our relationship was built on the carrying of this kuleana, and I have spent my life learning from her, taking on the lineage of knowledge to support my lāhui, the Native Hawaiian people.

Consequently, when the pandemic brought on school closures, my role as a music educator and cultural practitioner prompted me to ask a question that served as the guiding compass in supporting and coaching Hawaiian language and culture-based charter schools, and as the central hub of this chapter: How does one create a virtual choral curriculum that is culturally responsive to Hawai'i's host culture, and can engage students with limited access to technologies and limited space within Kanaka Maoli multi-generational living environments? I drew upon decolonial approaches framed in Native methodologies for multi-generational storytelling and song sharing that we call mo'olelo and kanikapila, respectively. These methodologies exist and thrive in multi-generational communities as the stories and song sharing require the presence of mo'okū'auhau or an individual's lineage (Wilson-Hokowhitu 2020, 118). Noting the limited access to western ideations of technology, I applied a decolonial view of digital artifacts, intervention, and resources to reframe a western gaze of what we consider as access. With this in mind, I positioned the curriculum to view our kūpuna, our elders, as the equivalent of a technological resource to ensure that all students could be allowed to develop their musical skills through a Hawaiian perspective. In responding to the challenges of the pandemic within our K–12 Kānaka Maoli choral community, I sought to assist choral educators in developing a curriculum that decolonized western perspectives of ensemble and drew repertoire from one's living community.

A DECOLONIAL APPROACH TO THE PANDEMIC

A guiding philosophy in Hawaiian culture–based education is to decolonize existing structures and curricula for K–12 learners. Beginning in the late eighteenth century, American colonization of the Hawaiian islands brought an entire curricular ecosystem of subjecting Native Hawaiian learners to educational practices incompatible with fundamental Indigenous beliefs. After centuries of low academic achievement and poor material-economic, social-emotional, and physical well-being, the 1970s brought an era that ignited a movement for Native Hawaiians to begin reclaiming their languages, traditions, and rituals. During this decade, Hawaiian educators also started to decolonize K–12 educational institutions that educated students in the Hawaiian language with a curriculum rooted in Hawaiian knowledge (Wilson and Kamanā 2001, 149). As Hawai'i continues to examine curricula responsible for educating Hawaiian language speakers and cultural practitioners, decolonization continues to be a driving force in Hawaiian language and culture-based education. Therefore, noting that decoloniality continues to be a driving force behind Hawaiian language and culture-based education, it was integral to continue the legacy of decolonization within creating the choral curriculum amidst the pandemic.

Initial curriculum planning for the choral students was guided by Hawaiian proverbs that are called 'Ōlelo No'eau. The planning took course with my initial design with continued conversations with K–12 educators through collaborative talkbacks and professional learning community environments for two weeks. Once finalized, I led three synchronous Zoom sessions around implementation. These proverbs, passed down from generation to generation, frame and articulate a Hawaiian worldview and root action in Hawaiian values. Therefore, many Hawaiian serving institutions select these proverbs to serve as integral guideposts in decolonizing institutional mission, vision, and curricula. Noting the institutional ties of choral educators and the population of learners, finding an 'Ōlelo No'eau to serve as an ancestral compass in crafting a curriculum for Kanaka Maoli learners in the pandemic was an essential step in my ideating and was rooted in the mentorship I received from kūpuna (elders) in my community. I was drawn to one particular proverb throughout this process:

> "He wa'a he moku, he moku he wa'a."
> A canoe is an island, an island is a canoe (Pukui and Varez 2018, 162).

This proverb seemed fitting because it provided ancestral insight to situate our conceptualization in decolonial thinking regarding a core concept within Hawai'i's geographical positionality. When the communities and lands you serve are located within a series of islands separated by a body of water, a fundamental divide between settler-colonial and decolonial perspectives arises. A potential settler-colonial perspective situates this phenomenon of water as an issue to be solved. The ocean becomes a boundary and a resource to manage and conquer to give all learners access to Wi-Fi and technological devices to engage with. However, several seemingly insurmountable barriers arise through this perspective, including the sheer number of students, the fact that most learners are situated in multi-generational households, issues around quality of Wi-Fi, differences in financial means to secure a technological device for each learner, and ensuring access to a designated space for study.

However, the proverb "He wa'a he moku, he moku he wa'a" situates the water between our islands not as a boundary but as a site of infinite connection. In Native contexts, water is the source of life, a revered deity, and an integral component in Hawaiian storytelling. Water is the center of the Hawaiian ecosystem, the site of wayfinding in the Pacific, and an infinite provider to the Hawaiian people. Water was the opposite of a boundary. Water was the answer. The result of planning within this decolonial headspace of water led to the idea that noting water's connection to the lineage of Polynesia—because of water—we as Hawaiians can draw our story of wayfinding to Kahiki, the origins of Polynesia, and therefore the entire world. The original approach to access operated from the premise that we were at a disadvantage because of how our islands were separated by water. However, if we operate from the Hawaiian understanding that we are infinitely connected because of our waters, as the waters are looked upon as a source of ancestral stories and genealogy, then access to an immersive educational experience was infinite throughout our islands. Our framing of the curriculum, then, must also be around lineage. Perhaps the answer was opening the western perspective of choir toward the decolonial perspective of communal vocal music, in which each household was to share the stories of their lineage through song sharing. Therefore, the household becomes a wa'a, a canoe of song, and the family's stories are the land and points of arrival. My role immediately became clear then: to provide the elders in the house with an asynchronous curriculum to help guide the family, to connect the households of Hawai'i together, and to offer resources and support as each household began a journey to sing together, share together, and reclaim their lineage. This proverb was our impetus to decolonize a curriculum to ensure all our learners received access to culturally responsive music education.

MO'OLELO AND KANIKAPILA AS CHORAL CURRICULUM

Communal vocal music is foundational to all Hawaiian language and culture-based charter schools. A Hawaiian choral class is flexible and broad.

Foundational concepts within the K-12 Hawaiian choral curriculum include song sharing, poetic analysis of ancestral songs and chant, pre- and post-western contact styles of singing, songwriting, and formal performances. Singing and sharing ancestral songs is a guiding learner outcome for all Hawaiian language and culture-based charter schools.

In the fall of 2020, following a summer of planning, families of 6th–12th grade choral students in Hawaiian language and culture-based charter schools were given access to a video accessible by Blu-ray, Vimeo link, and YouTube link. This video was divided into individual modules organized in the following way: (1) an introduction that outlined the scope and goals of the course, (2) a module outlining the role of the student, (3) a module outlining the role of the other members in the living environment, and (4) a module outlining the role of kūpuna (elders) of the house. Once these modules were viewed, each household was asked to dedicate an hour each week for moʻolelo and kanikapila situated on their own time. At the end of the quarter, each household was asked either through a pre-recorded video or a synchronous Zoom call within each respective institution hosted by the school's choral educator to share moʻolelo that the families discussed and perform selected songs they shared during their kanikapila sessions. The decision to prioritize moʻolelo and kanikapila as primary skills to foster within the choral curriculum was based upon how these two phenomena are situated upon crucial ancestral skills of storytelling and song sharing, which decolonized the colonial choral skills of western vocal technique and song analysis.

Moʻolelo, commonly translated as "a story" or "the act of storytelling," is the contraction of two Hawaiian words—moʻo, which is translated to "lineage" or a "sequence" and ʻōlelo or "talk." According to Hawaiian education experts Katherine Wurdeman-Thurston and Julie Kaomea (2015) "the idea of storytelling goes far more deeply; that is, moʻolelo serve as repositories of ancestral wisdom and a means for passing down cultural truths and values (426)." Ancestral wisdom is integral within a decolonial perspective as it actively decenters whiteness by honoring an elder's life, Hawaiian values, and legends while positioning these stories as a teacher.

Translated as "playing music together" and interpreted as an informal jam session, kanikapila similarly combines multiple Hawaiian words— kani (sound or noise), ka (the or a definite singular article), and pila (instrument). The practice of kanikapila in a decolonial sense is integral to sharing moʻolelo through mele (song). Kanikapila is an all-encompassing word, which can be used as a verb and a noun in a Hawaiian context. According to celebrated Hawaiian music educator, Kainani Kahaunaele (2020), "The kuleana and practice of mele in my household is essential. It's a training in mele language, 'ōlelo Hawai'i, perspective, creation, mo'olelo, and delivery (130)." Kanikapila is a practice through which people come together, share and sing songs, open themselves to the possibility of improvisatory harmony, and delve into flexible ways of instrumental accompaniment. I believed that kanikapila would be an effective, asynchronous, low technology, culturally responsive foundation of a choral curriculum to share and center mo'olelo, bringing households closer together through music.

The opening module of the course articulated an open-ended curriculum. Every week, households would come together to kanikapila for an hour with live instrumental accompaniment, pre-recorded accompaniment tracks, or a cappella. Each household was asked to record each kanikapila so that the families could have access to family history for future generations. They were not required to turn in these weekly recordings.

The student module was made for the individual enrolled in the chorus class. This module was separated into 30-minute sub-modules for each week of the quarter. The student was asked to watch one module each week before the family kanikapila. Each week contained an interactive lecture that discussed concepts around the development of musicianship, score analysis, poetic analysis, musical improvisation, and vocal technique. Each sub-module increased in detail and complexity throughout the quarter. As the students engaged with each skill, specific attention was spent on teaching the skills the student learned to family members. This idea of an immediate connection between learning content and teaching content centers in on another 'ōlelo no'eau:

> "E lawe i ke a'o mālamama, a e 'oi mau ka na'auao."
> They who take their teachings and apply them increase
> their knowledge (Pukui and Varez 2018, 171).

The idea of positioning the child as both student and teacher is a driving concept in Hawaiian culture-based education. Therefore, positioning the student as a resource for building skills in kanikapila for the family was an intentional act to build upon the student's skills through the preservation of mo'olelo. Students were called upon as teachers, or kumu, in this pandemic, as an extension of the legacy of their kumu, the choral educator who was supporting their leadership from afar.

The module for other house members outlined their role in being active members of the weekly kanikapila session. This level of involvement was a familiar concept as the entire household was asked every week to attend a monthly meeting to discuss the progress of the child enrolled in the school. Members were asked to reflect on the following 'ōlelo no'eau:

"E lauhoe mai na wa`a; i ke ka, i ka hoe; i ka hoe, i ke ka; pae aku i ka `aina." Paddle together, bail, paddle; paddle, bail; paddle towards the land (Pukui and Varez 2018, 181).

As family members reflected on the 'ōlelo no'eau, we stressed in the module that regardless of their musical skills, they are essential to the kanikapila process and in supporting the choral learner in the house. Members were told that this was not necessarily a choral rehearsal but rather a way to bring the house together, share stories, and sing in connection to the stories discussed. We ended the module by stating that this work is not about judgment and critique, but about bringing the 'ohana (family) together through ancestral song.

Kūpuna Wisdom as Technology

The role of kūpuna within the education of a child, within the context of a family, and within the decolonization of a people is integral. Defined by Hawaiian language expert Mary Kawena Pukui (2018) as an "elder, a source, or a starting point (190)," kūpuna can be many things within a family. We were intentional in articulating this sentiment within the module. Depending on the household members, kūpuna can take the form of grandparents, parents, guardians, aunts, uncles, and elder siblings. From a Hawaiian perspective, the kūpuna are crucial starting points to family memories, traditions, and mo'olelo that shape and lead the household.

Noting the limited support in providing Wi-Fi and technological devices for all households during the pandemic, it was essential to decolonize how we interpreted technology. Hawaiian thinking propelled us to view the kūpuna as a technological resource that all of our students could access. In the absence of internet access, there were stories and songs of grandmother's childhood; in the absence of a laptop, there was a parent's wisdom told through melody; and in the absence of a choral rehearsal, there was kanikapila led by kūpuna. Consequently, our curriculum was led with the understanding of the kūpuna wisdom as a treasured technological resource. The kūpuna of the household would be the navigator of the curriculum. Each member of the household would kanikapila as the choral students taught the household the concepts they were learning in their sub-modules using the kupun's repertoire of the kanikapila.

The kūpuna of the house would be responsible for scheduling and overseeing the kanikapila as well as supporting the choral student when they taught the concepts from their sub-module. The kūpuna would also be responsible for selecting the repertoire of mele and introducing the mele with particular mo'olelo that connect the mele to their personal lives, the lives of the family, or the stories of Hawaiian history. The module provided assistance in prompting the kūpuna in programming the mele and moʻolelo for the household kanikapila. Therefore, we encouraged the kūpuna to reflect on these questions:

- For programming mele
  - What are mele that hold significance to the ʻāina (land) of your ʻohana (family)?
  - What are mele that hold special memories in your upbringing?
  - What are mele that hold special memories associated with the people in your household?
  - What are mele that hold special memories of family members that the members in your household may not know?
  - What are mele connected to ancestral legends that you connect with personally?
- For moʻolelo and kanikapila
  - How can the moʻolelo and kanikapila connect the concepts the choral student will be teaching?
  - Is there a way to incorporate Hawaiian values and the values or mission of my student's school through the mele I program and the moʻolelo I tell?
  - Is there a way to build confidence and pilina (connections) among the members of our household within the kanikapila session through my moʻolelo?

The module also discussed considerations of finding a suitable background for the household for the performance, scheduling and running a dress rehearsal with the household, and coaching the choral student on introducing the pieces on behalf of the household for the performance. The nature of the performance was entirely up to the household. Finally, the module also provided kūpuna with instructions and guidance on how to select and prepare repertoire from the kanikapila sessions to share for the live performance or previously recorded performance for the school hōʻike. The results were often very powerful. For example, one particular family consisted of a 6th-grade student whose household consisted of their grandmother and father who all sang a traditional song called *Pua Sakura*. They shared that this song was special to them because it honored the sakura flower and wove elements of Japanese culture and Hawaiian poetics in the Hawaiian language. They recently lost their mother to COVID who was residing in Japan, and this song was a way to honor her life.

Kākoʻo: The New Role of Choral Educator

With most of the curriculum housed within the family or household, the role of the choral educator or school needed to be redefined throughout the quarter, as most of their instruction and planning was done in crafting the asynchronous modules. Recognizing that the system of institutional schooling is a colonial idea, the role and concept of a teacher within that framework are contextualized through colonization. Because the institution or school as a site of education was no longer part of a student's learning and the learning happened instead in the household community led by the elder, we had an opportunity to reframe the teacher within our decolonial ideation as a kākoʻo.

Translated as a "supporter" or "assistant", kākoʻo in a Hawaiian community are content area specialists who use their skills to support the unique needs of each household or individual. Kākoʻo are known to consult, check in, lead small group interventions, and coordinate activities that support the learning of the household (Pukui and Varez 2018, 35). These roles are ones that students and teachers take on often in a Native learning environment. During a time of social distancing, this was still possible. However, our kākoʻo needed to be flexible in how they communicated to each ʻohana. Depending on the house, the kākoʻo supported one household with conversations over a house phone and others households on Zoom; some households even invited the kākoʻo to their kanikapila by having the kanikapila outside, socially distanced, and masked. In the absence of weekly synchronous instruction, the kākoʻo became an instructional coach supporting the unique needs of each kākoʻo and household involved in the school's program.

KAUHALE: A RADICAL FUTURE FOR HAWAIʻI'S CHORAL PROGRAMS

A kauhale is an organizational structure of how Hawaiians lived before western contact. Defined as a village, a kauhale consisted of a community organized in a way that actualized each community member's skills, knowledge, and experiences toward the running of a thriving community. As I reflect on the experiences and successes of the curriculum created for our Hawaiian language and culture-based charter schools here in our islands, the idea of kauhale will remain in our work as we transition toward in-person learning. For when we teach in a kauhale in a Hawaiian context, lineage and land must be at the center from which we build. When we teach with lineage and land in mind, we give students the opportunity to form right relationships with their identities and surroundings and use these components toward building community while honoring the nuance of the collective whole. As I move forward with my practice in working with my community of K–12 educators and undergraduate and graduate students in choral conducting and choral music education, land and lineage will be at the heart of our practice.

A crucial takeaway in the reflection of the choral educators who facilitated this curriculum was the impact of well-being. As I led a reflection on Zoom among the kākoʻo, there was a consensus on how we engage with the role of kūpuna and families in the music-making process going forward. Kāko'o suggested, for example, continuing to program and rehearse repertoire connected to the lives of the kūpuna in the program, and inviting them to share mo'olelo as they transition to in-person learning. Kāko'o also discussed the concept of re-thinking practice or homework as applying the skills and concepts learned in rehearsal to teach to their household using a mele of their choice in coordination with the kūpuna, amplifying the concept of kauhale and moving away from a repertoire-to-performance approach. Finally, they had the idea of rethinking the hō'ike or performance to follow a model that included prepared pieces by the choir, prepared pieces from family or household ensembles, and a group kanikapila led by several elders of the choral students' families to which the entire school is invited, amplifying the idea of kauhale for an entire school community.

I end with a mo'olelo. Hawai'i is no stranger to pandemics. In the late 1800s, Queen Lili'uokalani, Hawai'i's last monarch before the wrongful occupation of the United States and prolific musician and composer in her own right, led her kingdom through the smallpox epidemic that wiped out 10 percent of the Native Hawaiian population. Her solutions in ending community spread were mirrored over a century later in the choices of our state and national leadership during the COVID-19 pandemic: inter-island travel was banned and a quarantine was put in place. However, one idea struck me that I did not come across until after the employment of our choral curriculum during the pandemic. Queen Lili'uokalani tasked each house to continue singing in their homes led by the elders of the house so that the youth could continue musicking (Kauanoe 2020). This information was incredibly affirming, noting that the goal to reach as many students as we could throughout each island had roots in the past. It was a reminder and an affirmation that the 'ōlelo no'eau that drove our planning, "He wa'a he moku, he moku he wa'a" (Pukui and Varez 2018, 2016), continues to guide us. Our curriculum was a way to guide our students back to their kūpuna, to center kūpuna as an island. Our curriculum, through making our work in educating the choral students of Hawai'i's future culturally responsive, decolonial, and a radical act of healing through music, was also a way to guide our choral programs back to our mo'olelo—and unknowingly back to the wisdom of our Queen.

REFERENCES

"Hawaii DOE: Memos & Announcements." Hawaii DOE Memos & Announcements. Accessed July 5, 2021. https://www.hawaiipublicschools.org/ConnectWithUs/MediaRoom/PressReleases/Pages/HIDOE-COVID-19-Memos-Guidance.aspx.

Kahaunaele, Kainani. 2020. "The Value of Mele." In *The Value of Hawai'i3: Hulihia, the Turning*, edited by Goodyear-Ka'ōpua Noelani, Howes Craig, Osorio Jonathan Kay Kamakawiwo'ole, and Yamashiro Aiko, 127–130. Honolulu, HI: University of Hawai'i Press.

Kauanoe, Ku'u. 2020. "What We Can Learn From Hawai'i's Past Pandemics." In *Civil Beat*. Accessed July 6, 2022, https://www.civilbeat.org/2020/11/what-we-can-learn-from-hawaiis-past-pandemics/.

Pukui, Mary Kawena, and Dietrich Varez. 2018. *'Ōlelo No'eau: Hawaiian Proverbs & Poetical Sayings*. Honolulu, HI: Bishop Museum Press.

Wilson, William H., and Kauanoe Kamanā. 2001. "'Mai Loko Mai O Ka 'I'Ini: Proceeding from a Dream.'" In *The Green Book of Language Revitalization in Practice*, 147–176. https://doi.org/10.1016/b978-012349353-8/50020-0.

Wilson-Hokowhitu, Nālani. 2020. "Colours of Creation." In *Routledge Handbook of Critical Indigenous Studies*, 114–128. https://doi.org/10.4324/9780429440229-11.

Wurdeman-Thurston, Katherine, and Julie Kaomea. 2015. "Fostering Culturally Relevant Literacy Instruction: Lessons from a Native Hawaiian Classroom." *Language Arts* 92, no. 6: 424–435.

Chapter 7

The Playlist Project

Exploring Culturally Responsive Practices through Online Learning

Tamara T. Thies

We had just begun working with foundations of culturally responsive teaching in our upper-division Introduction to Teaching Music course during the fall 2020 semester when a very thoughtful student connected his own large ensemble experiences: "I feel I'm a part of the group, but I don't feel seen"—a comment so clear and, simultaneously, jarring.

... *I don't feel seen.*

Several heads in the little Zoom windows bounced up and down with this comment. It opened a larger conversation that led students to consider their own experiences in differing musical settings. While students enjoyed making music with "like-minded" people who promoted a sense of belonging and community (Kokotsaki and Hallam 2007), several individuals described acculturating to the norms of the European large ensemble setting which is most often grounded in the Western canon and practices. Story after story indicated that differing styles and ways of knowing diminished and, at times, segregated individuals from their personal identities.

... *I don't feel seen.*

While these conversations spotlighted in-person experiences, I quickly turned my attention to our online learning platform. How was I going to navigate learning engagement in a mode of muted faces in boxes which were, literally, not seen at times? With the sudden transition to online classes in March 2020, several students indicated that their initial online learning experiences were negative. They fundamentally lost their "conventional" version (Turner 1978) of their college student identities (Collier 2000, 2001) with this forced transition to an online platform, and they needed to establish a new student identity; otherwise, they could and would simply turn off their cameras.

. . . I don't feel seen.

Like several of my colleagues, I spent the summer learning techniques and skills to develop and engage students online from several different perspectives, but I quickly noticed that the individuals guiding these sessions taught courses grounded in reading, writing, and speaking that more easily transferred to online platforms. When I requested alternative ways to engage students beyond the ways that worked for these content-area instructors, one individual instructor told me that she just provided the information and I needed to figure out how to use it in my area.

. . . I don't feel seen.

As opposed to becoming discouraged, I was still excited about the creative possibilities to teach and learn through an online platform. Because most of the courses I teach are grounded in implementing pedagogical practices, redefining the in-person expectations of these courses into meaningful online learning challenged the students practically and philosophically, especially students taking Instrumental Methods and Literature courses that I taught. These courses are historically grounded in the Northern European cultural framework (Chávez, Ke, and Herrera 2012; Ibarra 2001; Rendón 2009) that focuses on the skills and strategies for a director to rehearse large ensembles. This European framework often marginalizes the unique cultural complexities every individual brings into a classroom . . . including the instructor.

. . . I don't feel seen.

The monocultural learning environment in academia alongside students fractured college identities due to the online learning paradigm shift created a need for students to develop another identity in order to establish some stability and familiarity. Navigating student expectations alongside a platform that was not conducive to particular skill sets proved to be more challenging than I expected. In this chapter, I explore how teaching preservice instrumental music educators, in Instrumental Methods and Literature I, forced me to deepen my culturally responsive practices, teach across cultures, and assist students in identifying and developing the complex layers of their own identities.

Tapping into Cultural Responsiveness

> "I'm a work in progress . . . I've never arrived . . . I'm still learning all the time."
>
> Renée Fleming

As a music teacher educator, I strive to guide each preservice music educator's transition to their own, individualized teaching identity. This means students explore their own values, beliefs, customs, and actions as learned through their own intersecting identities (e.g., race, ethnicity, gender, religion) and how these cultural underpinnings intersect with their future students. Pedagogies grounded in cultural responsiveness assist in guiding preservice teachers to integrate their own identity with the content of teaching music. That said, guiding each student is a challenge in a face-to-face setting, but guiding students into their own identities through an online platform poses an even greater challenge.

The forced shift to online learning impacted how music students interacted with me and course content as well as challenged students' transitions to becoming independent, critical and creative thinkers and implementers (Hammond 2015)—a pillar of culturally responsive practices (Ladson-Billings 1994, 1995). Students more easily tackled challenging learning tasks during in-person settings than through the online platform. During the first fall 2020 class of Instrumental Methods and Literature, several students shared that their initial online learning experiences in spring 2020 were fully lecture-based with little input or direction from students. As I observed the little windows with visible and invisible faces, I realized that these initial experiences set their expectations for online learning which added another layer of difficulty to guide students. How was I going to guide preservice teachers toward becoming independent learners when students' previous experiences determined that the professor provides all the information and students fundamentally reproduce the information for a grade?

I also realized how much I depended on in-person social interactions and body language of students to guide my scaffolding with students' progress. Because I was an introverted student, I rarely volunteered answers nor liked being called upon to answer a question; however, I was always fully engaged in learning and rarely missed a detail. I believe all students learn in different ways, and I do not expect every student to answer a verbal question or provide comments in a discussion if this is not their way of learning; therefore, I read body language. This was more than challenging in an online platform, especially with students who had their cameras off. While I provided opportunities to respond to prompts in the chat, used breakout rooms for small group discussions and discovery, and attempted to provide a safe platform to share without judgment, I found it difficult to navigate the pacing of online learning when silence penetrated what is normally my active, engaged, and creative in-person environment.

After several missteps in online teaching during the first semester, I was grateful to have a second semester with the same set of students to redevelop the online experience. Needless to say, I fundamentally abandoned the written and unwritten traditions and expectations higher education imposes on teaching students and student learning in favor of grounding students' online experiences, projects, and learning styles in their current settings and cultural underpinnings. To do this, I had to learn and get to know my students in different ways that altered my own ways of interacting with students.

   . . . *I am a work in progress.*

Student Class Portrait

Cultural responsiveness is often related to student backgrounds and interests when we are designing assignments, but I needed to be fully present to understand the students' needs during this virtual time of learning. Knowing that there were eight female and ten male students in the class or that seven students identify as Hispanic, two as Asian, and nine as white, Western European only provides a small demographic window into their lives. The online component they were adding to their individual lists of cultural identifiers was missing.

   Almost all students in my class were on some form of scholarship or financial assistance in order to attend the university. This financial assistance generally did not cover living expenses, so most students taught lessons or worked at least one additional job to make ends meet each month. For example, one of these students worked night shifts at Amazon and attended classes during the day so they could purchase a computer . . . a necessity for online learning and recording/mixing music for classes. Another student would start class from their car coming back from their job then switch to the computer at home when they arrived. Commitment to attending class was not an issue but adapting to students' needs became a priority.

   The time our class met posed issues for several students. Because the Instrumental Methods and Literature II course was scheduled and taught on Tuesday evenings from 7:00–9:45 p.m., students shared that they would disturb family members if they played their instruments. One individual shared that this was the time his father slept since he worked a night shift. Another student indicated their younger siblings would be in bed. Those living in apartment complexes expressed concerns that they could be cited or evicted for noise violations if they played their instruments in the evenings. To respect their settings, I redesigned several projects in the course.

   Due to living expenses, most students' learning environments were in their childhood homes. Finding a space to focus was difficult for several students. One student spoke of sharing their room with two other siblings while their siblings were online at the same time. Another student shared that their family divided the apartment into sections in which they rotated based on their needs (e.g., the closet was for practicing, one room was for attending class, and outside the bathroom door was another place to take meetings). One first-generation college student indicated they set up their camper and locked the door for their learning space; otherwise, their family would constantly interrupt, and the student would not have a possibility to focus. Realizing the differing issues and environments from which these students were attending class, collaborating, developing projects, and internalizing learning was a fundamental turning point for me.

... *I am a work in progress.*

Using a redesigned, pre-pandemic assignment as a project framework, I will describe the changes I implemented using student input and realizations that freed our learning environment for students to become independent, critical, and creative thinkers and implementers who experience and embrace culturally responsive practices.

THE PLAYLIST PROJECT

Music literature drives the curriculum for music instruction in large ensemble band and orchestra settings; it is common to engage preservice teachers in this topic through discussions and projects in undergraduate instrumental methods courses. My approach to the topic of music literature selection is a discovery-based learning project where students explore scores of band and orchestra literature that are considered *the standards*, compositions written by historically underrepresented composers, and large ensemble compositions of personal choice that they like or would like to perform with their future ensembles. *The standards* expose students to traditions, compositions written by historically underrepresented individuals are intended to expand their curricular platforms, and compositions they like inform personal preference. When forced into online learning, student access to scores became significantly limited; therefore, I shifted the approach from score study to analysis through listening; hence, the music literature project transformed into *The Playlist Project*.

This project unfolded organically as I set the environment for students to discover their own tendencies, and often, their own biases when selecting music literature. Initially I introduced *The Playlist Project* outlining a process for selecting music literature that required students to reflect on their choices. Second, I supported their personal selection process through mini-lessons that required students to question, compare, and analyze music literature during class while I implemented strategies so every voice had an opportunity to be validated. Finally, I opened opportunities for students to share their projects in a manner that reflected their own choices and personalities. *The Playlist Project* and process is fully grounded in student discovery of their own progress in culturally responsive practices.

114   Tamara T. Thies

To begin the project, preservice teachers choose a total of fifteen compositions they believe their students should experience in their own future band or orchestra programs—five compositions from *Standard Band/Orchestra Repertoire*, five compositions written by *Composers from Historically Underrepresented Populations*, and five compositions of *Personal Choice*. In addition to the title, composer/arranger, difficulty level, and instrumentation of each composition, students aurally analyzed each composition for compositional benefits (how the composer manipulated musical elements to create interest) and technical benefits (instrument-specific challenges and techniques needed by young musicians) that drive the teaching of musical content.

After students choose their top five compositions for each category, they analyze their choices to write a reflection for each category and answer the question, "How does your analysis of your selections relate to your past learning experiences, content, life experiences, and future goals?" (figure 7.2). The culminating question, "What have you learned about yourself, your personal teaching philosophy, and your future goals through this format of music literature selection?" reveals each preservice teacher's priorities and values, cultural competence to assist in developing positive ethnic and social identities, and critical consciousness to recognize and critique societal inequities and challenge the status quo (Ladson-Billings 1994).

Student feedback in the first semester revealed that the students developed more thoughtful submissions and content when I presented information in multiple ways as well as offered choices throughout projects. Figure 7.1 offers a glimpse into how I visually engaged and grabbed students' attention

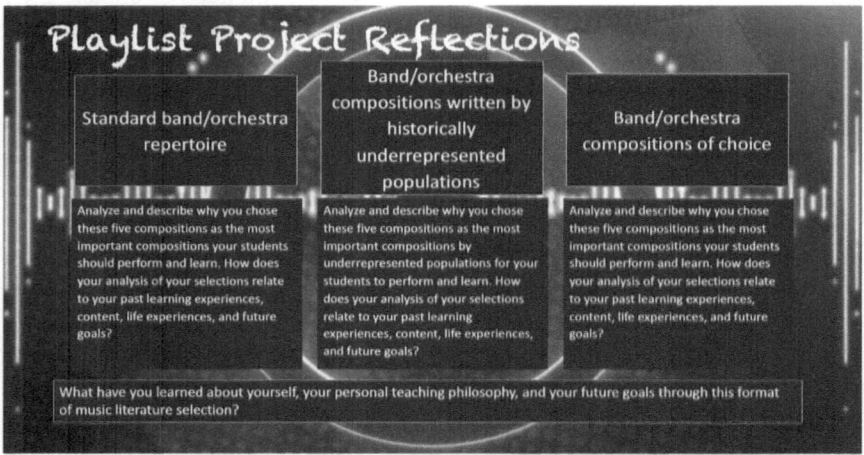

Figure 7.1   PowerPoint Slide Outlining Playlist Project Reflection Expectations.

to bring them into the learning environment. The more thought and creativity I used to present content, the more students appeared to be meaningfully involved with the content.

Each iteration of this project reveals how undergraduate preservice teachers engage with the challenges that accompany an ever-changing society and how these challenges impact their priorities as future music educators. Rewind to 2018, and most submissions from students' initial engagement with this project focused on compositional content followed by cursory reflections that brushed the edges of the questions. These instrumental students appeared fearful to share themselves or provide insights into how the project impacted their priorities as music educators. Fast forward to spring 2021, and instrumental music education students seemed open to self-analysis and willing to share their personal discoveries within the context of this project. While I am continuously finding ways to integrate culturally responsive practices into my own teaching and learning, the online learning platform forced me to adapt in ways that I may not have attempted or experienced.

... *I am a work in progress*

WEAVING A CULTURALLY RESPONSIVE TAPESTRY

Students' learning environments and their sharing of online experiences were a driving force for adaptations I embraced and implemented during the second semester of online learning. By the spring semester of 2021, several normally positive, energetic, and engaged students appeared exhausted and depleted in their little boxes on the screen. As I checked in with them, students shared that almost every class was requiring significantly more graded writing within and outside of classes. Students were writing more papers, weekly discussion boards, and weekly responses to peers with little engagement outside of this way of knowing. Realizing that these students tend to express themselves more naturally through music making, I was determined to engage students in learning opportunities that offered alternatives to writing that included recorded discussions via Zoom, partner interviews based on readings, individual verbal (and sometimes pictorial) reflections, and student choice. Once students engaged with several alternative ways to share their learning, I opened the possibility for students to determine how they wanted to share their learning. By reframing online barriers and addressing an overused format related to online instruction into opportunities, I opened a more accessible world for students to infuse their own interests, perspectives, and identities.

Personally, I pushed back on the established higher education traditions and expectations of perfectionism, timeliness, and efficiency. The combination of singular ways to express learning and unwavering deadlines appeared to be creating significant stress and anxiety, a familiar trait of undergraduate music students that intensified during the forced transition to online learning. By using deadlines to guide student learning and not determine grades, student learning transitioned from content perfection and timeliness to student's personal construction of learning. Interestingly, this shift assisted with productivity, independence in learning, and even depth of how students interacted with content. In addition to repurposing deadlines and ways to demonstrate learning, I reframed how students interacted with content through mini-lessons content and construction in addition to freedom of choice in how to present their learning.

Mini-Lessons

As the semester progressed, students more frequently expressed feeling overloaded by their coursework. Because this course met for three hours beginning at 7:00 p.m., students appeared and stated that they were exhausted by the time I would see them in the evening. One student indicated that his schedule required him to be in online classes for eight hours in one day not including homework. Students were mentally drained by the time I would work with them, so I engaged students in shorter lessons at the beginning of class then opened breakout rooms for students to use as they needed to complete projects. I remained available until the end of class if anyone had questions, concerns, or just wanted to chat.

While I know the students in this course were more than capable of finding resources and making connections on their own, I designed interactive synchronous mini-lessons that focused on foundational information so students' mental capacity would focus toward their personal interactions with the content and, ultimately, more thoughtful responses. These mini-lessons tapped into students' prior knowledge, provided initial resources from which they could explore further, and set students on a path to personally informed decision-making practices.

The first interactive, synchronous mini-lesson within *The Playlist Project* focused on "what" determines our music literature choices and "how" students can analyze music literature to make their personal decisions. This lesson tapped students' prior knowledge while empowering their personal choices through analysis. After introducing the question, "What criteria do you use when evaluating music by listening?" students shared their thoughts after discussing their thoughts in small group discussions via Zoom breakout rooms. By tapping into students' prior knowledge from other classes and experiences, students made connections across contexts (Chávez and Longerbeam 2016).

I then provided teacher-designed considerations in the form of questions for students to use while evaluating compositions for educational purposes:

- Does the composition create interest to continue listening? How?
- What kinds of musical complexities are involved in the composition? How does the composer manipulate those elements?
- How many "voices?" How do the "voices" interact with each other?
- Does the composition create images as I listen? Is the musical material being used respectfully and responsively?

Even though the criteria were formed as questions, I provided additional considerations for students to ponder and infuse into their analyses (Chávez and Longerbeam 2016). These questions assisted students to develop their own thoughts and, consequently, voices in determining criteria that is important for their own selection processes.

Another interactive, synchronous lesson addressed "why" one of the categories focuses on historically underrepresented composers. At the time of writing this chapter, instrumental students with whom I worked never intentionally engaged with recognizing composers from historically underrepresented populations. Even during in-person instruction, students struggled with finding compositions within these contexts; therefore, this mini-lesson established a foundation to assist students in exploring resources. That said, I also engaged students in questioning why I chose to have one category fully devoted to music literature written by composers from historically underrepresented populations.

Using Jodie Blackshaw's "ColourFULL Music" YouTube video (2019), I set a framework for why we explore compositions written by composers from historically underrepresented populations, and how to access these composers' compositions. Blackshaw brilliantly addresses and dispels the standard argument, "I want my students to play quality music," by simply stating, "I do, too." By sharing multiple ways to access diverse composers' compositions using databases, her website assisted these preservice teachers in exploring newer and alternative possibilities for performing ensembles.

To further support the "why" of focusing toward historically underrepresented composers, I supplemented her energetic video with her Texas Music Educators Association Clinic/Convention presentation with Carter Biggers (2021). Using signature compositional approaches to create musical works, Biggers and Blackshaw compare "standard" composers' compositions with compositions written by composers from historically underrepresented populations as evidence that *quality music* is being written by diverse, contemporary composers. These comparisons brought another perspective to students by focusing on the musical elements indicative of each composer; in turn, these musical elements laid a foundation to teaching musical concepts across literature.

Laying a foundation from which students could develop their own paths also required participation during the mini-lessons. I built in polling and *forced* students to share their perspectives during class. It is very easy to become passive and disconnected in an online learning environment, so I developed activities where every student needed to respond to prompts that required personal insights followed by supporting their thought processes.

Over time, students became more comfortable sharing their thoughts and taking chances.

An interactive, synchronous listening lesson engaged students by applying criteria from previous activities then formulating their own opinions. Students listened to two different compositions of the same grade level and individually pondered this prompt: "Listen to these two compositions and determine which composition would be more musically interesting. In other words, which piece would provide more educational content for your students?" I polled students to see who chose the first listening example and who chose the second listening example. I asked for volunteers to explain their reasoning for their choices. Because the intent of *The Playlist Project* was for students to discover why they chose particular compositions, I would normally not offer my thoughts. However, students indicated they needed more clarity, so I provided my insights and reasoning for the listening example I chose as an example for students to dig deeper into their own listening experiences. By providing how I process and evaluate by listening, I modeled criteria I wanted students to consider and, ultimately, infuse in their own analyses (Chávez and Longerbeam 2016).

Because students requested additional activities that focused on clearer scaffolding, content, and direction for projects due to the online learning platform, I developed a new interactive, synchronous lesson and layered in the consideration of cultural respectfulness when choosing music literature for ensembles. In this learning activity, students evaluated music by comparing two listening examples—*Danza la Habana* by Ruth Brittin and *Byzantine Dances* by Carol Brittin Chambers, responding to the following prompt: "Listen to these two compositions and determine which composition would be more educationally sound, which would be more musically interesting, and which you believe would be more culturally respectful. In other words, which piece would provide a more authentically educational experience for your students?" This activity offered practice for students to evaluate music aurally. Again, I polled students then asked individuals who I had not heard in class yet that evening. Student discussion focused on how each composer infused stylistic characteristics, represented authentic instruments in a concert band setting, shaped the complexities within the musical style, and finessed compositional techniques to honor the cultural underpinnings. I reinforced their thoughtful perspectives and interpretations by honoring their personal analyses. This focus toward cultural respectfulness initiated students' exploration into cultural competence—a pillar of culturally responsive pedagogy (Ladson-Billings 1994, 1995).

Personalized Project Presentations

Due to students' inconsistent access to resources, I opened a platform for them to present their work in a manner that reflected their interests and personalities. They embraced this opportunity of choice and developed very creative and memorable products. Some individuals designed colorful PowerPoints and magazine interviews that visually exposed the inequity and lack of diversity in composers of band and orchestra literature through photos of and interviews with their chosen composers. One student designed and developed the "Piece Picker Podcast" which offered a contemporary platform for this student to develop his analyses and thoughtful reflections. However, two individual submissions surfaced as highly original, personalized projects that provided a window into their worlds—iPhone app video by Morgan Paddock and a video game designed by Evan Wicks.

Presented as a video, Morgan organized a series of iPhone apps into a conversation with a colleague. Initially set at a concert, Morgan is in the role of a first-year teacher texting with her new colleague about her thoughts and challenges of selecting music literature for her new ensembles. Figure 7.2 offers a snapshot of the texting conversation Morgan had with her colleague.

As their texting conversation progresses, different iPhone apps, like Spotify, are used to address content and reinforce her thoughts for music literature choices. After her exploration into differing music literature that is influenced by the concert she is attending, suggestions by her colleague,

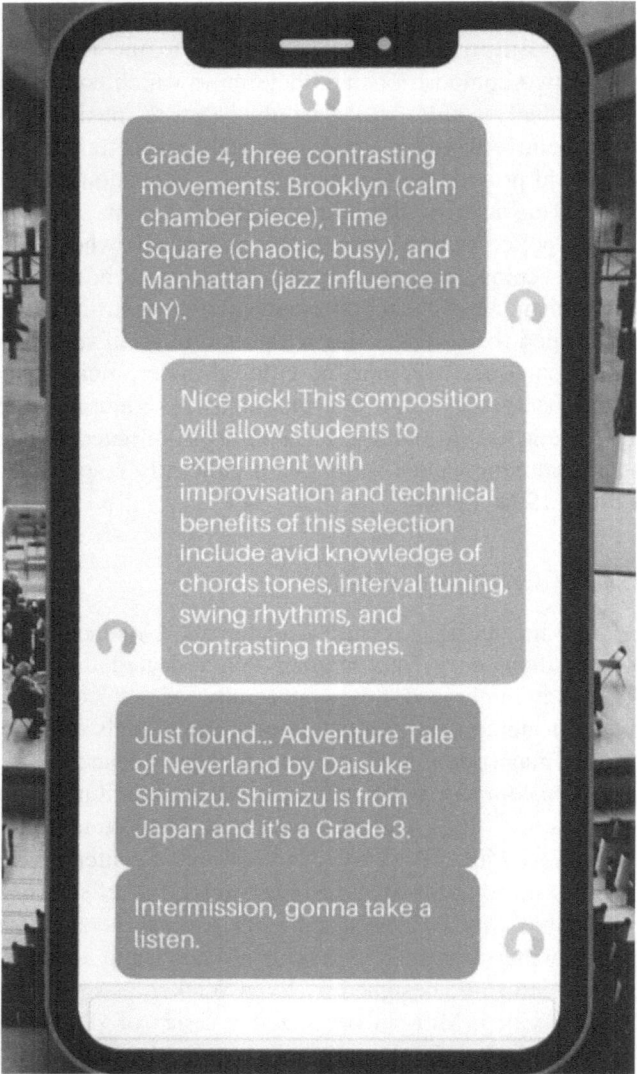

Figure 7.2 Screenshot of Morgan Paddock's Video Project—iPhone. Credit Tamara Thies. 2021.

and exploring music on different platforms, she thoughtfully reflects on her process and choices through a phone conversation with her colleague in her new band room after her first day as seen in figure 7.3. Morgan reveals that she desires to develop fluency in her students' cultures while engaging their expertise in her classroom.

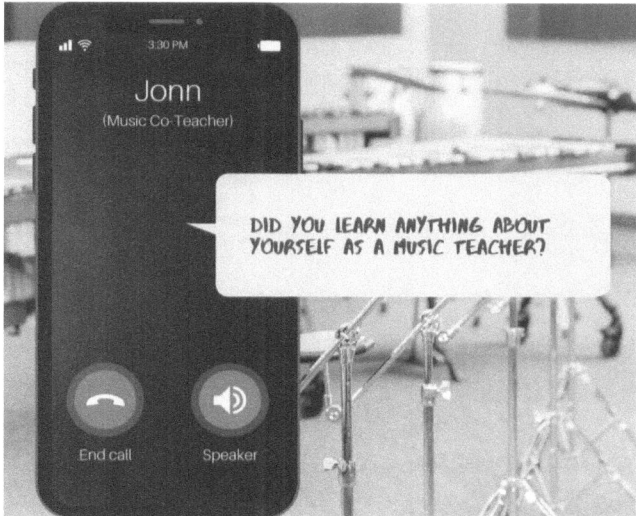

Figure 7.3 Screenshot of Morgan Paddock's Video Project—Conversation. Credit Tamara Thies. 2021.

Using the ubiquitous platform of the iPhone, Morgan designed a creative project that addressed contemporary ways of developing insights and knowledge that would be considered responsive to the current culture of many individuals and, more importantly, to her own cultural underpinnings.

Indicative of Evan's personality, the video game offered a fun, interactive way to access the information outlined for the project. Thankfully, Evan provided a full video for non-gamers like me who could not make it past the first composition! The gamer chooses a composition to play in the background, serving as the video game music, while they clear obstacles to access the analysis of each composition. Figure 7.4 offers a stop-action screenshot that illustrates Evan's Level I visual content from his game.

Each category of the compositions is a level in the game: *the standards* is level 1, *compositions by historically underrepresented composers* is level 2, and *personal choices* is level 3. As seen in Figure 7.5, the prize at the end of each category is presented as a reflection until the gamer reaches the final level.

Evan's reflection prize at the end of level 2 highlighted his personal journey through his music selection process. Adding another layer to his teaching philosophy through this project, Evan shared, ". . . there is a treasure trove of wonderful music written by composers who have not been given a spotlight. Purchasing, practicing, and performing these works isn't to show that the standard rep isn't great music; it's to show how much great music we have never heard."

We all are works in progress.

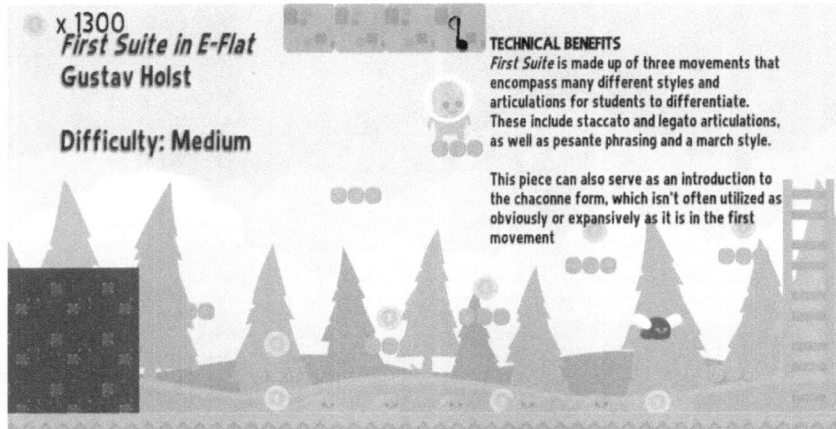

Figure 7.4 Screenshot of Evan Wicks's Video Game—Level 1. Credit Tamara Thies. 2021.

Student Discoveries

The platforms students chose to present their projects may have contributed to a deeper interaction with culturally responsive practices. Originally, *The Playlist Project* was a written paper; however, student control over the product platform appears to have more significantly impacted their interactions with the content. While reflecting on their own compositional choices required students to question and interrogate their own established beliefs, the choice of how the content was presented seems to have internalized their

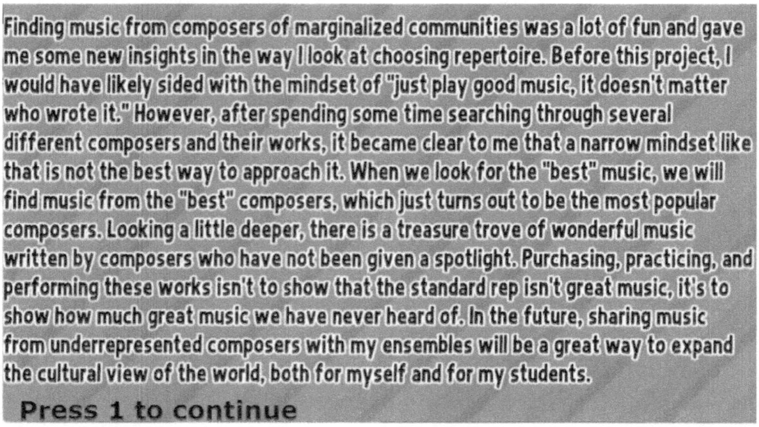

Figure 7.5 Screenshot of Evan Wicks's Video Game—Level 2 Reflection. Credit Tamara Thies. 2021.

discoveries and learning more than a prescribed collegiate paper—an assessment that was overused during online learning.

Initially, students tapped their prior knowledge to find music literature. While most were exposed to compositions that fit *the standards* or their personal choices, many were challenged with composers from historically underrepresented populations. One student expressed, "When I started looking into underrepresented composers, I got excited about the possibilities and I was surprised at how few female composers, composers of color, and LGBTQ+ composers I could think of . . ." Another student was "disheartened and disappointed" that he spent a considerable amount of time finding compositions by historically underrepresented composers, because he normally has several compositions in mind when discussing music literature. Yet another student realized "how sheltered" she was because the compositions she performed in high school and collegiate orchestras "were written predominantly by white men . . . It's a little disappointing how dominated the wind band composition community is by white males, so researching underrepresented communities made me realize how much fantastic music is out there that we don't often hear in our ensembles."

Almost every reflection articulated a variation of each student embracing critical consciousness as they discovered inequities of their own performing experiences that were dominated by white men compared to compositions written by historically underrepresented composers.

Over the last few years, I have prioritized guiding students into embracing their unique identities and sharing themselves with their communities. The impact of this work is best seen through the epiphanies of two students with Hispanic backgrounds. Derrick Nuño shared:

> When I first began this project, I was so eager and thrilled to select some of my favorite music and discover new music, but I found a tendency that I think was introduced subconsciously. All my standard rep and personal choice composers were white men who had written masterworks for the wind band. The issue I discovered was why did I only select these composers? Why do I consider them standards or my favorites? I had to do a bit of digging and I realized that my former band directors' repertoire selections heavily featured white males. I was only getting exposure to that and that's why my selections were skewed.

Similarly, a first-generation Latina commented that her compositional choices were highly influenced by the compositions that her instructors and directors chose, ". . . the main difference I notice is the representation of myself as a person. My choices in this project were all based on the choices by my past teachers or professors where I had to find ways to connect with each piece, if any connection happened at all." As students realized that their directors guided them, whether subconsciously or unconsciously, toward a particular cohort of composers, most of the students in this class resolved to challenge the status quo and guide their future students to develop positive ethnic and social identities through musical choices. These preservice teachers embraced their cultural competence by articulating that their future students will experience music and musicians that are representative of the differing cultures in their classrooms. While most of these preservice teachers were embracing cultural competence and recognizing the societal inequities through critical consciousness, Bryce Hansen recognized the current status but made a plan of action to redefine the status quo:

> Over the course of my teaching, I hope we get to a point where composers who may currently be underrepresented do not have the same systemic obstacles, but for now that is certainly not the case, and I will not approach it that way in my classroom ... Moving forward, I hope to not just implement this music into my classroom but pressure my peers into doing the same so their students will not have the same realization I had.

We are all works in progress...

CONTINUING THOUGHTS

By embracing barriers involved with online learning and challenging the traditions and expectations often experienced in higher education, I redesigned student learning opportunities to reflect student needs for learning as well as opened opportunities for students to express themselves in ways that may have not been designed and implemented if we had not been forced into an online learning platform. Online learning was never going to offer a "business-as-usual" experience, so I chose to upend my online classrooms based on my students' first-semester feedback. I opened a plethora of possibilities for flexing with students' class expectations and schedules, access to technologies and materials, and work/home/school/life balance. This flexibility opened a door that deepened my experiences with culturally responsive practices which, in turn, impacted my students' understanding and experiences with culturally responsive practices.

The extent and depth to which instrumental music education students were grounded in the ensemble traditions of director-centered teaching and perfectionism was one of my greatest realizations during online teaching. My initial attempts, in the online platform, to use discovery methods and constructivist lessons and projects were challenging for students even though I had used similar learning opportunities during in-person instruction. Once I realized that students' personal preferences and needs for learning were intensified with online learning, I adjusted to the needs of individual students by offering a significant amount of choice within their own learning environments (i.e., choice of presentation product, personal preference regarding music literature, choice of working alone or with others, and the like). Students' personal choices led them to broaden their differing ways of knowing and provided a foundation for self-discovery and analysis.

Additionally, I generally needed to provide more intentional scaffolding and practice for students to feel open to construct and share their personal learning. While I provided content in the mini-lessons, the focus toward practicing a process of analyzing in conjunction with opening a nonjudgmental platform impacted student learning. While scaffolding and practice are not new to education, implementing these concepts in a manner where students are empowered to share their thought processes drives their personal discoveries into cultural responsiveness.

Since returning to in-person learning, my own teaching practice has changed significantly. While I believe that I have always been a concept-based and constructivist instructor at heart, I more intentionally scaffold activities that focus toward multiple and differing student interactions and products through musical concepts and content. My focus is not just the content but the processes by which individual students internalize learning. Not only do I continue to open opportunities for students to make choices, I challenge students to consider how their choices are impacting their future students and communities. This next step is guiding students more effectively to culturally responsive practices as they explore the communities in which they interact.

I am a work in progress . . .

As music teacher educators, we must consider our priorities in our profession and how we engage students to meet those expectations. Are the traditions in higher education truly embracing the diversity within each of our students into the classroom? Are we setting students on a path that embraces the ever-changing populations in our country? Are the only validated ways of knowing, performing and writing? If we set our students on a path toward understanding their own beliefs and biases then have them analyze how these impact their future students and communities, we are serving future music educators by empowering their individuality, tapping their unique qualities, and encouraging them to consider each of their students as unique individuals who add to the cultural tapestry of their classrooms.

The online platform offered all of us a unique window into another world of learning. Entering the unknown required a great deal of analysis and flexibility in order for students and instructors to thrive. By challenging the written and unwritten traditions of teaching and learning in higher education, we can develop stronger individuals where learning becomes personalized and, ultimately, more meaningful.

We are all works in progress and deserve to be seen.

REFERENCES

Biggers, Carter, and Jodie Blackshaw. 2021. "Whose Ears Are You Listening With? Repertoire that Matters." 2021 TMEA Clinic/Convention. https://www.colourfullmusic.com/tmea-2021.

Blackshaw, Jodie. 2018. "ColourFULL Music." https://www.colourfullmusic.com/.

Blackshaw, Jodie. 2019. "ColourFULL Music." YouTube video, 4:35, January 7. https://www.youtube.com/watch?v=XuRVfJHgZsc&t=2s.

Chávez, Alicia Fedelina, Fengfeng Ke, and Felisha A. Herrera. 2012. "Clan, Sage, and Sky: Indigenous, Hispano, and Mestizo Narratives of Learning in New Mexico Context." *American Educational Research Journal* 49, no. 4: 775–806. https://doi.org/10.3102/0002831212441498.

Chávez, Alicia Fedelina, and Susan Diana Longerbeam. 2016. *Teaching Across Cultural Strengths: A Guide to Balancing Integrated and Individuated Cultural Frameworks in College Teaching.* Sterling, VA: Stylus.

Collier, Peter J. 2000. "The Effects of Completing a Capstone Course on Student Identity." *Sociology of Education* 73: 285–299. https://doi.org/2673235.

Collier, Peter J. 2001. "The Differentiated Model of Role Identity Acquisition." *Symbolic Interaction* 24, no. 2: 217–235. https://doi.org/10.1525/si.2001.24.2.217.

Hammond, Zaretta. 2015. *Culturally Responsive Teaching and the Brain: Promoting Authentic Engagement and Rigor Among Culturally and Linguistically Diverse Students.* Thousand Oaks, CA: Corwin.

Ibarra, Robert A. 2001. *Beyond Affirmative Action: Reframing the Context of Higher Education.* Madison, WI: University of Wisconsin Press.

Kokotsaki, Dimitra, and Susan Hallam. 2007. "Higher Education Music Students' Perceptions of the Benefits of Participative Music Making." *Music Education Research* 9: 93–109. https://doi.org/10.1080/14613800601127577.

Ladson-Billings, Gloria. 1994. *The Dreamkeepers.* San Francisco, CA: Jossey-Bass Publishing.

Ladson-Billings, Gloria. 2000. "Fighting for our Lives: Preparing Teachers to Teach African-American Students." *Journal of Teacher Education* 51, no. 3: 206–214. https://doi.org/10.1177/0022487100051003008.

Rendón, Laura I. 2009. *Sentipensante (Sensing/Thinking) Pedagogy: Education for Wholeness, Social Justice and Liberation.* Sterling, VA: Stylus.

Turner, Ralph H. 1978. "The Role and the Person." *American Journal of Sociology* 84: 1–23. https://doi.org/10.1086/226738.

Chapter 8

Learning to Be Human

The Art of Care, Compassion, and Empathy in Music Education

Nicholas Ryan McBride

> We do not automatically see another human being as spacious and deep, having thoughts, spiritual longings, & emotions.... It is an achievement to see a soul in that body, and this achievement is supported by poetry and the arts, which ask us to wonder about the inner world of that shape we see—and, too, to wonder about ourselves and our depths.
> —Nussbaum 2010, 102

In the preceding quote, philosopher Martha Nussbaum (2010) notes the important role the arts and humanities play in providing entry points to explore our individual and collective humanity. Recently, our ability to see one another, to wonder about and examine our depths as human beings has been tested in unprecedented ways. In this new and socially distant reality brought about by the COVID-19 pandemic, music and arts programs have been similarly tested, as have the teachers and artists who lead them. Out of necessity, we, as music educators, have adapted to the best of our ability. Our computers have served as conduits for real human interaction. The creative synergy and empathic response ignited by physical proximity have been dulled by partitioned Zoom boxes, slow internet connections, and silent conversations in chat windows. For many artists and teachers, this type of engagement has felt anathema to the very soul of who we are and what we do. There is much to learn from our experiences navigating teaching through a pandemic, but a central one for us as music educators is that the relationship between music, community, and human connection is invaluable and dependent on our collective desire to be, learn, and create together.

Like many teacher educators who situate art and music within humanistic and empathic learning domains (Hendricks 2018; Laird 2015; Yob 2020), I have spent the last eighteen months worrying about my college students as they entered virtual classrooms as novice teachers; particularly those who student taught while positioned in their childhood bedrooms, some, hundreds of miles from the children in their care. Beyond learning the day-to-day mechanics of effective instruction and how schools function, how would these teacher candidates come to understand and cultivate in their own students and classrooms "the role of the arts in human life as, above all else, that of nourishing and extending the capacity of empathy" (Nussbaum 2010, 101)?

Compounding these new concerns are somewhat older challenges, conditions that took shape far before the pandemic but have similarly tested our ability to make meaningful human connections in classrooms. As digital platforms replaced in-person learning, narratives of accountability and high-stakes testing had already begun to replace discourses of human well-being in schools. Concepts such as *community* and the *public good* have been sidelined, while neoliberal narratives of individual responsibility have been foregrounded with little resistance from policy makers (Giroux 2014; Ross and Gibson 2007). Preservice teacher curricula have been vulnerable to this trend. The adoption of edTPA as an evaluative measure of preservice teacher readiness has required college teacher preparation programs to refocus their values on efficiency and measurable outcomes (Bernard and McBride 2020; Parkes and Powell 2019). As any experienced educator knows, more tests, standards, prepackaged curricula, and teacher evaluation models leave less opportunity to develop human connection, communication, and provide care to our students. The global pandemic seemed to only intensify the already challenging landscape of teacher education. At an unprecedented moment of isolation, with our students at their greatest need for compassion, the shift in values was stark. Preservice teachers were tasked with not only completing a high-stakes, state-sanctioned teacher evaluation portfolio but also addressing the immense pedagogical and emotional needs of their students during a global health crisis.

Watching my students struggle to take on challenges that would overwhelm any veteran educator, particularly at such a formative stage of their career, disconcerted me greatly. In response to these conditions and my own frustration with the inflexible and unreasonable requirements for state teacher licensure, I took action the only way I knew how: by creating a course that, if successful, would not only mitigate some of the damage but also passionately and unapologetically explore how music and the arts help us learn to be human.

In this chapter, I embrace John Macmurray's (2012) theory of learning to be human as a framework to examine the relationship between curriculum and student experience in a new undergraduate pedagogy course: Fostering Community & Human Connection in the Music Classroom. Macmurray's philosophical basis for a person-centered approach to education is structured through two types of encounters with other human beings: the functional and the personal. For the purposes of this chapter, I align the functional encounter with the neoliberal ideology. I explore the personal encounter through the course content, which focused on engendering a sense of human connection and community through collective musical engagement, artistic disposition, and passionate teaching as modeled by an in-service teacher and music teacher educator. Through an instructional framework known as community, awareness, reflection, and empathic action (CARE) I sought to help preservice music educators balance and foreground the personal, empathic, and humane qualities of teaching as they navigate the functional, neoliberal, and increasingly inhumane landscape of public education.

A VIGNETTE: I DON'T BLAME THEM

It is 8:41 p.m. I have just wrapped up my third one-on-one Zoom meeting with a student in Student Teaching Seminar. Like them, I have been in front of a computer screen for close to twelve hours today. My eyes are tired and red. I am exhausted, as are the students, but I am kept awake by a sense of urgency and anxiety in our conversations. In addition to those who have remained after class, several in the course have requested to meet with me individually throughout the week to discuss concerns over effective teaching practices for Zoom, the latest confusing shift in their district's COVID protocols, the challenges of teaching music virtually, and of course their immense fears over completing and passing the edTPA during a global pandemic.

Only four students asked to stay this week: the fourth seems to have given up and left the waiting room after an hour and twenty-minute delay as I shuffled between his peers. I don't blame him. I'll send an apologetic e-mail—right after I apologize to my husband for missing dinner again.

Two of three students I have spoken with tonight have broken into tears—one expressed genuine concern over how prepared she will be to actually become an in-service teacher after a semester of online student teaching. I try to hide the fact that I share her concerns, instead sharing a story about how my own student teaching experience at a high school did not prepare me adequately for my first teaching job as a middle school general music teacher. My story provides little comfort to her, and in response, she says something that sticks with me: "If I had known it was going to be this bad, Dr. McBride, I would have taken the semester off." Honestly, I don't blame her.

The last meeting of the evening feels more like a 60-minute interview. Frustrated over having to complete the edTPA in a virtual environment and the unclear guidance from Pearson Education (n.d.) and our state's Department of Education on accommodations for virtual teaching environments, the student grills me with rapid-fire questions I don't have answers for:

> So wait, if my school stays asynchronous, what do I do? It says asynchronous teaching won't be accepted by edTPA. Why weren't we told about this sooner? Why was I even placed at this school if I'm not going to be able to get certified to teach? I don't know what to do! Are we going to get our tuition back for the semester if I don't get certification? Dr. McBride, I've been at this school now for 4 weeks and I've never even had a live conversation with one of the students. What am I supposed to do?

This student is angry and scared. Again, I don't blame her.

THE FUNCTIONAL: UNLEARNING NEOLIBERALISM

The conditions depicted in the vignette above may seem familiar to students, teachers, and teacher educators. Teaching and learning during the age of COVID-19 proved to be, at best, an exhausting and frustrating process and, at worst, a once-in-a-career experience that impacted teachers and students on a profound professional and emotional level. A record number of educators in K–12 schools and higher education retired after the 2021 school year, and even more mid-career educators left or have considered leaving the profession permanently, compounding an already problematic retention trend for teachers in American schools (Morgan 2021; Reilly 2020). In addition to these troubling metrics, the global pandemic exacerbated an even more disturbing and undoubtedly related trend: the diminishing role and value of humanity in schools as an outcome of the neoliberal ideology in action.

Within educational settings, neoliberalism is often discussed in reformative contexts, particularly in regard to reshaping the relationships between privatization and public service and the individual and society. As Au and Ferrare (2015, 5) noted, "Within the neoliberal framework public goods and services that were once provided by the state are converted into new markets ripe for exploitation and profiteering by private/corporate interests." Until recently, many states issued teacher licensure based, in part, on the recommendation of college teacher preparation programs. The adoption of edTPA shifted this responsibility to private entities, standardizing a notion of teacher readiness and supplanting the role of the college supervisor.

Giroux (2014, 12–13) posited a more troubling interpretation of the term: "Not only does neoliberal rationality believe in the ability of markets to solve all problems, it also removes economics and markets from ethical considerations. Economic growth, rather than social needs, drives politics. Long-term investments are replaced by short-term gains and profits, while compassion is viewed as a weakness and democratic public values are derided." Giroux's definition highlights the problem I witnessed in my classroom: as my students struggled to navigate the expectations of student teaching during a global health crisis, their social needs, and by extension their students' social needs, were not met with compassion. Pearson Education's (n.d.) inadequate modifications for completing edTPA in virtual learning environments did little to quiet my students' fears as they faced unprecedented personal and professional challenges in their classrooms.

As the fall 2021 semester progressed and frustrations over capturing teaching videos in virtual and asynchronous learning environments began to mount, members of my department and I raised objections. My colleague and I wrote a letter detailing the outrageous expectations edTPA had for our students and an entreaty for a waiver of the edTPA requirement for the 2020–2021 academic year. We sent it to New Jersey's Governor and the State Department of Education. Colleagues from five other New Jersey institutions signed on to the document (see the Appendix for the letter).

Our position was clear—policymakers and field leaders should have been developing solutions to support students' success, not forcing teachers, students, and student teachers to perform impossible tasks with seemingly no consideration for the traumatic conditions under which we were all burdened. My response to these conditions was to create a course that aimed to refocus my students' attention toward humane ends in teaching, what Macmurray (2012) referred to as the *personal*, and to respond decisively against the neoliberal ideology that conceived of evaluation models like the edTPA.

THE PERSONAL: LEARNING TO BE HUMAN *IN THEORY*

The chaos occurring in many school contexts throughout the pandemic presented an opportunity for conversations about empathetic and compassionate teaching approaches and curricula in music classrooms. The course I developed focused on teaching and learning music through a humanistic philosophical lens, or "learning to be human" (Macmurray 2012, 1).

John Macmurray's (1891–1976) theories of humanistic education, in contrast to neoliberal discourse of educational reform, resurged when educational philosopher Michael Fielding (2000) cited his work examining a person-centered approach to education. In summarizing this humanist-centered theory of education, Fielding (2012b, 661) drew attention to key themes in Macmurray's arguments: "For Macmurray the most important double fact about our human nature is, first, its mutuality: we can develop our humanity only within the context of our reciprocal care for each other. Secondly, what he calls the 'paradox of human nature' is that whilst we are born human we also have to learn to become human." It was clear to me—and more importantly, to my students—that the educational establishment had not been designed to enact or support reciprocal care. Nor could my students learn humanity from within a bureaucratic iron cage. Within this context, I continued to think about how we might react, what routes we might take to enkindle the humanity Macmurray championed.

The publishing of Macmurray's seminal Moray House lecture in 2012 solidified his place in contemporary educational debate. In the 1958 lecture, Macmurray (2012, 670) argued that the priority in education is "learning to live in personal relation to other people." Fielding (2004, 209) explored the difference between what Macmurray calls "functional" relations and "personal" relations:

> "Functional" or instrumental relations are typical of those encounters that help us to get things done in order to achieve purposes: indeed, functional relations are defined by those purposes. . . . We do not reveal our deeper fears and aspirations to each other. By contrast, "personal" relations exist in order to help us be and become ourselves in and through our relations with others and part of that becoming involves our mutual preparedness to be open and honest with each other about all aspects of our being.

A critical distinction to the theory of learning to be human is Macmurray's belief that "the functional is for the sake of the personal. . . . Within systems of compulsory public education, schooling (the functional) is for the sake of education (the personal). . . . Within schools themselves, administrative, management, and other organisational arrangements (the functional) are for the sake of a vibrant and creative community (the personal)" (Fielding 2014, 210). All the bureaucratic requirements, the lists of documents and media, the applications and licensures, the years of dutiful study and practical engagement are meant to support not the institutions or the government agencies, but the students, the teachers, and the school communities. They are meant to support human growth, but they are failing at this.

Fielding warned of dilemmas faced by students and teachers whose encounters are increasingly defined by the high-performance model of schooling, a model that, in his view, shifts the priorities of the functional/personal modes of relations. He stated,

> The crisis we currently face has its roots in the fact that our dominant practical and intellectual frameworks reverse the very relation I am advocating. In what I term the "high performance" model of schooling the personal is used for the sake of the functional: students are included or excluded, valued or not, primarily on the basis of whether they contribute to organisational performance of the school. The pressure they and their teachers are put under to raise standards and improve performance marginalises the very educational aspirations that gives schooling its justification and its purpose. (Fielding 2007, 210)

Fielding's language in regard to the high-performance model of schooling is strikingly similar to the discourse of dehumanization and educational reform that regards human contribution as capital gain and that works to replace concepts such as the public good or community with narratives of competition and individual responsibility (Ross and Gibson 2007). Fielding (2004, 210) warned that if schools become "impersonal" organizations, then the "functional marginalises the personal."

THE PERSONAL: LEARNING TO BE HUMAN *IN PRACTICE*

How do music educators and music teacher educators avoid marginalizing the personal for the functional in schools? How do we, as a profession, privilege the humane over the transactional? To approximate answers to these questions, I identified four curricular focus areas, collectively CARE, that broadly connect to compassionate pedagogies and humanistic philosophies on teaching and learning: community, awareness, reflection, and empathic action. I detail below how I developed the CARE framework and implemented it as part of a new course entitled Fostering Community & Human Connection in the Music Classroom (FCHC).

Community

My perspective on what a community is or means in the context of schooling is predominantly shaped by the work of two individuals: Maxine Greene and Fred Rogers, legendary teachers in their respective domains. I begin with

Greene (1995, 33–34), who cited Dewey in her vision for what communities within schools might look like:

> To imagine a democratic community accessible to the young is to summon a vision of the "conjoint experience," shared meaning, common interests and endeavors described by John Dewey (1927 [1954], 153). Interconnectedness and communion . . . characterize such a community. A continuing search for intellectual freedom of articulation . . . give vibrancy and energy to the possible community.

Although approached from a different vantage point, Greene's concepts of interconnectedness and communion align with Rogers's work, which famously characterized community as a neighborhood, a point made obvious by the title of his PBS Children's Television Show, *Mister Rogers' Neighborhood*. Maxwell King (2018, 12) passionately documented Rogers's vision for a neighborhood as a community of friends and helpers:

> So, where do we find the strength of neighborhood today, in a world of dramatic globalization, an environment of rapid technological change, a planet increasingly consumed with fear of others? . . . In his work, Fred Rogers himself pointed the way back to the neighborhood. He used the cutting-edge technology of his day, television, to convey the most profound values—respect, understanding, tolerance, inclusion, consideration—to children.

Inspired by Greene's vision, Rogers's pragmatism, and Karin Hendricks's (2018, 17) models of compassion, I asked Dr. Lynnel Joy Jenkins—an in-service music educator who epitomizes a person-centered approach to music teaching and learning—to co-teach FCHC. Jenkins is a music educator, conductor, and teacher educator; the Artistic Director of the community-based Princeton Girlchoir; and a middle school choral director in New Jersey public schools.

Via Zoom, my college students observed her Monday evening rehearsals with the Princeton Girlchoir, and in real time, generated reflective notes and written dialogue with one another using a shared class Google Doc. Select observations from my students follow that exemplify the impact Jenkins had in communicating and embodying community in a music classroom. (All of the observation reflections were framed in the course literature, which I discuss in detail in the Awareness and Reflection section.) Greene's (1995, 39) thoughts on community supply a framework for the observations:

> In thinking of community, we need to emphasize the process words: making, creating, saying and the like. . . . Community is not a question of which social

contracts are the most reasonable for individuals to enter. It is a question of what might contribute to the pursuit of shared goods: what ways of being together, of attaining mutuality, of reaching towards some common world.

Making

Dr. Jenkins always prioritizes including her students and making them feel valued. One inclusive practice that I find so valuable is including the individual students as well as their interests throughout the lesson. Dr. Jenkins is continuously giving her students the opportunity to lead the class and choose their own way to implement the curriculum. This not only allows the students to feel important, but it celebrates their own unique ideas and interests.

Creating

I believe that as educators we need to be deliberate in creating situations where our students feel encouraged. By allowing the singers to take responsibility, to lead in different areas of the rehearsal, such as when they act as "vocal models," she creates an environment where every student feels as if they matter, and that their opinion and voice is important. This should be practiced in every classroom. A very noticeable result of this culture is that, even virtually, a huge portion of her singers are engaged in the rehearsal at all times. She has created an environment where her students model her habits of empathy and inclusivity in the chat and with each other at all times. They are constantly thanking and praising one another, and it seems very genuine and real.

Saying

Dr. Jenkins does an incredible job at being inclusive throughout her lessons, even within the virtual format. She calls people individually by their names and makes a point to use correct pronouns. If she does not know the pronunciation, she asks the student to "teach us your name," which provides the student ownership and ensures we are communicating our care for them. Moreover, she actively reads EACH message in the Zoom chat when she asks them to participate. Although this seems like such an insignificant concept, this small gesture makes students feel seen and valued. She reinforces such a healthy and supportive environment with her very intentional language choices, such as when she affirms when they help one another in the chat, gives unsolicited positive feedback, and empowers them with phrases like "rise up," or "alright, let's do this my sisters." Her language choice is extremely inclusive!

One of the most rewarding aspects of Jenkins's involvement in FCHC was the inspiration she provided in allowing the teacher candidates to see themselves in her work, to imagine their own approach to building community in music classrooms. Jenkins's personable approach to teaching music was never about an arrival point; it was about a journey toward what is possible in a community of musicians. As Hendricks (2018, 30) reminded, "I invite all of us (myself included) to keep an open mind to possibility, with a belief and understanding that each of the qualities of compassion is attainable by all of us."

Awareness and Reflection

In taking up Macmurray's (2014, 210) charge of repositioning "the functional . . . for the sake of the personal," I sought to shift the teacher candidates' focus from the quantifiable, evaluative, and impersonal toward an awareness of humane ends in music teaching and learning. We accomplished much of this perspective-taking through the course readings and discussions. Karin Hendricks's (2018) *Compassionate Music Teaching: A Framework for Motivation and Engagement in the 21st Century* served as the course text. Hendricks beautifully explored the intersections between research, practice, modeling, and action in chapters that focus on the qualities of compassion: trust, empathy, patience, inclusion, community, and authentic connection. She carefully situated these topics within psychological and sociological research domains, allowing for a comprehensive examination of compassionate pedagogies while also avoiding the pitfalls of an overly sentimental or cursory approach to social and emotional learning.

To broaden students' perspectives, I paired the Hendricks (2018) chapters with readings from various artists, psychologists, politicians, and activists, who, in a variety of contexts, explored the importance of self-awareness, social awareness, and reflection. For example, I paired Hendricks's chapter on "Trust" with an excerpt from then U.S. presidential candidate Pete Buttigieg's (2020) text of the same name, *Trust: America's Best Chance*. Her chapter "Authentic Connection" paired with a chapter from Maxwell King's (2018) biography of Fred Rogers, entitled "Fearless Authenticity." Weaving together the literature on humanistic teaching with the work of individuals both from within and outside of music education, provided an opportunity for the teacher candidates to draw connections between the arts, other disciplines, and perspectives they may not usually encounter in music education discourse. This wider lens allowed for a more empathic process to unfold while engaging with the course literature; one in which the students could better understand the importance of "recognizing and validating the Other, the individual who is different from us, and at the same time, fully appreciating the commonalities and the wholeness of humankind, as if there is no Other" (Yob 2020, 26).

As is common in many teacher preparation courses, I asked the students to maintain a weekly reflection journal; however, for FCHC I asked them to consider responding via video instead of in a written discussion board. The video journal functioned as a dialogue between me and the students; it created a space for them to privately discuss their joys, curiosities, and insecurities about teaching, providing a unique and expressive window into students' thinking. I encouraged them to situate their video journal responses within the context of the course literature but also to speak openly, honestly, and candidly. Most were appreciative of the opportunity to respond not only through words, but also through facial expressions, tone of voice, cadence, and gestures.

The students engaged in a more organic process of deep reflection with the course topics because the strictures of the conventional course reading response no longer bound them to word or time limits. In class discussions, students spoke of the importance of the video journal as a reflective tool in their own self-supported inquiry, a type of meta-analysis where they could reflect *on* their reflections for the benefit of their peers and students, as well as their growth as teachers. Notably, as the following reflection from a student in the course, Amanda, demonstrates, the teacher candidates became aware of—and interested in—the nuanced and meaningful acts that yield unmeasurable outcomes:

> One quote that really resonated with me in the Mister Rogers reading is . . . "The white spaces between words are more important than the text, because they give you time to think about what you've read." One of the key factors to being an authentic teacher is appreciating silence, and being comfortable with it. Those so-called "white spaces" allow you to reflect on what you've read, and the same goes for speaking and teaching. Silence allows you to reflect on your teaching, and allows the students to reflect on what they have learned. I definitely know a lot of teacher friends who are terrified of silence in their classrooms, and feel as if they always have to be speaking, running around, etc. I personally feel somewhere in between in terms of my comfortability in front of students, which I believe can be improved slightly by appreciating silence.

Empathic Action

In a 2016 *Atlantic* article aptly titled "Learning to Be Human," Sophie Gilbert argued that the diminishing position of the humanities in schools may, in part, correlate to the speed with which human beings now engage with information. Gilbert referred throughout the article to a conversation between Leon Wieseltier and Drew Gilpin Faust. During the conversation, Faust argued, "The humanities are such an important vehicle for widening the world, for seeing through other people's eyes, . . . and developing a kind of empathy for people outside yourself" (Wieseltier and Faust 2016, 16:35). Wieseltier blamed the decline of the humanities on "the immediate intellectual gratification . . . of Google," stating that "all knowledge has in some way been reduced to the status of information. . . . Information is highly inferior. . . . Knowledge requires inquiry, method, and above all, time" (Wieseltier and Faust 2016, 20:00). Revisiting the work of Fred Rogers, King (2018) emphasized that part of Rogers's success derived from the time and patience he applied to all aspects of his work. Rogers's approach was "so painstaking that some of his friends and coworkers referred to time with him as 'Fred-time': Whenever one sat down to talk with him, urgency seemed to dissipate, discussion proceeded at a measured, almost otherworldly pace, and the deepest feelings and thoughts were given patient attention" (King 2018, 8).

Given the rapid pace of change and shifting modalities of instruction during COVID-19, I aimed to prioritize *time* as an essential part of the culminating project for the course. The assignment was to write "the lesson plan you've always wanted to write," which was meant to move my students from theory to practice in generating curricula that addressed the issues of the course; most significantly, empathy. In contrast to the time-bound and rigid expectations of edTPA, the CARE Lesson Plan Project led to fascinating results: having the students reflect upon the confines of their student teaching experience ignited a type of creative autonomy in how they approached the project. Many relished the opportunity to deviate from the traditional in teaching: rubrics were tossed aside for critical reflections and open dialogue, student rapport was discussed in the context of care and compassion, the traditional lesson plan served as a malleable framework for compassionate pedagogy, learning experiences could be developed and nurtured for weeks at a time, and evaluation was reframed as an opportunity for empathic action.

The students' final submissions boldly tackled issues such as race relations in the United States, the LGBTQIA+ rights movement, the history of protest songs, teen suicide, and gun violence in schools. One student commented, "I would have never come anywhere near this subject for my edTPA lesson plans, there just wasn't enough time to do it right." Those who wished to take on less controversial topics still managed to explore complex and deeply personal themes in their work. For example, one teacher candidate, Emma, who wanted to explore mindfulness and music as tools for helping elementary school children navigate the emotional difficulties of the pandemic, shared the following as part of her final project, entitled "Exploring Mindfulness through 'Chasing Sunlight' by Cait Nishimura":

> I chose the piece "Chasing Sunlight" because of the wonderful meaning behind the title. The composer, Cait Nishimura, was inspired to write this piece while

driving along, trying to chase the last rays of sunlight. The piece is about making the most of every opportunity life throws at you. I think this concept is especially important now during the COVID-19 pandemic; we have lost so much. We've lost the ability to do things we often took for granted like going to school, working in person, and seeing people every day. We've lost opportunities to make music together. I want my students to play this song and think about how special it is to make music with one another, and how special it is to live in the moment. Teaching children how to be mindful and present is so important, I believe. So often, children are told that their lives haven't really begun yet. Their lives do not suddenly start in adulthood, their lives have already begun, and, through music, they should be able to appreciate where they are in life right now, and be present.

In taking time to explore these issues in a meaningful way through music, the teacher candidates truly embraced the creativity Allsup (2020, 37) espoused: "I have found that the greatest possibility for mutuality occurs through an open curriculum, one that is enacted, which means that it is local and immediate, but foremost actively creative."

CONCLUSION

In his biography of Rogers, King (2018, 11–12) revealed another important fact about him that may be unknown to most people:

> Rogers turned down offers from the major networks to take his show from PBS to commercial television, where he could have earned millions as scriptwriter, songwriter, and star. . . . In this and in most other ways, Fred Roger's life offers an interesting contrast to a twentieth-century world consumed by rapid change and inexorable growth. . . . His legacy lives in the concept of a caring neighborhood where people watch out for one another.

Fred Rogers knew that the personal should *always* come before the functional, that a child's education should never be considered a for-profit enterprise. His is an example to live by, to emulate not just in our work, but in our relationships, our mindsets, our everyday lives. We can—and we must, despite neoliberal policy—affect humanity from within. We must foster growth and understanding and empathy and passionate, creative thinking in order to change the ideological direction from the functional to the personal.

A curriculum of care and compassion is simply a starting point for deeper and more pointed conversations about the structures of power in education, the policies that shape our pedagogy, and ideologies that privilege profits over passion. Although the creation of FCHC grew out of my own deep frustration with Pearson, the New Jersey Department of Education, and their reluctance—and at times refusal—to respond compassionately to the needs of our next generation of teachers, I also recognize the good that came out of this moment. While my student teaching seminar would, at times, serve as space for my students and I to commiserate over the flawed assessment process they were about to undertake, the pandemic presented an opportunity to respond and act. We took a step forward and moved theoretical conversations about humane teaching practices into practical contexts.

My FCHC course and the CARE framework was a first step in establishing a precedent and realigning educational expectations for humane pedagogy. Absent a practical model, I believe policies like edTPA will become further entrenched and cultures of accountability and high-stakes testing will continue to erode humanity in schools and society. The immense challenges of the COVID-19 pandemic underscored some of the deepest flaws in the field of education—flaws we must address. For myself, and for my students, this course served as a small and imperfect act of subversion in addressing those flaws, and in reorienting our vantage toward humanistic ends in music teaching and learning. In closing, I present a few words from one of my students, Keith, who beautifully bookends the opening statement from Nussbaum (2010) on the use of the arts as a means for humanity:

> Music is often seen as a vehicle of communication. It can serve as a supplement to the words and the verbalizations of emotions. I hesitate to say as a substitute because I think that having a wide array of tools for the students to process and utilize their emotions is important and will serve them in the long run. As music educators, we must be more creative with our ideas, avoid the superficial in our teaching, and explore multiple avenues while utilizing various resources, or asking for help from other teachers; all are great ways to initiate a more emotionally engaging experience for our students. Emotions are not easily shared. It will be up to us as educators to initiate difficult conversations, be vulnerable, and show our emotions before our students feel comfortable doing so. If accomplished, we can provide an authentic experience for students; one that makes them feel comfortable just being themselves.

REFERENCES

Allsup, Randall Everett. 2020. "On the Perils of Wakening Others." In *Humane Music Education for the Common Good*, edited by Iris M. Yob, and Estelle R. Jorgensen, 29–39. Bloomington, IN: Indiana University Press.

Au, Wayne, and Joseph J. Ferrare, eds. 2015. *Mapping Corporate Education Reform: Power and Policy Networks in the Neoliberal State*. New York: Taylor & Francis.
Bernard, Cara, and Nicholas McBride. 2020. "Ready for Primetime." *Visions of Research in Music Education* 35 (March). http://www-usr.rider.edu/~vrme/v35n1/visions/Bernard%20and%20McBride_Hyperreality%20Manuscript.pdf.
Darling-Hammond, Linda. 2012. "Real Teacher Ed Reform." Inside Higher Ed. https://www.insidehighered.com/views/2012/08/13/essay-argues-real-teacher-education-reform-going-led-profession.
Dewey, John. 1927 [1954]. *The Public and its Problems*. Athens, OH: Swallow Press.
Fielding, Michael. 2000. "The Person-Centred School." *Forum* 42, no. 2 (January): 51–54.
Fielding, Michael. 2007. "The Human Cost and Intellectual Poverty of High Performance Schooling: Radical Philosophy, John Macmurray and the Remaking of Person Centred Education." *Journal of Education Policy* 22, no. 4 (June): 383–409. http://doi.org/10.1080/02680930701390511.
Fielding, Michael. 2012a. "Education as if People Matter: John Macmurray, Community and the Struggle for Democracy." In "Learning to Be Human: The Educational Legacy of John Macmurray." Special issue, *Oxford Review of Education* 38, no. 6 (December): 675–692. https://doi.org/10.1080/03054985.2012.745044.
Fielding, Michael. 2012b. Introduction to "Learning to Be Human," by John Macmurray, in "Learning to Be Human: The Educational Legacy of John Macmurray." Special issue, *Oxford Review of Education* 38, no. 6 (December): 661–664. https://doi.org/10.1080/03054985.2012.745958.
Gilbert, Sophie. 2016. "Learning to Be Human." The Atlantic. https://www.theatlantic.com/entertainment/archive/2016/06/learning-to-be-human/489659/.
Giroux, Henry A., ed. 2014. *Neoliberalism's War on Higher Education*. Chicago, IL: Haymarket Books.
Greene, Maxine. 1995. *Releasing the Imagination: Essays on Education, the Arts, and Social Change*. San Francisco, CA: Jossey-Bass.
Hendricks, Karin S. 2018. *Compassionate Music Teaching: A Framework for Motivation and Engagement in the 21st Century*. Lanham, MD: Rowman & Littlefield.
King, Maxwell. 2018. *The Good Neighbor: The Life and Work of Fred Rogers*. New York: Abrams.
Laird, Lynda. 2015. "Empathy in the Classroom: Can Music Bring Us More in Tune with One Another?" *Music Educators Journal* 101, no. 4 (June): 56–61. https://doi.org/10.1177/0027432115572230.
Macmurray, John. 2012. "Learning to Be Human." In "Learning to Be Human: The Educational Legacy of John Macmurray." Special issue, *Oxford Review of Education* 38, no. 6 (December): 665–674. https://doi.org/10.1080/03054985.2012.745958.
Morgan, Chandler. 2021. "'Everybody Loses' Study Finds Nearly a Third of Teachers Consider Resigning, Retiring Early Due to Pandemic." WIS News. Accessed

February 16, 2021. https://www.wistv.com/2021/02/17/everybody-loses-study-finds-nearly-third-teachers-consider-resigning-retiring-early-due-pandemic/.

New York Times Magazine. 2019. "The 1619 Project." August 14, 2019. https://www.nytimes.com/interactive/2019/08/14/magazine/1619-america-slavery.html.

Nussbaum, Martha C. 2010. *Not for Profit: Why Democracy Needs the Humanities*. Princeton, NJ: Princeton University Press.

Parkes, Kelly A., and Sean R. Powell. 2015. "Is the edTPA the Right Choice for Evaluating Teacher Readiness?" *Arts Education Policy Review* 116, no. 2: 103–113. https://doi.org/10.1080/10632913.2014.944964.

Pearson Education. n.d. "Requirements and Considerations for Candidates Completing edTPA in a Virtual Learning Environment." edTPA. Accessed July 11, 2021. https://www.edtpa.com/PageView.aspx?f=GEN_PlacementInAVirtualSetting.html.

Reilly, Katie. 2020. "With No End in Sight to the Coronavirus, Some Teachers Are Retiring Rather Than Going Back to School." *Time*, July 8, 2020. https://time.com/5864158/coronavirus-teachers-school/.

Robertson, Katie. 2021. "Nikole Hannah-Jones Denied Tenure at University of North Carolina." *New York Times*, May 19, 2021. https://www.nytimes.com/2021/05/19/business/media/nikole-hannah-jones-unc.html.

Ross, E. Wayne, and Rich J. Gibson. 2007. *Neoliberalism and Education Reform*. Cresskill, NJ: Hampton Press.

Scherer, Marge. 2012. "The Challenges of Supporting New Teachers: A Conversation with Linda Darling-Hammond." *Educational Leadership* 69, no. 8 (May): 18–23. http://www.ascd.org/publications/educational-leadership/may12/vol69/num08/The-Challenges-of-Supporting-New-Teachers.aspx.

Wieseltier, Leon, and Drew Gilpin Faust. 2016. "Humanities in Decline: A Cultural Crisis." In *Aspen Ideas to Go*, August 30, 2016, podcast, 55:00. https://podcasts.apple.com/us/podcast/humanities-in-decline-a-cultural-crisis/id702896920?i=1000374741815.

Yob, Iris M. 2020. "There Is No Other." In *Humane Music Education for the Common Good*, edited by Iris M. Yob, and Estelle R. Jorgensen, 17–28. Bloomington, IN: Indiana University Press.

Yob, Iris M., and Estelle R. Jorgensen, eds. 2020. *Humane Music Education for the Common Good*. Bloomington, IN: Indiana University Press.

Chapter 9

From Wide Roots to Connected Branches

Perspectives on Early Childhood Music Education across Brazil during the Pandemic

Tiago Madalozzo, Vivian Agnolo Madalozzo, Angelita Vander Broock, and Regiana Blank Wille

FOUNDATIONS: OUR IDEA OF MUSIC IN CHILDHOOD

Schools in Brazil had been open for only four weeks in 2020 when the COVID-19 pandemic shut everything down. Many music programs for children migrated to the online mode. In this chapter, we share our practices in different early childhood music education settings across three different states in Brazil. We raise questions, ideas, and perspectives on how we reframed the way we plan and teach early childhood music during the pandemic and how these ideas may impact our future, in-person teaching formats. We explore the challenges imposed by the need for reinvented pedagogies and reflect on what we learned through this process, outlining implications for early childhood music teaching and learning.

In Brazil, we use a specific word, *musicalização*, referring to collective music education programs for children with music and movement activities. The word derives from the verb *musicalizar*, which means "to make someone musical" (Ilari 2010, 57). Madalozzo (2021) defines musicalização as a process of sound sensibilization in which children gradually understand the meaning of musical concepts through active music practice, engaging with music in meaningful ways.

Before the pandemic, this might include one or two teachers working with groups of children, with or without their parents/caregivers, in weekly in-person classes that involved dance, singing, active listening, improvising, creating, and playing instruments. During remote teaching, the diverse learning contexts within the family home setting positioned parents and caregivers as a crucial part of the music teaching and learning process more than ever before. As the sounds of household objects melded into music practice, and the omnipresence of music in the daily routine broadened repertoire, new teaching strategies came to the fore.

In this chapter, we use Sarmento's (2013) concepts of childhood and childhood cultures. Through this lens, childhood is a structural and generational category of society: a permanent component of culture and society from a holistic and interdisciplinary perspective (Sarmento, 2013). For Sarmento, Childhood (with a capital "C") is a macro structure through which different generations of children undergo. Moreover, children are biopsychosocial beings—individuals located in a specific historical time and space that is a combination of a multifactor context involving biological, behavioral, educational, and social conditions. This definition promotes the idea of multiple childhoods (with a lowercase "c"), as each child's social environment involves family, school, and society-specific relationships. Therefore, multiple micro childhoods exist across a macro *Childhood* that is a fundamental part of society.

Sarmento (2004) presents childhood cultures as ways in which children understand and intentionally act in the world, a process that is defined by alterity in relation to the adults, as children produce their own culture (Madalozzo and Madalozzo 2021). Among the products and forms of childhood cultures, which include representations and symbolizations of the world specific to children, Sarmento (2004) theorizes four principles of childhood cultures: interactivity, playfulness, fantasy, and reiteration.

According to Sarmento (2004), interactivity in childhood takes place in two ways: with adults and in a peer relationship. Play is a condition for learning and accompanies the construction of social relationships. Fantasy defines the way children build their worldview and attribute meaning to things, thus being the "intelligibility mode" of childhood (Sarmento 2004, 16). Reiteration characterizes the nonlinearity and the possibility of restarting and repeating time for children: it is a "recursive time" (17).

In this chapter, we integrate this theory with music education to explore the ways in which children engaged with music in online settings. We present three vignettes from our work as coordinators and educators in different teaching and learning settings in Brazil. These vignettes reflect critical teaching and learning moments during the pandemic and demonstrate our newfound understanding about early childhood music education. Sarmento's four principles of childhood cultures are key to reading these narratives and lead to three discoveries that emerge from the stories.

We discuss these experiences and observations in relation to our foundational understanding of early childhood music education—the *wide roots* in which our work is based. We then reflect upon the challenges and creative solutions that shape our current practices—the *new branches* that emerged during this period, and that connect our narratives and thoughts, in the same way as the online musical practices have connected all the participants and childhoods involved in musicalização. Finally, we highlight implications for the training of music educators.

WIDE ROOTS: LEADING THREADS FROM TEACHING AND LEARNING SETTINGS

We, the authors, coordinate musicalização programs across Brazil in three different contexts: (i) Alecrim Dourado Formação Musical, a music school in Curitiba, state of Paraná; (ii) the Program of the Integrated Center of Musicalização at the Federal University of Minas Gerais (UFMG), in Belo Horizonte, state of Minas Gerais; and (iii) the Musicalização Program at the Federal University of Pelotas (UFPel), state of Rio Grande do Sul. Most of Alecrim Dourado's students come from upper-class families, whereas children who attend Musicalização at UFMG and UFPel come from a variety of sociocultural contexts, as these are outreach programs offered by the universities. Alecrim Dourado's teachers hold at least an undergraduate degree in Music Education, while the teachers at UFMG and UFPel's projects are music teachers in training. We will further refer to these student-teachers as *instructors*.

The initial context for each vignette is the same: none of the programs were prepared for the sudden demand for online teaching and learning. The starting point is temporally located in March 2020, some weeks after the shutdowns imposed by the COVID-19 crisis.

Vignette 1: Through the Screen

It is a sunny, cold Saturday with blue sky in Curitiba. The teachers, wrapped up with warm clothes and masked, keep themselves at a distance from each other, but it is possible to see that their eyes are watery. It is "Musical Drive Thru" day: all the children come with their caregivers by car to get musical materials for the next weeks of online classes. In bags there are materials for the construction of an instrument, a handwritten letter from the teachers, and a bunch of rosemary, the fragrant herb that lends its Portuguese name to the school. When they receive the bags, children are surprised by its content and mention: "Look: there is rosemary, a letter, and materials for an instrument!". The teachers' eyes overflow.

> *This is the first face-to-face meeting that takes place after the suspension of the school's activities due to COVID-19 in 2020. Children, locked in their cars, exclaim amazed when they see their teachers gathered: "Look! The teacher who has a dog named Bono is here too!"; "Look, this is the teacher that I saw on the computer!". We all have fun with their reflections, in a clear perception that the boundary between face-to-face and online is too thin for them: this encounter is an important moment of breaking through the barrier of the screen and seeing each other in person. A mother parks her car to receive the musical kit. When opening the window, she accidentally unlocks the car door and Cecília, a four-year-old girl, quickly unbuckles her seat belt, opens the back door of the car, and rushes out as if she were running away. Finding her teacher, she grabs her by the legs, keeps her eyes closed, and locks herself in a hug that feels, at the same time, long and hopeful.*

Alecrim Dourado Formação Musical is a music school for children from infancy to eight years old. The school organizes classes by age: infancy to 6 months, 6 to 12 months, and so on. It has a staff of 10 teachers and an average enrollment of 150 children per semester. Classes take place weekly, lasting 50 minutes, and two teachers facilitate each class (Ilari 2010). However, in 2020 the school had to reinvent itself.

Based on initial guidelines from municipal administration, we believed that within a few weeks everything would be back to normal and so our first idea was to offer temporary musical activities, using YouTube, where the aim was to nurture the bond among children, their families, and teachers through musical activities. We created *Music with Family*, a program in which the teachers organized and broadcasted 30-minute daily live-recorded classes to families. Though 100 teaching videos were created, this proved insufficient. Without the real-time interaction of the children, they did not fulfill the aims of the program.

After three weeks, the team of teachers met online to answer pressing questions: *Are we going to teach online? How will we do that? How will children engage? What do the parents expect from us? What instruments will they use?* One key word emerged from the discussion: *interaction*. The question then became: *How could we promote interaction and engagement through digital screens?*

We decided to study the use of screens by children (Sociedade Brasileira de Pediatria 2020), to learn more on emergency remote teaching, and to investigate which digital platform would be more appropriate for online musicalização. However, we found no resources addressing online musical practices for early childhood in Brazil (Souza, Broock, and Lopes 2020). Using information gleaned from literature about older children, we designed a new course based on synchronous, online classes that took place via the digital platform Zoom. The class time was reduced from fifty minutes to thirty minutes. The teachers adjusted all instructional materials so that they could be facilitated using household objects. An idea for students to build their own musical instruments and a desire for a short in-person meeting led to the *Musical Drive Thru* described in the vignette above. Figure 9.1 shows the team of teachers distributing the kits with materials for making musical instruments. Highlighted in the center is one of the students receiving the yellow bag with the rosemary branch.

Figure 9.1 Pictures of the Musical Drive-Thrus at Alecrim Dourado. Credit Tiago Madalozzo. 2020.

Our major challenges were: (i) to maintain the engagement of adults, especially with young children who did not yet have the autonomy to handle electronic equipment and (ii) to attend to concerns about excessive exposure to screens in children's lives. Despite the fact that class participation was a weekly commitment by caregivers before the pandemic, many teachers reported that, due to the heavy home-office workload, the caregivers were too tired or busy to take part in online classes with their children. Although parents currently spend more time with children than in other generations (Dotti Sani and Treas, 2016), the pandemic required a readaptation from everyone, especially in the family setting.

The team also sought solutions to problems brought forth by parents and caregivers regarding difficulties in accessing digital platforms and reports that children "did not sit properly to attend the class." We needed to make caregivers aware that there was no need for the children to sit down or to indeed participate or even watch the class; that making music at home during the pandemic was more than interacting with a teacher online. The team discussed the modeling concept proposed by Bandura (1977), guiding the caregivers to place themselves as observers of their own attitude toward online classes; in other words, teaching the caregivers how to interact and have fun with the children, even if they were not static and "paying attention" in front of the screen.

One strategy was to design colorful, instructional cards that were shared with the families via the class's WhatsApp group. The goal was to develop a fun yet direct way of informing parents and organizing the practices. Card titles included: *Prepare the space for the activity*; *Establish the rules before the class*; *Leave at sight only the necessary materials*; *Have fun with your child*; and *Keep supporting Alecrim!* Card 1 read: "Find a space in your house that is free for the child to move, well lit, and with little noise. No musician likes to play his/her show competing with the washing machine, or with a neighbor who is not an Alecrim student and likes to sing in the shower." Card 4 read: "We are all under social isolation and tired. What if you leave everything behind and just make music with your child? Only two things are necessary to a successful music learning process: a good teacher—something you already have!—and family support. Enjoy!". These messages sent through curricular materials resulted in greater engagement and continuity of family participation in online activities. These instructional cards can be found at rowman.com/ISBN/9781793654144.

This reflection on Alecrim's activities throughout the pandemic highlights an important aspect of the remote classes: that music happens not only inside the school's walls. Through these experiences, both teachers and caregivers opened their eyes and ears to children's musical expressions in their houses as extensions of the music school.

Vignette 2: Challenges for Teacher Training

"Hey! Psiu! Psiu! Psiu! Psiu! (interjection to call someone's attention)."

"Você sabia que o sabiá sabia assobiar?" ("Did you know the rufous-bellied thrush knew how to whistle?"—a Brazilian tongue twister).

"Sabiá! Sabiá! (pun with the words "sabiá"—thrush—and the past form of the verb "to know": "sabia")."

It was a remote music class for 3–6-year-old-children in a Zoom synchronous meeting. Everyone had their cameras and microphones on. Two teachers-in-training led the group with autonomy and joy, in front of their computer, isolated in their houses. Students and teachers had plastic pots and spoons; the song was "Sabiá," by Luiz Gonzaga, a great icon of Brazilian music.

When introducing the song, one teacher played a game with the lyrics of the song, singing a verse and asking the children to say "Psiu! Psiu! Psiu!" every time he stopped. All the children were engaged with the music. In the second part of the song, the challenge was to "call the thrush" between one stanza and another. Plastic pots and spoons had been used in a previous class, so children spontaneously used again the resources at hand. One child started to "call the thrush" singing inside the pot. The teacher noticed the student's action and imitated her, suggesting that everyone did the same. The children connected even more with the activity and interacted creatively by exploring various ways to sing and express themselves.

The CMI—"Centro de Musicalização Integrada" (Integrated Musicalização Center) at UFMG is a complementary department of the School of Music, which brings together teaching, research, and outreach. The CMI is a teacher training laboratory, and offers outreach programs for babies, children, and teenagers, with musicalização and instrument classes. All the teachers-in-training are students at the university's BA in Music, and are supervised and accompanied by their professors, who teach specific courses for planning, and hold weekly follow-up meetings. In the in-person mode, these practices take place in a building attached to the Music School. Classes are divided by age. For children up to 6 years of age, musicalização classes are offered once per week. From age 7 onwards, classes are held twice per week—one for musicalização and the other for a musical instrument.

Starting in 2020, with the suspension of in-person instruction, classes took place remotely, with synchronous meetings and provision of support materials. Because of this new teaching format, many families canceled their enrollments, and the CMI went from 470 to 185 students. With this significant dropout rate, children were organized in a more comprehensive way with groups from 6 months to 3 years and from 3 to 6 years. The new format also led to many challenges regarding teacher training. Coordinators wondered how they would train student instructors to teach in such an unfamiliar setting. Another challenge concerned the perceptions of the community, which did not know what to expect from the new format.

As in the previous vignette case, everyone initially believed that in-person practices would soon be viable. But over time, it became necessary to develop strategies for online classes. The first step was to carry out open experimental meetings. Families needed to understand how the classes would work. Instructors needed to explore the resources they had at hand. The platform Zoom was chosen for these meetings. After a 4-week trial period and many meetings with the instructors, the coordinators decided that the platform chosen, the adapted format of the classes, and the interactions with children were a viable approach to the online experiences and the classes restarted.

We designated two instructors for each class so that they could take turns leading the activities and share in *paying attention to the responses* of the children and their caregivers. Additionally, if any instructor had technical problems, the other could take over the class without interruption. Co-instructors could also exchange experiences and debrief together. This strategy worked well in ensuring robust engagement of children and families. Still, according to the instructors, creating bonds and establishing clear and efficient communication with students was very challenging. Additional challenges included: dealing with technical limitations and not being able to play music together because of sound latency issues.

Practices that made room for *musical play* were the most successful during this period, as shown in figure 9.2. This screenshot of a Zoom meeting displays interactions and engagement between instructors and families, instructors sharing experiences and testing Zoom's tools (such as switching their background), and instructors and families exploring household objects, like spoons. As in the previous vignette, children appear in different places and spatial configurations: alone or with a caregiver, interacting or not with the suggested sound object; engaging with their whole body or even in a static position; in the living room, in a bedroom, and even inside a bus.

Figure 9.2   Screenshot of a CMI/UFMG Project's Online Class. Credit Angelita Maria Vander Broock-Schultz. 2020.

Buckets, pans, wooden spoons, and other household objects were great allies of children's online music classes. As everything became potential sound sources, children explored the objects around them and their sounds in inventive ways. Many times, even the CMI instructors were challenged to deal with unexpected situations in creative ways, looking for innovative solutions. Some positive aspects raised were the possibility of exploring audiovisual resources with ease, the use of digital resources such as backgrounds and filters, the convenience of not having to leave home to go to the CMI building to teach the classes, and the possibility to use virtual games. Another point raised was the opportunity for student-teachers to learn through collaborative work with a peer.

CMI coordinators sought to offer instructors support for classes, guiding them to articulate musical practices with students, to produce musical content, and to understand the entire teaching-learning context (Oliveira, 2015). As a result, the team was increasingly aware of the children's responses and was able to highlight and use them creatively, establishing a musical and artistic communication as seen in the vignette above.

Vignette 3: Reflecting on Interaction and Participation

In Portuguese, the official language of Brazil, there is a word called "saudade," which means "sentiment of sorrow, nostalgia and incompleteness, caused by the absence, disappearance, distance or deprivation of people, times, places or things to which one was affectionate and happily connected and that one would like to be present again" (Infopedia, n.d., Definition 1).

That feeling seems to describe the emotion of one mother who took part in the Musicalização Program at UFPel: "The class was awesome, teachers! It was great to have participated in the class! The kids loved it. This mom here has been touched. But, I miss going to the meetings!". This statement reflects a yearning to return to in-person meetings after a whole year of the COVID-19 pandemic. It brings out a feeling of nostalgia for something that was abruptly taken away from everyone, and which they wished to have back.

This "missing" generated emotion by parents and children, who in some cases have participated in the project since the first months of life and had their four-year birthdays in a context of social isolation. Until the beginning of the pandemic, weekly music classes were part of their daily routine, but in 2020 this changed. This memory of pre-pandemic, in-person classes highlights the absence of interaction, music, being with others, and sharing joy.

The Children's Musicalização Project at UFPel is a free university outreach project offered since 2007. Until the suspension of classes, it worked at LAEMUS—Music Education Laboratory. The facility has a specific space for musicalização classes, with materials, sound toys, and musical instruments that are specifically for musicalização practices. There are several instructors, a scholarship-holder instructor, and undergraduate students from the BA in Music at UFPel and other programs such as Pedagogy, Bachelor's Degree in Composition, and bachelor's degree in Piano.

Following lockdown in March 2020 there was no activity until mid-April, when the academic calendar was reorganized. The project started again with weekly, remote meetings between the coordinator and the instructors teaching in a digital context. The discussions centered on the idea that for Musicalização Infantil the priority was interaction and making music in person. After May, the team produced recorded music classes and made them available on a YouTube channel to the participants of the program. The team was split into pairs, and each established a recording schedule and ways to inform the parents about the classes.

Unlike the in-person mode, the groups of children were reduced and merged into two large groups: infant to 2 years, and 2 to 4 years. Almost three months later, the project started its online version and from August until November, weekly pre-recorded classes were made available to the families.

There were many initial challenges. As most of the materials remained in the university building, not all instructors had musical instruments, sound objects or children's musical instruments at home. Many instructors had little to no experience in video production. Many of the children's caregivers did not have a place specially prepared for the classes, with instruments or musical objects. In addition, there were shared challenges of both instructors and families such as internet connection issues and difficulties with the use of technologies.

Given that the classes were pre-recorded, instructors worried about how to know if children were interacting, making music, and taking part with their parents/caregivers. The difference between *watching* and *interacting* became an important question for the coordinators. A solution raised by the group was to ask caregivers for a report of musical practices in a text message, photo or video. The hope was that children would see their teachers in the videos and feel the enthusiasm and energy of the team.

The caregivers provided feedback about classes after direct requests. After receiving the last recorded class in 2020, one of them sent this message, referring to the video: "We really, really, really appreciate it. Araúna loved the mess in the music! By the end she took the guitar to accompany teacher Regiana (laughs)." Feedback like this acknowledged the children's and families' enthusiasm toward the activities. And yet, at the weekly planning and study meetings, the discussions always centered around the same questions: *How are the children really receiving lessons—with the enthusiasm and dedication we seek to show, or are they just watching our performance? Are we carrying out the interactions we are looking for between children and parents/caregivers? What are the musical responses like?*

Considering the alternatives available in November 2020, the team decided to start offering online synchronous classes. As the project is public, there was no budget to use platforms with technical resources (backgrounds, filters or games), and the instructors had technical difficulties (some used cell phones with weak internet connection). The remote synchronous classes brought new challenges: providing equal access to children and caregivers with their different connected devices; providing a pleasant place to participate in the activities; the impossibility of playing and singing together with unmuted microphones (even if some children accidentally left them on). These were all similar to the issues that the team from UFMG had to deal with on their first attempts at online classes. Once again, the instructors wondered, *Is the interaction between instructor and students, between students and caregivers, and among themselves, really happening?*

The two teaching and learning modes—recorded asynchronous materials and synchronous live classes—are illustrated in figure 9.3. The first picture, sent by a caregiver, shows children interacting with a pre-recorded class. The second is a screenshot of a pre-recorded class featuring the teacher singing. The third picture was sent as feedback from one of the caregivers, showing a girl interacting with the teacher during a live class.

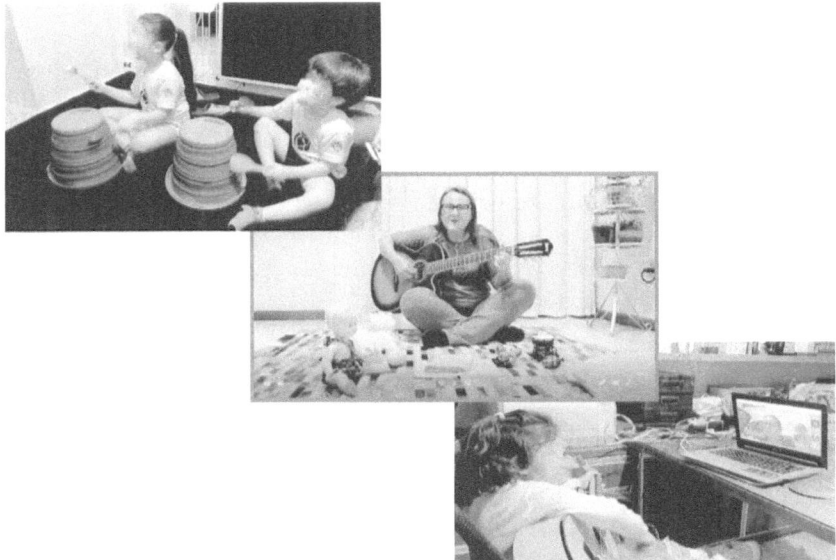

Figure 9.3 Two Pictures and a Screenshot of UFPel Project's Classes. Credit Priscila Garcia, Henrique Wille Buss, and Joseane Canez. 2020.

The 2021 school year started in February, again with remote synchronous classes. Feedback from the caregivers continued to highlight the idea of interaction as a crucial part of musicalização. As one commented: "Hi guys! I was happy with the return of classes, even if it is not yet possible to meet in person. Olivia really liked it, too. It's great to be able to meet up with friends and the teacher. Kisses full of affection for everyone!"

Many challenges remained, whether technical, educational, or musical. Yet, while many children and parents left the project at the time of remote classes, there were also many that remained enrolled in the project. There were many possibilities for learning about the use of platforms, digital resources, and recording applications. As an outreach project that has a history of several years offering musicalização practices, one sentiment presided: remote classes are possible, but not substitutes for in-person classes. They cannot replace the beauty of having partners to play with live and making music together.

CONNECTED BRANCHES: EMERGENT THEMES

The narratives shared above reflect some common experiences across contexts: each team's ability to adapt, glance at possibilities, and face challenges; the sensitive focus of coordinators and teachers/instructors on children and different childhoods across the projects; and an attention to featuring children and their participation, which is the starting point of every planned action.

When we look back at the *wide roots* of our pre-pandemic work, the definition of musicalização, and the concepts of childhood and childhood cultures, these stories reveal a larger narrative of early childhood music education during the pandemic that highlights three important themes: (i) the use of screens and the resulting interactions in musicalização; (ii) the ways in which teachers/instructors recognize children's musical expressions; and (iii) the centrality of an interactive process among children, caregivers, and teachers. In this section, we explore each of these themes, describing strategies for reframing practices that grow out of them.

The Use of the Screen

Based on the unprecedented need for interaction with digital resources through screens during these classes, we suggest that such interfaces act as distance shorteners, which was a vital aspect of establishing relationships during the pandemic. None of these courses used any technology-based resources before, and that was not unusual in Brazil. For that reason, we argue that it is a potential turning point in musicalização classes from now on.

Historically, The Brazilian Society of Pediatrics tends to publish strict guidelines limiting or even completely discouraging screen-time, especially for younger children. However, the guidelines manual published by the Society in 2020 suggests that, taking social distancing into consideration, the digital world offers alternative solutions for the restrictions on people living together, where the use of screens offers possibility for education. Unlike previous guidelines, the new document argues that, besides the use for school assignments, there is also an "affective use" of screens that can ensure the "presence," even if only a virtual one, among the children's relatives and friends (Sociedade 2020, 3). This affective use of screens implies a direct management by the parents or with some level of monitoring.

Our work revealed the vital role of electronic interfaces in encouraging collaboration with musicalização at home. We discovered the inefficiency of screens as a one-way means of communication such as lessons produced and addressed to the children, who would watch them passively. Digital content is a way to promote interactions but learning itself doesn't happen *on* screen rather through the relationships between children and caregivers. Our goal became, then, to engage caregivers in the music learning process; an invitation to interact: a *co-sharing* of possibilities.

Connecting with Children's Musical Expressions

Broock-Schultz (2013) points out the game-like quality of musicalização pedagogy. Improvisation and spontaneous actions happen all the time, requiring constant changes in pedagogy in order to "take advantage of children's situations of discovery" (48). As such, teachers are the main agents in guiding the music teaching and learning process. This was seen in the UFMG's project story, where the instructor was alert to the children's musical responses, mimicking them and incorporating these expressive elements into the lesson.

Beyond this, we discovered that interactions with the children's family through multiple digital resources (WhatsApp groups, exchange of pictures, messages, audios, and videos) made it possible for teachers/instructors to have continuous access to the different ways children produce and respond to music. This widened the context when compared to a traditional situation, where such family engagement would have happened away from the teachers' gaze. It is essential that caregivers are considered in their important role as *facilitators* in musicalização. In live classes it can be difficult for teachers/instructors to pay constant attention to the children's bodily expressions. Establishing paths for continual communication with caregivers offered us, the facilitators, a view of the musical and social elements that emerged from musical interactions in the family context even when the camera or microphone did not record them. Training caregivers to recognize and capture these musical moments became a core goal in the projects discussed above.

Meaningful Music Learning Through an Interactive Process

Meaningful music learning involves shared action between children, their teachers, and their families. This interaction is made possible by caregivers participating, singing, and improvising in the process of musicalização. the construction of meanings in musicalização takes place through "interactions constituted with other partners in real and tangible practices, through an environment that brings together circumstances, elements, social practices and meanings," in an action shared with all parties—children, teachers, and caregivers (Wille et al. 2018, 60).

Remote learning revealed even more clearly that we cannot think of one childhood, but rather, multiple childhoods (Sarmento 2013) since social and affective conditions, and technological access among children in their different family contexts can differ greatly. For infants, the online class was not designed to engage them directly but rather be a resource for the caregiver to guide and interact with the child. We often asked caregivers to have their babies' backs to the screen, in a position to interact with the caregiver and not with the phone or computer. As such, the screen was, ironically, a way to get children *out* of the screen.

Within a family context, online musicalização was a practice where parents/caregivers were in a way *forced* to see their children making music. The teachers/instructors were framed on the screen, whereas the co-habitant adults witnessed the children's musical expressions. We emphasize that, being the *eyes and ears* of the teachers/instructors at home, the caregivers got a very new and deep role in the process, as the entire musicalização practices depended on their involvement and participation.

In the end, the main agents of the musicalização process are the children. In each of the three projects discussed above, we noticed that children seemed to show their participation and expression more clearly than in face-to-face settings restricted to the space of school rooms. This was supported by accounts from caregivers who were more attentive to the musical expressions of their children in different times and spaces in the home routine. Such accounts emerged with the use of communication technologies. Caregivers' sharing of out-of-class musical moments was no longer restricted to passing conversations at the classroom door.

IMPLICATIONS FOR FUTURE PRACTICES

Our experiences in these three contexts have caused us to rethink our basic definition of musicalização as *wide roots* and introduce the notion of *connected branches*. With this in mind, we connect our discoveries to Sarmento's

(2004) four structuring axes of childhood cultures: interactivity, playfulness, fantasy, and reiteration. Although Sarmento did not develop his theory in regard to music, we borrow these concepts to broaden them in light of musical education during the pandemic.

We understand that *interactivity* is central to children's relationships with music, peers and adults (teachers and caregivers). Screens served as shortening elements in these relationships, as the presence of technological interfaces and digital resources was crucial so that musicalização became viable. Musicality in early childhood education takes place through musical and social interactions (Madalozzo 2021). Yet, inclusion appears to widen comprehensively in the remote mode. Children's musical expressions happen, and are seen, not only by the teachers but also by the caregivers. Interactivity now occurs in two ways: through the screen and within the family.

This point leads to an expansion of the concept of *playfulness* in musicalização. Play is a creative experience that permeates a significant part of children's actions, and which can also generate learning experiences, especially when it involves children and their peers and the adults with whom they engage. The music, the gaze, the movement, singing, and speaking we witnessed were all parts of this musical *play* and generated new possibilities for engagement. The screen became an extension of what happens in a broader and more complex way in the in-person mode. Recall the musical drive-thru in Alecrim Dourado; the children's surprise when they saw the teachers they had been making music with in recorded classes; their joy at receiving the *affective* objects in their bags. All of this suggests that face-to-face contact interfaces with the relationships built through the screens.

Musicality happens in a time, a space, and a reality that are particular to each child. The notions of *fantasy* and *reiteration* also help to understand what we witnessed in musicalização online activities. The remote teaching experiences demonstrated that children do not need to respond musically only when teachers allow them to activate their microphones. They don't need to limit themselves to imitating the teacher's suggested body movements. Experiencing music with the family through the screen is, above all, free, fun, and musical. It does not have to be from a physical presence or in a sitting position. Children engaged with the musical experiences by being *present* even if in constant movement, out of the frame of the camera, or listening and expressing themselves musically in another room in the house.

As a result of our online experiences, we have reimagined our former practices, connecting and expanding them into *new branches* of musicalização. Just as the roots provide nourishment for each branch of a tree, we recognize that a wide and consistent concept of childhood cultures in musicalização provides the basis for new, yet connected, aspects of early childhood music education. Examples are many in the stories we relate above: the interaction that emerges from the whole community being involved; the different, yet complementary, roles of the in-person and online settings; the widening of the concept of *presence*; and an understanding that music making happens in the most unexpected places and spatial configurations. Our powerful experiences in these online projects have impacted our notions of in-person music classes and what we always considered the most appropriate, even sole way of making music with young children.

FINAL THOUGHTS

The remote mode reframes topics in music education that are not new. While these topics originate in face-to-face teaching, they are highlighted exponentially in interactions mediated by screens and by the adults in a closer way. What we have seen, because of the pandemic, is that music is one element that indisputably penetrates children and families in their homes, enabling new teaching approaches based on a very new way of doing music.

Despite very real logistical issues of access to technology for all, we advocate a respect for children's music expressions, taking advantage of technology to rethink music as a fundamental part of childhood, especially after an entire year of social distancing. In the coming years, we hope to highlight three important considerations. First, the potential of teaching music to children in the hybrid mode, considering the active and affective use of screens, reaching families in a most engaging way. Online musicalização classes can provide an opportunity for families located in other cities, states, and even other countries to experience Brazilian culture through music. We discovered that the online format worked well for many families. Thus, remote learning is one more possibility for musicalização, capable of bringing the entire family together in musical learning and including children from anywhere in the world who can benefit from this format.

A second consideration is the valuing of professionals who work with young children's music education. In a country where musicalização is viewed as recreational activities without learning goals and where most of the music teacher-training courses do not focus on early childhood, online classes contributed to helping parents and caregivers become aware of the learning processes involved and shifted their perspectives on the specialized work of early childhood music teachers. Online teaching and learning experiences will likely impact teacher training and future careers as well. The urgent need to learn new ways of producing content, editing music and video, operating computers and other equipment to facilitate online classes, handling virtual platforms, and at the same time to interact more than ever with the students' families, discovering ways to promote musical dialogues during the classes, developing innovative and creative proposals to engage students through the small frame of a digital interface—all of these issues are now part of teaching and learning in musicalização. They change not only the way we will make early childhood music from now on, but the way in which the curriculum of undergraduate courses on music education must be rethought for the training of future teachers.

A final consideration is the acknowledgment of children's musical expressions observable in online musicalização settings, which seem to be more accessible now than in previous in-person 50-minute classes. We hope that parents and caregivers will come to value musicalização in a more evident way and look for courses that engage the whole family in music making, beyond weekly meetings in the music school.

As coordinators and professors, we assume that we work on behalf of a creative, expressive, and wide musical life for children in musicalização. Musicalização is a tree that has grown on account of the deep efforts made during the pandemic by music teachers across the country. We hope that children are the ones who get the most from the multiple lessons we have learned.

REFERENCES

Bandura, Albert. 1977. *Social learning theory*. Englewood Cliffs: Prentice Hall.

Broock-Schultz, Angelita Maria Vander. 2013. "Formação de professores para musicalização infantil: o papel da extensão universitária." PhD diss., Federal University of Bahia.

Dotti Sani, Giulia M., and Judith Treas. 2016. "Educational Gradients in Parents' Child-Care Time Across Countries, 1965--2012." *Journal of Marriage and Family*, 78, no. 4, 1083–1096. https://doi.org/10.1111/jomf.12305.

Ilari, Beatriz Senoi. 2010. "A community of practice in music teacher training: the case of Musicalização Infantil." *Research Studies in Music Education*, 32, no. 1, 43–60. http://doi.org/10.1177/1321103X10370096.

Infopédia, s.v. "Saudade." Accessed July 15, 2021, https://www.infopedia.pt/dicionarios/lingua-portuguesa/saudade.

Madalozzo, Tiago. 2021. "'I want [to hear] it again!': 5-year-old children's creActive involvement in music education." *Revista da Associação Brasileira de Educação Musical*, 29, 120–136. http://doi.org/10.33054/ABEM20212907.

Madalozzo, Tiago, and Vivian Dell' Agnolo Barbosa Madalozzo. 2021. Childhood cultures on early childhood music and movement: constellations at play. *RELAdEI - Revista Latinoamericana de Educación infantil*, 10, no.1, 45–57. Accessed June 6, 2022, https://revistas.usc.gal/index.php/reladei/article/view/7790.

Oliveira, Alda. 2015. *A Abordagem PONTES para a Educação Musical: aprendendo a articular*. Jundiaí: Paco Editorial.

Sarmento, Manuel Jacinto. 2004. "Childhood cultures in the crossroads of second modernity." In *Crianças e Miúdos. Perspectivas sociopedagógicas sobre infância e educação*, edited by Manuel Jacinto Sarmento and Ana Beatriz Cerisara. 9–34. Porto: Asa.

Sarmento, Manuel Jacinto. 2013. "A sociologia da infância e a sociedade contemporânea: desafios conceituais e praxeológicos." In *Sociologia da infância e a formação de professores*, edited by Romilda Teodora Ens and Marynelma Camargo Garanhani. 13–46. Curitiba: Champagnat.

Sociedade Brasileira de Pediatria. 2020. "*Alert note: recommendations on the healthy use of digital screens in the time of the COVID-19 pandemic.*" Last modified May 21, 2000. https://www.sbp.com.br/fileadmin/user_upload/22521b-NA_Recom_UsoSaudavel_TelasDigit_COVID19__BoasTelas__MaisSaude.pdf.

Souza, Isaac, Angelita Broock, and Helena Lopes. 2020. "Musicalização on-line para a primeira infância em tempos de pandemia: reflexões sobre práticas em construção." Paper presented at *XII Encontro Regional Sudeste da Associação Brasileira de Educação Musical, 2020*, 1–12. Accessed June 6, 2022, http://abem-submissoes.com.br/index.php/RegSd2020/sudeste/paper/download/613/422.

Wille, Regiana Blank, Gabriela Cintra, Andréia Lange, Tamiê Pages Camargo, Luana Medina de Barros, and Leidiane Borba Feijó. 2018. "Consolidando ações entre música, infância e inclusão." In *Infância cidadã*, edited by Francisca Ferreira Michelon and Matheus Blaas Bastos. 57272. Pelotas: Ed. UFPel. Accessed June 6, 2022, http://guaiaca.ufpel.edu.br/handle/prefix/4144.

In Dialogue

The Courage to Change—A Dialogue of Experience

In this dialogue, Dr. William L. Lake Jr. and Dr. Albert R. Lee reflect on the impact of COVID-19 and social justice awareness, and their impact on music education and music performance.

WL: If anyone had told me at the start of the COVID-19 pandemic two years ago that we would still be wrestling with this health crisis, paired with the flames of the awareness of social inequity in our country, I *would* have believed them. Everything in our world has changed (although we work hard to deny this truth), including the world of music education and performance. How did we get here?

AL: I will start with the big picture. I will talk about music education through the lens of race, gender, sexuality—a myriad of intersectional points and thinking broadly about music education as K-DMA/Ph.D. because I think we have to deal with the entire educational landscape to understand where we were, where we are, and where we are going. Before the pandemic, we were horrifically disjointed. We talked about collaborations between institutions, programs within institutions, and educational levels but, there weren't any in all honesty. There wasn't anything tangible that we could say was happening, and *if* there was any collaboration, it was because individual people decided that coming together as artists was important.

WL: I totally agree. For institutions in the public and private sector, that's horrible.

AL: Yes, that *is* horrible. I am learning, as a scholar, however, to assess and not judge.

WL: That's not easy to do.

AL: Yes, I may know that circumstances are not excellent or what they should be, however, I evaluate things for *what they are*. Once I have an emotional reaction, my ability to do what I do at the highest level goes out the window because I'm angry. The anger manifests because the solutions have always been there. The answers have been offered –but it's *the powers that be* that aim to preserve and sustain power at all costs that limit the advancement of our society and profession (this isn't solely about race—it includes gender, class, and all the—isms that plague our country). The classical music field, like most, was not without influence of these ills. The profession is incredibly elitist and thus also plagues formal music education training in our country. The pandemic exposed these problems.

WL: I have become more and more aware that although there is advancement in music education in the area of inclusive pedagogy, forward motion is often stifled such that power is preserved by gatekeepers. These moments appear when faculty members and students present issues regarding admission requirements and expanding the curriculum to only be met with shallow solutions that don't really address the core of the problems.

AL: Control. Control is a significant factor that we must see with clarity. I think it's so important to understand that as humans, the lower the stakes, the more ferocious the politics around power, because—*If I don't have a lot of money, I must at least run something.* Before the pandemic, a few high-level K through 12 programs and college programs were consistently producing at a high level because the infrastructure was set up for them to produce (the fiscal infrastructure, the personnel, everything they needed). This is a privilege. There are many institutions where leadership desires to preserve a sense of power to inhibit capacity and infrastructure.

WL: What's alarming to me is that so many ideas and visions are marked dead on arrival—we won't try new ideas; new visions seemingly repulse us. We can't pretend that the issues of society are not also here in our creative and performance space.

AL: Problems we want to solve—we solve. Evaluating issues and problems in departments you've worked in—you'll notice specific problems get solved—and others are allowed to fester for ten years; we need to call a committee together for discussion—those that are immediately remedied.

WL: There are also these moments where committees are charged with huge tasks with no frameworks to do these tasks. Let's rewrite the curriculum!—*How are we going to do this? Are you going to provide a framework to do this?*

AL: So, here's what we have as we consider the expediency or the glacial pace of change. We come back to power. We could discuss white supremacy; however, that term creates deflective responses—so we will just underline that classical music supremacy means—that unless it fits this aesthetic, we aren't even going to assess your music, study it, we're not going to consider it, we're not going to even look at it. I'll add that this false supremacy is equivalent to false freedom—one must seek to control you to be supreme. Even as a classical singer, I realize that the genre closes off everything else—classical music refuses to compete in the broader musical sphere; thus, it closes off everything else, pandering to those with wealth and power, creating an insular paradigm.

WL: This makes the genre often anti-Black, anti- *other*, unless it's based on white cis-gender heteronormativity. The music becomes a soundtrack for that space.

AL: When I was working for my previous institution, I saw the traps—State University, R1-Institution, and a smaller music department. Why were we not advocating for music education curriculum with the state legislature to improve the K–12 music experience? One, it would aid K–12 teachers to have a foundation to execute their work. Two, it would ensure that a large body of prepared musicians are ready for post-secondary training (liberal arts degree, performance, commercial music, etc.) It makes sense, right? As I surveyed the programs, including some that I worked for before attaining my advanced degrees, there were programs advertised. Still, significant competencies were unaccounted when you surveyed the course of study.

WL: Did we work for some of the same institutions? I found myself asking quite often at a previous institution, "How are students getting this degree when this major experience is missing from the program?" This was when I realized even more that the same degree from two different institutions does not equal the same acquired experiences: significant ensemble experiences with only two concerts a year versus four; programs with chamber music experiences, others with none.

AL: Yes! To make matters worse, what we offer is also racist, sexist, and exclusive. It's understandable, then, why people would want to *blow the whole thing up and start over.*

WL: . . . which still wouldn't change much because the powers that decide what gets included are still biased and often lack the formal training to execute a diverse curricular experience.

AL: We must look at music, competencies, and exposure. For instance, we must determine, at the end of elementary school, what programs should be produced at this level for our students at the end of elementary school. *What should a student who has completed music middle school know about the musical world around them?*

WL: . . . the diverse and inclusive world around them (even if in aspiration).

AL: K–12 teachers are stretched so thin, paid so poorly, and have so little actual oversight and so little power to fight for their programs. The education provided for students lacks growth as a living art form.

WL: . . . and the resources to be inclusive are all around us—specifically . . . our students who don't identify with musical traditions of Western European influence.

AL: Before formal music training, I was a Black church kid. I could learn anything. If you sang it to me. I could sing it back to you and if I sang it two more times, not only was it learned but it was also memorized.

WL: . . . and you probably added a little *something* to it. You had very advanced aural skills; you lacked the knowledge of how what you sang would be labeled in a tradition outside of your own.

AL: I was successful before the labels. My mother, however, raised me never to make an excuse for a lack of achievement.

WL: Did we have the same mom?!

AL: I learned quickly what I didn't know—and figured it out. I had a teacher tell me about two-thirds of the way through my first semester that I should drop and try again next year. My mother would *kill* me!- I figured it out! By the time I was navigating my doctoral program, I had tested out of theory requirements.

WL: While we both navigated the space, I uniquely grew up as a gospel and formally trained musician due to the myriad of music I experienced in church upbringing. Classical style anthems intertwined with the gospel, spirituals, contemporary gospel, and hymns sung in multiple styles set me on this unique course to appreciate such a wide variety of music. It became a fluid vocational experience. Improvisation, creativity, expression existed in my life in amazing ways in and outside of the classical, jazz, and gospel worlds. Essentially my upbringing *disrupted* the norms and isms (to some extent).

I feel that COVID-19 as a *disruption*, the pause, the caesura brought our profession to a place of hearing the music and voices around us that were smoldered by domineering cultures. Right before the pandemic, many classical institutions were poised to celebrate the 250th birthday of Beethoven. COVID-19 canceled these plans due to the health concerns of amassing so many people together in a health crisis we didn't understand. As a result, music directors were forced to consider other repertoire, some overlooked, and commissioned "hot off the press" composed for smaller forces.

AL: In many cases, the inability to do the more significant well-known works disrupted the traditional obsessions with specific works (hint: around Christmas and Easter) and explore new and insightful programming that resonated and proved relevant to communities beyond the 55 and older crowd. We've always had the infrastructure to do this—those in power have chosen not to. As we consider infrastructure, if the body of knowledge culturally, musically, and artistically is streamlined, everyone can benefit from each other (K–12, Community Colleges, Four Year Institutions, and Graduate Degree-Granting Institutions).

WL: This lack of community within our field is bringing about a slow death in terms of sustainability. This resistance to the magnitude of music that makes up the unique cultural and life soundtracks that exist in our communities can't last with favorable results. The merging of a health crisis and social injustice is but one pandemic in itself. How we relate to each other, and the world abroad has brought us to travesty. It is an outward symptom of an inward disease.

AL: To cure this illness, we can't go after what is necessarily easy. Some illnesses require difficult procedures. Because we are underpaid, overworked, and under-resourced in education, we are always looking for what is most efficient—"How do we cure this with the cheapest, less obtrusive initiative?"

WL: You can't microwave great art.

AL: You've got it—At the highest level, you have to burn the midnight oil. People may not know this about me, but I sing on the praise and worship team at Love Fellowship Church. My favorite rehearsals were the ones where Bishop Hezekiah Walker came in. He wouldn't do all of the rehearsals, just special ones from time to time. Bishop Walker was a taskmaster! He knew exactly how he wanted every single note, syllable, and phrase to be constructed. There was an electric energy to those rehearsals such that you'd look at your clock all of a sudden and realize that three hours had passed.

WL: I relate a lot to that experience and find that the unique myriad of cultural experiences I've had have allowed me to have a unique flair to rehearsing, performing, interpretation, and style. However, I lament for many of our students who only know music through a very narrow lens. My students don't have the unique aural knowledge of how expression, text, and interpretation in genres like gospel can fuel their interpretation of even classical aesthetic works. Music never was an *or* for me—it has always been *and*.

AL: I hope that we develop a sense of collaboration in music education and performance in the years to come. There are so many intersections and much to learn from all disciplines. When I was in my master's program at Juilliard, I will never forget going to a dance concert. It was truly inspirational seeing how this particular dancer moved to spoken poetry. At the moment, I wasn't sure why I needed to experience this and how it would apply to my career as a singer—but I knew that I needed it.

WL: We need teachers that will say to their students, "You need to go to a dance concert. You need to go to that lecture; you need to go to the museum and check out this new exhibit." Unfortunately, we don't consume culture, we don't consume the arts, and then we have the nerve to call ourselves *artists*. Our period of social reawakening demands that we strive evermore to be more authentic, more accountable, and sincere in the art that we create. The social requirement for us, as artists, is that we do our homework and move from mere appropriation to performances of appreciation. There are so many idiosyncrasies in a culture's music that are available to us for study and informed practice—we have to do better.

AL: Because of COVID-19's isolation and quarantine, we are closer than ever before. Through Zoom, webinars, and other interactive sessions—our access to each other has increased. The excuses to be more authentic in our practice are over. Relating this to education, teachers must consider that they are the leader of the change we want to see as we go forward through, and hopefully, post-pandemic. I think of myself as the classroom leader, where I am accountable for my studio's contribution to the changes that we need to see in our institutions.

We need leaders in our institutions who will be more vigilant in the changes our institutions need to survive. I see the resistance to expanding performance repertoire and reimagining curricula as *refusing to work* as we are charged. Until our leaders hold our programming and syllabi against diversity, equity, inclusion, and belonging standards, the change that could come from these moments will be stuck. This isn't a threat to any professor's research interests; however, the institution's mission, vision, and core values should be apparent.

WL: I'm excited about the disruption actually; I believe that we are witnessing and helping correct the course of our profession and society at large. It won't come without its conflicts and resistance; however, we will be better people because of this experience. The question is, "Do we have the courage to change?"

Part III

DEMOCRACY AND DUMPSTER FIRES

Chapter 10

Remodeling Choral Experiences

Historic Preservation or Gut-Job Renovation?

Andrea Maas

In fall 2018, I bought the 100-year-old home I currently reside in. As I write, more than half of my life in this home has been some version of COVID-19 quarantine or the like. Living so intimately and intensely within these walls and under this roof with my family has given me ample opportunity to appreciate the sandstone foundation, the worn but beautiful woodwork, and the strength and endurance of the cast iron radiators. The single-paned windows are impossible to open in the summer and incredibly inefficient in the long, frigid winters. I'm convinced that the plaster walls and ceiling are being held together by paint, and yet, the time spent in this space, and the experiences shared with my family, have afforded me a truly aesthetic perspective, shaping this structure into a home. At times, I have considered the improvements we could make to the house to respond to the needs of a growing family living in contemporary society. I respect the craftship while becoming acutely aware of how its age has required significant updates and renovations over time. I'm sure the original builders of this house never imagined that it would need grounded electrical outlets or that we would all benefit from double-paned glass windows in the middle of winter. Or, that a dishwasher would not only be more efficient but also help keep a working mother sane. Certainly, there are newer, innovative technologies that another person might integrate into this home that I don't even know exist.

I like to think that the educational spaces I move through benefit from my experiences in this house in the ways that I value the *good bones* while recognizing a need for updates. The COVID-19 pandemic moved me to see this old house and the choral spaces I inhabited differently than I had before and compelled me toward an ongoing process of remodeling choral experiences in music teacher education.

On Tuesday, March 11th, 2020, the governor of New York announced that all SUNY (State University of New York) schools would move to a distance-learning model for the remainder of the semester to reduce the spread of COVID-19. I had a sense that we might close for a short period, but it was somewhat shocking to hear we would be online through May. There was a lot of work to do to figure out how I would facilitate a large choral ensemble and serve as a model to my students for teaching music online! The inability to sing together in-person would certainly require a reimagining of what my students and I intimately knew as choir. I recalled the potential that Randall Allsup (2016) described for reimagining large ensembles as a *remixing* of the old and new, the familiar and unfamiliar, making space for possibilities we may have not previously considered. Yes, please! I was ready. Then I realized I had just twelve days to plan for how I would conduct choir online for the remainder of the semester.

Days turned to weeks and the charmingly crooked floors in my house became more noticeable during the daily dance parties my husband and I held to keep ourselves and our toddler sane. I thought nonstop about my work and my students, and I wondered: *How would the foundations of what we knew as choir stand up to such extraordinary disruption?*

Three weeks of online learning turned into three semesters during which, the students and I were challenged with deciding which traditions and values of choral singing we would cling to, "keeping the old warm" (Allsup 2016, 64) while learning to "flip, dip, and serve"-up new approaches to ensemble music making (1). This chapter describes the joint pursuit between myself and the members of my choir as we sought possibilities for group singing in online settings.

I'll be playing with the metaphor of remodeling choral spaces and the ways such renovations impacted my students' experiences and my own roles. I find myself looking beyond the facade; scrutinizing form and function, questioning who these experiences and the specific spaces in which they take place are intended to serve, and what changes, if any, might better serve their needs. I begin by reflecting on my own process of coming to terms with disruption and what choral singing might look (and sound!) like in online settings. I then describe the ensuing collaborative endeavor with singers to rediscover meaning in our work and determine how these meanings would manifest in pedagogy, curriculum, and music making. Finally, I discuss the implications of remodeling choral experiences in music teacher education in post-pandemic landscapes.

SITUATING OURSELVES IN A GLOBAL PANDEMIC

As a music teacher-educator in New York State, I experienced the shift to distance learning before having a concrete sense of what this would mean for teaching and learning music. Like many, I was asked to make the sharp turn to teaching music online with less than two weeks' notice. The shock of the pandemic and the immediate isolation of quarantining were reflected in every choice I made. We were all—teachers, students, staff, and families—literally in survival mode. At the time I was teaching multiple field experience courses in both general and choral music, and I also led a fifty voice SATB choir which was comprised mostly of second-year music education majors. This choir became a focal point for how I would respond to the pandemic as a music teacher-educator and is the subject of this chapter.

At first, the students and I "made it work" together, trying to stay connected, desperate to find ways to continue to make music together using collaborative, digital, music making tools like Soundtrap, GarageBand, and Acapella. We converted the repertoire we had been preparing into various projects that the students could choose to engage with. The projects were framed by questions and prompts designed to engage them in four artistic processes: Respond, Connect, Create, and Perform/Present (National Core Arts Standards 2015). Their final presentations included slide presentations, music videos, and audio recordings of their work. I was astounded by the students' engagement and creativity at a time when most of us had little energy to take a shower or don a real pair of pants.

At the same time the students in my field experience courses were struggling to find meaning in their work now that their ability to teach children had evaporated overnight. They expressed losing their sense of purpose—that they had only just begun to identify as music educators and without children to teach they felt "at a loss" for why they would continue their work. After some reflection to relocate our core values and principles as music educators, the students and I discovered that caring for students through the design of meaningful, musical experiences was where we found meaning in our work. This new clarity of what our work was about was one of the most important lessons I learned during pandemic teaching, and it became the foundation for how I would approach my own teaching with my choir. Although this first semester often seemed like mere survival with little time for planning and reflection, I felt incredibly fortunate to have found some meaning through the experience.

Reorientations

As the fall 2020 semester unfolded and our classrooms remained too dangerous to enter, the physical spaces the singers and I inhabited continued to take on new definitions. Rehearsal halls were now online meeting rooms, personal living spaces, cloud-based software applications, and digital audio workstations. Distanced learning during a global pandemic challenged the notion of equitable and inclusive learning spaces. Previously (Maas 2021), I have considered the ways in which rehearsal configurations impacted perceptions of power, how nongendered concert attire could acknowledge and validate the identities of the singers, and how privileged experiences would inform our work as ensemble members. Now, students were participating across a variety of spaces and formats. Some students were on campus with limited access to practice rooms where they could sing and make music without worry about roommates and dormitory policies. Some were off campus, either living in total isolation, or back home with all of their family members in close quarters. In some cases, students were sharing their physical space, internet bandwidth, and digital devices with large numbers of people or they didn't have access to adequate digital devices at all. Tragically, many were caring for sick family and friends or were ill themselves. I needed to be flexible and open to all possibilities for music making and collaboration if I was going to adequately provide opportunities for these students to be heard—both literally and figuratively.

Our shift in physical spaces also impacted the interpersonal relationships between myself and my students where opportunities for care manifest. As I continued to plan, I was reminded of Nel Noddings' descriptions of relational care in which the carer is both attentive and receptive "to understand what the cared-for is experiencing—to hear and understand the needs expressed" (Noddings 2012, 772). Ethically, the teacher as carer must go one step further, so as not to assume the needs of the student but understand the "*expressed* needs of the cared-for" (772, original emphasis), so as to respond to their needs appropriately. One might further associate notions of care with Maxine Greene's description of "connected teaching" in which, "the caring teacher tries to look through students' eyes, to struggle *with* them as subjects in search of their own projects, their own ways of making sense of the world" (Greene 1988, 120, original emphasis). This act of caring for students would allow me to better understand how I might adapt my pedagogy and curriculum to respond to my students' needs. And, while I knew that being flexible with students was important, I also learned that my students benefited from my ability to be consistent and reliable. I remembered the announcements made on airplanes before take-off instructing me to put my oxygen mask on before putting on my child's. It goes against every instinct in my body, but it's true: one can't take care of another if one doesn't have the oxygen they need to breathe. I became keenly aware of my own well-being, specifically in the context of my identity as a mother of a small child. Self-care became critical to my ability to care for others.

Between February 2020 and January 2021, the world witnessed an exodus of over 2.5 million women abandoning the workforce to care for their families as compared to just 1.8 million men (Bateman, Nicole, and Martha Ross 2020; Marte, Jonnelle, and Aleksandra Michalska 2021). Like many other parents at the start of the pandemic, my son's in-home daycare provider retired to manage her own health needs. Thankfully, just before the fall 2020 semester we learned that we had acquired a spot at the University's childcare facility for which we had been on the waiting list for over 2 years. I was ecstatic. Then I was terrified. I grappled with the idea of sending my three-year-old to what felt like the *front lines* of the pandemic—putting him back in school so that I could teach more effectively—even though I, myself, would not and could not teach in person. It was devastating to consider.

What would it mean for me as a teacher-educator to model self-care, resilience, and caring for my family while also fulfilling my work obligations and attending to students' needs? All at once, I realized bell hooks' rejection of the idea that we must compartmentalize and disconnect from "life practices, habits of being, and [our roles as] professors" (hooks 1994, 16). It became clear that there would be childcare challenges beyond the usual, with no possibility of support from an outside caregiver. I knew that I would be better able to serve my students in a consistent and stable manner, within a virtual space. I also understood that it was an incredible privilege to be able to choose how I would teach my classes for the next year. My decision to remain fully virtual was grounded in principles of well-being, equity, and inclusion, a desire to reduce chaos, and an aim toward consistency and stability to make room for the flexibility and creativity we would need to carry out whatever experiences we were afforded. Much like parenting, I made critical choices based on unique and constantly changing circumstances, using my best judgment at any given moment. There was, and would continue to be, little guidance for how best to proceed.

SEEKING OPENINGS

When I adopted my choir two years earlier, B.C. (before COVID), I felt I needed to do something to set this choral experience apart from the other mixed choir experiences they would have during their time in our program. I decided to intentionally integrate practices that would help these singers, who were largely second-year music education majors, begin to analyze and evaluate their ensemble music making in the context of their future work as music teachers. I was simultaneously terrified and thrilled to embrace these aims with these students in the upcoming year. The fall 2020 semester brought a new group of singers who would work together for the entire academic year in an online setting. The students were skeptical, to say the least, about holding rehearsals online, and debated whether we should approach our classes from a business-as-usual stance or if a reconceptualization was necessary. We all felt inclined to hold fast to what we knew and loved about singing in choirs, but it was clear that if we were going to be successful, we would need to step outside our comfort zone. I wondered: How far would we need to go? How far were we willing to go? I determined that we had two distinct challenges before us. First, the students and I needed to establish a working conceptualization of what it meant to be in a choral ensemble, and then, we would need to consider the pedagogical and curricular implications of these ideas. I was excited to present these challenging questions and hear their responses, but I was also fully aware that this was not what the students were accustomed to in a class called *choir*.

Reconceptualizing Choir

To stretch the remodeling metaphor—pandemic protocols and the nature of singing online had essentially stripped choral spaces as we knew them, down to the studs. We struggled as an ensemble to imagine what our choral experience would be in this new setting. I found that although I was confident in my principles and values of teaching, I lacked confidence for how my students and colleagues would perceive my choices for carrying them out. I have long believed in facilitating ensemble music making experiences that invite musicians to be active participants in a process-oriented endeavor. Particularly for preservice teachers, this is an opportunity for them to find agency in how they conceptualize ensemble music making and develop their own philosophies and approaches which they might take with them into their teaching. Now more than ever, the need to question and problem solve what, why, and how we would sing together presented an opportunity for such engagement. However, the traditions and assumptions we held about choirs were a burden, especially when confronted by technical and logistical barriers to carrying them out. In online spaces, the physical walls of the rehearsal rooms were nonexistent, but the expectations and traditions of large choral ensembles weighed heavily on each decision I made. Randall Allsup's concern that "the ideology of achievement, excellence, and Mastery makes more nuanced considerations feel subordinate" (2016, 12) resonated loudly with me in this moment. Realizing that the students seemed to be facing similar ideological and perhaps, existential conflicts, I decided to invite them into this process of reconceptualizing choir with me so that we could collaboratively reconstruct the meaning of our work for a new choral experience.

I initiated the process by asking the singers of the choir what they had hoped and expected to get from this course. This launched a vibrant, and somewhat heated, conversation about what it meant to be in a choral ensemble. Some students held very tightly to the idea that they must learn and perform traditional choral repertoire and yet, they understood that doing so would be challenged by our inability to rehearse and perform in person. Others believed it was possible to stretch the notion of choral ensemble to simply mean making music together using their voices. They weren't quite sure how we would go about it but they thought this might open the door to more possibilities. This quickly ignited a discussion about performance and outcomes. Some wondered, how can we possibly perform if we can't stand on a stage and sing together? Others suggested a reimagining of performance as a presentation of their work, prioritizing processes over products since we were uncertain about what the products could and would consist of. We set forth on a quest to experiment with a variety of approaches to doing choir online.

The students began by drawing on the practices of singing in large groups that were familiar to them. We tried working together in online sectionals using breakout rooms to learn and perform Samuel Coleridge-Taylor's "Summer is gone." Debates over the pros and cons of working to construct a *virtual choir* video project, as so many others were doing, resulted in the decision that this would not be the best path for us. We did not have the technical or fiscal resources to carry out a finished project similar to some of the examples they had seen shared via social media. Instead, we decided that working in smaller groups in collaborative, online spaces would be preferred. The students understood that this work would require some exploration of new digital tools, and an engagement with audio or video editing, which was a new skill for most. They also realized that any final product would likely be less polished than a professionally edited video, but they preferred to work on material of their choosing and to have autonomy over their expressive and artistic choices. We set deadlines and presented unfinished, *works in progress* to one another during class time. It was not what many imagined as their collegiate choral experience but in their final reflections and course evaluations, some remarked on the positive surprises they encountered through this work: "It was great to do something creative with my friends even if it's not chorus. I loved playing my bass again too on the backtrack. I don't usually get to play at school. Maybe I should start a band after COVID!"; "I'm so impressed by my classmates! We came up with so many interesting and different interpretations of the same piece."; and "I didn't know I could edit video and audio! I actually had a lot of fun putting our recordings together with the photographs we took." Others were clearly exhausted, frustrated, or downright angry: "I don't know how much longer I can do this." and "I want my money back!" We agreed in our final class discussion that most of all, we missed the intimate and spontaneous interactions that come with in-person music making. We knew we could not solve all of the challenges we faced but we decided on several parameters for moving forward in the spring 2021 semester:

1. Students would work in smaller groups.
2. We would collectively be more flexible with deadlines and outcomes.
3. Students would identify interests and possible topics to pursue with their small ensembles.
4. Students and I would collaboratively develop project plans with reasonable expectations.

The first and second parameters specifically addressed obstacles presented by distance learning and pandemic life. We simply could not navigate the constantly changing needs of fifty individuals and expect to engage in any kind of productive, artistic process. One another's physical and emotional health were at top priority. Quarantining, isolating, financial barriers, limitations of technical resources, all posed challenges that became exponentially more difficult to overcome with a larger group. Parameters 3 and 4, addressed our desire to not only overcome such challenges but to make the experience manageable and meaningful. We used a questionnaire, an online discussion forum, and class conversations over Zoom to identify possible topics and peers with common interests. After some negotiation and reorganization to address remaining logistical components such as project formats and timelines, we had fifteen small ensembles that were ready to work.

There was no question that singing together was the most important aspect of our choral experiences. Yet, in these moments, this was the most challenging to accomplish by traditional means. We had to work toward a version of "keeping the old warm by providing an understanding of the new" (Allsup 2016, 63). Technological barriers such as latency prevented the satisfying, synchronous singing we had hoped for and even presented minor challenges in recording to cloud-based software programs. Singing together, synchronously, in online environments remains significantly challenged despite exciting developments in low latency software programs such as Reaper and Sonobus. Unfortunately, the costs of some digital tools and resources continue to pose barriers to equitable participation by all ensemble members. When the students broke into smaller ensembles, however, the possibilities for solutions expanded. Now students could more easily share media and other files that were not cloud based, had more flexibility in the software choices they engaged with, and could more directly address and solve barriers in hardware or other access issues. The ability to self-select small ensembles was key in enabling students to sing together in person when it was safe to do so. When this was not possible, students identified the aspects of singing together that they could achieve using innovative, problem-solving approaches. Students prioritized collaboration to reach a collective expression of musical ideas which they discovered they could carry out in a variety of ways that did not look or feel like choir in its most traditional forms.

Discovering Creative Possibilities

To facilitate a process-oriented experience from a distance, I adapted Creative Music Strategies (CMS) (Robinson, Bell, and Pogonowski 2011) for online settings. CMS suggests a series of steps to help guide groups through a collaborative and creative music making process:

- Identify a springboard for the strategy
- Develop an open-ended musical question
- Large-group brainstorming: Aural/oral analysis—set musical parameters
- Personal exploration: Aural/oral analysis
- Large-group conducted improvisation and small-group planned improvisation (composition)
- Record for reflection
- Reflective aural/oral analysis

As we rehearsed online, I found that the students and I benefited from a collaborative space where we could document the creative process thus, I created a template presenting the CMS steps using a Miro board—a cloud-based whiteboard. It was free to use, reproducible, and accessible via a link. I used elements of the Miro board such as shapes, post-it notes, and text boxes to create a visual map of how they could proceed through the steps. I intentionally placed the springboard at the center with the possible steps for engagement around it in a circle, rather than in a sequential list to make it a more flexible and fluid process. When music educators facilitate a CMS in an in-person setting, the teacher typically serves as a guide, listening and responding to the students' work during each of the steps. She might ask a question to challenge the students to think differently and more deeply about an idea or encourage a musical exploration or experiment based on a student suggestion. More importantly, the teacher might observe something in the students' work that warrants skipping or repeating a step, taking them out of the presented order. To accommodate for our online circumstances, I incorporated numerous prompts and questions into the Miro board template to guide the students through the steps, as I would not be present during much of the work that would take place. I checked the boards between our synchronous meetings to see how the students were progressing, suggest additional resources or approaches, respond to musical artifacts, or to post follow-up questions to further guide analysis or focus a discussion.

The CMS template served as a valuable way for me to support students as I observed their work. It also became an important tool for responding to the regularly changing needs of these students who were still navigating the challenges of living and studying in the midst of a pandemic. It provided them the flexibility they needed to remain engaged with their ensemble in an online setting as well as a collaborative space to develop creative ideas beyond synchronous Zoom meetings. An example of the CMS Miro board template with my prompts and questions can be seen in supplemental materials at rowman.com/ISBN/9781793654144.

We applied the CMS to "Summer is gone" to develop an understanding of the process and imagine possibilities for using this template with smaller groups and new topics. We worked as a full ensemble during synchronous Zoom meetings to learn the music, share collective understandings and contextual knowledge, identify individual musical skills and assets, and brainstorm presentation ideas. We used the Miro board as a space to document this work so we could return to it during each rehearsal. The students then broke into smaller groups to plan and present the work. They posted links and embedded media to the Miro board, and we gathered to share the final products.

This collaborative Miro board contains artifacts of *musical brainstorms* or experimental ideas for voicing and expressive choices, images of the composer and his family, links to historical and biographical information, embedded videos and audio of other performances for analysis, audio recordings of rehearsals, links to individual parts for editing in a digital audio workstation of their choosing, images and backtracks to accompany their final performances, and a few final performances in the form of links and embedded media. The Miro board demonstrating the class's use of the CMS to explore and present Coleridge-Taylor's "Summer is gone" can be found in supplemental materials at rowman.com/ISBN/9781793654144.

Finally, I turned them loose to develop their own springboards and pursue topics of interest that they agreed upon as a small ensemble. They designed projects to reflect various genres and styles of music such as musical theater, vocal jazz and R&B. They investigated intersections of gender and musical traditions such as Sea Shanties and challenged gender normative roles in group singing. They composed original music inspired by visual works of art, and studied the potential of music to support and tell the stories of those suffering from mental and emotional health challenges. In many of these projects, the singers incorporated secondary, tertiary, electronic, and homemade instruments and they demonstrated their ability to apply digital skills using tools like Soundtrap, iMovie, and GarageBand. They became photographers, cinematographers, screen writers, and film score composers. The Miro board allowed for multimodal readings and responses to the materials they were engaging with. For example, during an analysis of one of the pieces they were covering, the students went beyond reading the notation and lyrics in the score to seek a variety of performances, posting links and embedding video, audio, and still images on the board. They were able to rehearse independently and then post excerpts of their work, sharing interpretations, and discussing expressive choices before recording. The students were able to move through the CMS in a flexible manner, skipping or revisiting various steps as needed. They could schedule synchronous times to meet or they could attend to elements on their own, asynchronously. Students' musical and extra-musical assets paved the way as they engaged in creative processes and arranged musical works across a variety of genres and styles. Some composed original works inspired by their personal interests in visual art, social justice issues, and literature. They also created backing tracks, video, and image slideshows to accompany their performances.

I built time into our planning to discuss what the presentation of this work would look like. The students decided early on that they did not want to livestream their work as if it were any other concert. They preferred to share it among peers and invited guests. Their insecurity and vulnerability were palpable but so was their sense of pride in their work and their eagerness to share it with those who had participated in this challenging experience. They chose to present their fifteen unique projects over four, final course meetings so that each group would have an equal opportunity to share their work and receive feedback. The students discussed the quantity and the quality of the time they needed for these presentations, generously considering their peers' efforts and their own interest in learning from one another's work. They thought carefully about what a performance of this music might require. Debates ensued about the purpose and value of performing in both online and educational settings and the students considered how this would impact their work. Many chose to incorporate video or still images reflecting the multimodal ways they listen to and experience music (Lewis 2020).

While there were certainly challenges for both the students and me throughout this process, there were also many unanticipated and positive aspects to this work. Many of the students in this ensemble were flexible and versatile musicians who play other instruments and have experience in various genres and styles beyond traditional choral repertoire. As such, many of the small ensembles engaged musically in a variety of other ways including electronic music making. Most importantly, the students seemed curious about their own learning, and all fifty singers were fully engaged through the end of the project. In discussion forums, students described their engagement with the work and were able to realize how they and their peers each contributed in meaningful ways throughout the artistic process. They described finding agency and independence in selecting materials, defining rehearsal processes, and engaging in creative and collaborative skills. I was surprised by the frequency with which many directly referred to their identities as preservice teachers. Several students identified areas for continued professional development in their final reflections and discussed elements of their work that they hope to carry forward as future music educators. The two quotes that follow are final reflections by singers in the choir at the end of the spring 2021 semester. Student names are pseudonyms.

May 5, 2021, Marcus Williams

> I hope to develop in the future as a learner as well as an educator by using some of the ideas I started focusing on through this project and incorporating them into my own classroom in the future. Throughout the course of this project, I was able to start thinking in the perspective of myself leading a classroom and encountered problems and tried to fix them as best I could. I would like to take this mindset into my further development in order to be constantly working on what I can in the future with my students.

May 7, 2021, Chiara Tomasi

> Watching my peers share their ideas openly and freely has inspired me to share myself unquestioned as well. I hope to also bring this creative process to one of my future choirs. Being able to choose our own projects and [the] pieces [we] performed, while still maintaining learning goals was so enjoyable to me. Too often, music can be too strict on its students. Embarking on a passion project, or something I truly enjoy was amazing. So, I hope to bring those ideals to my future career!

Re-Discovering Original Musical Ideas

Throughout the semester, much of our class time was used by students to work asynchronously on their small group projects with planned, synchronous meetings for sharing progress, resources, and discussing successes and challenges. I found through these discussions and observations of their work that, for many of the singers, creating music in an online setting seemed to be simultaneously daunting and exciting. They wanted to explore new music and even create arrangements of familiar songs, but they struggled to create original musical works. They were unsure how to begin, where to find inspiration, and how to shape an idea once it was born. We realized that distanced learning was providing us with many opportunities for forming thoughts *about music*, but forming independent, original, *musical thoughts* proved much more challenging. After an exasperated exclamation by one student of, "Making music is so hard right now!" I wondered, was it only distance learning that had caused this perception or was it the different, unfamiliar nature of the music making that was difficult? Learning vocal parts independently was more challenging for some students who needed to seek out support and resources. Combining their voices in digital spaces was understandably new and challenging, calling for skills and tools that they were not prepared to engage with. The uncomfortable revelation was however, that this setting may have revealed a deeply shrouded truth: *that we in music education had inadvertently been facilitating a learned helplessness for students when it came to imagining and articulating original musical ideas.* Had students become accustomed to having their music making directed in specific ways so that, without that structure, they simply did not know how to proceed? Were they so reliant on notated scores that without such a *script* they didn't know what to sing about? Making music in-person was impossible. Making music together was significantly challenged. Making music, especially original music, was right there—in our bodies, brains, voices, fingertips—but felt out of reach for many.

I hoped that through the small ensemble projects utilizing a Creative Music Strategy, students would begin to improvise and share musical thoughts as part of the brainstorming process. However, students expressed a fear, tentativeness, or vulnerability when it came to sharing original musical ideas. After some discussion, the students and I agreed that sharing musical ideas more regularly was not only an important skill that they wished to develop confidence in but could also contribute to our overall sense of community and satisfaction as musicians.

Monday class meetings became a time for gathering as a large group to sing and generate musical thoughts. We engaged in a scaffolded process for generating ideas, drawing from Pauline Oliveros' notion of expanding one's awareness of the musical environment and then using the voice to enhance, expand, and respond to the sounds heard (Oliveros 1971). We used our time together on Mondays to develop new understandings of what it could mean to generate original musical ideas and sing as a group. The students were challenged with learning to listen and forge new musical thoughts through improvisation exercises. We often sang muted so students could explore their musical ideas and vocal possibilities. I had learned from doing similar work with middle school singers in the past, that being able to practice as a group, provided them the space and time they needed to develop their ideas and the confidence to share them. In an online setting, we had the benefit of privacy via mute. We laughed (and cried) as we came up with topics to sing about and brainstormed words and phrases. Some days the topics were more serious in nature as they navigated personal responses to the pandemic, racial tragedies, and political conflicts unfolding. One theme for improvisation, "Pandemic Blues," offered a solid inspiration for text as well as a structural form for this work. Other days the students just needed to be silly and sing about the weather, their favorite quarantine food, or cleaning their rooms. I provided a variety of pre-recorded backtracks and played live piano accompaniments from my living room piano for them in different styles. Harmonic and melodic loops on Soundtrap and various blues backtracks found online gave the singers a chance to improvise over familiar progressions. We explored the effects of expressive choices on musical ideas, including the impact of text, meaning, vocal timbre, articulation, and phrasing. Throughout these sessions, numerous students began incorporating other instruments including percussion, electric bass, piano, flute, and french horn. Ultimately, some took the risk to unmute and sing in a call-and-response format, improvising in real time with their classmates.

The necessary and long-overdue updates through the integration of digital tools and resources were a key element of our ability to proceed with collaborative and meaningful musicking during distanced learning. The inability to gather together in a rehearsal space, pass out choral folders loaded with octavos, and sing together, in person, led students to find more accessible, digital materials to engage with musically. This included not only digital sheet music but more often video, audio, and alternative forms of notation. They could draw on various digital tools such as MuseScore, GarageBand, Chrome Music Lab, iMovie, FlipGrid, and Soundtrap to differentiate learning and acknowledge multiple literacies and ways of listening (Bernard and Abramo 2019; Lewis 2020). These tools helped students to engage regardless of their skills or musical experiences.

REMODELING ENSEMBLE EXPERIENCES IN MUSIC TEACHER EDUCATION

The disruption I encountered as a facilitator of choral ensemble experiences during the COVID-19 pandemic caused me to confront the uncomfortable realization that the existing format of choir might not be serving my students' needs not only in that moment, but also more generally as preservice music educators. It led me to ask challenging questions about all of the ensemble experiences they are afforded during their degree program such as: Who is included in these ensembles, who is left out? Whose needs do the ensembles serve? Which experiences are prioritized and how does that impact the learning experiences of ensemble members?

Deweyan thinkers may recall the familiar quote, "If we teach today's students as we taught yesterday's, we rob them of tomorrow" (Dewey 1916). This call to action, as I hear it, seems exponentially more urgent during times of rapid and dramatic change. More recently, Webster and Williams (2018) reminded us that leaders in the field of music education have been calling for fundamental curricular change for nearly fifty years, and the role of technology in curriculum reform has been considered for over thirty years! I realized that failing to integrate digital tools in ensemble settings would be to continue to ignore the ways students are interacting with music and to limit their creative potential during these experiences. Scholars posit that singular courses focusing on music technology are less effective than an overall integration of music technology across and throughout curriculum for preservice music educators (Dorfman 2016; Webster 2016).

I began to think that designing a more flexible ensemble experience could create potential openings for incorporating digital tools and other innovative pedagogies in applied settings. I noticed that our experiences integrating digital tools reflected a recent report by James Frankel (2021) who interviewed leaders in music education technology and identified key factors for selecting engaging tools such as points of access, learning curve, the ability to support curricular goals and foster creative work by students of varied skills and experiences. I also observed that while we selected digital tools largely to facilitate specific curricular aims and musical processes (Bauer 2014), the students benefited from the exploration of tools to help them imagine new and unanticipated curricular pathways that centered around creativity and diversity of musical experiences (Bauer and Mito 2017; Dorfman 2016; Webster and Williams 2018).

As I wrapped up a year of online teaching I could not pretend as though none of this happened and just go back to business as usual. I attempted to place myself as a player within the remodeling metaphor in specific ways: I recognized my potential to act as a *re-modeler* in the sense that I could directly reform my choral ensemble curriculum to look and sound differently. I could also serve as a *role model* to demonstrate dispositions of flexibility, versatility, and creativity in the learning environments I cultivated. This modeling, or remodeling, would occur through advocating for, and facilitating flexible spaces for music making.

In fall 2021 I returned to teaching fully in person. In preparation for this, I co-conspired with a colleague who had undergone their own transformational discoveries in choral settings, to design a new ensemble course which we called an *Eclectic Ensemble*. The course would be an experiment in group music making focused on democratic practices, flexible and versatile musicianship, and acknowledging the multitude of ways the singers in our choirs are musical.

Facilitating online choral ensembles during the COVID-19 pandemic demanded a resituating of my own roles and responsibilities. Teaching online repositioned me both literally and figuratively as I was aggressively *shoved off the podium* and sat down in my home office chair. Initially, it presented an opportunity for me to interrogate the form and function of choral experiences as a structural endeavor but through what became a collaborative and responsive process, I discovered that I could also model new ways of being with my students to help these preservice teachers imagine new possibilities for their own roles and their future students' musical experiences. It reminded me of the value of stepping aside and allowing students to re-create their [musical] worlds (Freire 1970).

We often teach as we have been taught. Leading a large ensemble is no different. Consequently, ensemble experiences in music education programs serve as models for teaching and learning which preservice teachers will likely adopt and re-enact in their own teaching. But what experiences are they afforded in these spaces? Borrowing the emphasis of the prefix *re* from previous scholars (Allsup 2016; Freire 1970) has helped me to understand how music teacher educators might open spaces for flexible and diverse musical encounters. When the pandemic offered a wide-open path with no instruction manual, I found guidance from my students, eliciting their musical assets, interests, and curiosities to sketch a blueprint for remodeling choral experiences. However, rather than codify and define our particular iteration of choir as a blueprint on paper, I think I would prefer to use an Etch-A-Sketch, so that I can shake it up, erase, and start over with the next group of students. Our new Eclectic Ensemble has, of course, distinct course aims and objectives that include among other things: engaging actively and critically in repertoire selection and rehearsal processes, experimenting with various stylistic approaches and performance techniques, developing dispositions of equity, diversity and inclusion toward ensemble singing and playing, and effectively communicating musical and extra-musical intentions to an audience through the performance of group music in a variety of styles, genres, and languages. As their instructor, I continue to seek ways to integrate digital tools to expand and enhance their collaboration and music making. I encourage them to *bring in* the apps, digital media, and other technology that they would normally engage with and not *leave it at the door.*

Of course, my colleague and I need to situate even this very openly formed ensemble within logistical parameters such as rehearsal schedules, concert dates, and space availability. Yet, we allow the needs, experiences, and interests of its members to shape the program and define the small ensembles within. We think carefully about the frequency of facilitated and independent rehearsals and how we will utilize our learning management system to mediate and share weekly progress through forum discussions and multimedia artifacts. We facilitate vocal and other warm-up activities to support the work of the individual ensembles and intentionally integrate improvisatory music making into these experiences. Occasionally the student ensembles take on the look and sound of what one might expect from a traditional choral performance: standing in semi-circles, holding scores, singing in four or more designated voice parts. However, their work also takes the form of modern bands, barbershop quartets, vocal jazz ensembles, free improvisation ensembles, and other groups that have no defined format but are instead driven by the topics and questions they choose to pursue. The musicians sing and play numerous other instruments, compose, arrange, and perform music in a variety of styles and genres. The students employ their musical and cultural assets and self-identify the gaps in skills and contextual knowledge they wish to fill. Together, we continue to explore the integration of digital tools in this ensemble setting. They are indeed *eclectic*.

The lockdown caused by COVID-19 dismantled large performing ensembles and catalyzed changes in a field that had remained largely the same for nearly one hundred years. I'm not sure how this rendering of choral experiences will be read in years to come. I'm not sure I can say whether it qualifies as historic preservation or gut-job renovation or somewhere in between. But much the same way that being with my family has shaped the making of our home and the experiences we've shared in it, putting the focus on being with my students has informed the remodeling of the choral experiences we've created together. It has been surprising, challenging, intimidating, thrilling, and rewarding. I'm grateful for the students who have been willing to put on their metaphorical hard-hats and join me in the difficult work of facing disruption, change, and the unknown.

REFERENCES

Allsup, Randall. 2016. *Remixing the Classroom: Toward an Open Philosophy of Music Education*. Bloomington, IN: Indiana University Press.

Bateman, Nicole, and Martha Ross. 2020. "Why has Covid-19 been Especially Harmful for Working Women?" Brookings (March). Accessed September 9, 2021, https://www.brookings.edu/essay/why-has-covid-19-been-especially-harmful-for-working-women/.

Bauer, William I. 2014. *Music Learning Today: Digital Pedagogy for Creating, Performing, and Responding to Music*. New York: Oxford University Press.

Bauer, William I., and Hiromichi Mito. 2017. "ICT in Music Education." In *The Routledge Companion to Music, Technology, and Education*, edited by Andrew King, Evangelos Himonides, and S. Alex Ruthmann, 91–102. Routledge.

Bernard, Cara and Joseph Abramo. 2019. *Teacher Evaluation in Music: A Guide for Music Teachers in the U.S.* New York: Oxford University Press.

Dewey, John. 1916. *Democracy and Education.* New York: Free Press.
Dorfman, Jay. 2016. "Exploring Models of Technology Integration Into Music Teacher Preparation Programs." *Visions of Research in Music Education* 28: 1–24. Accessed January 19, 2022, http://www.rider.edu/~vrme.
Frankel, James Thomas. 2021. "Choosing Engaging Tools for the Music Classroom." In *Creative Music Making at Your Fingertips: A Mobile Technology Guide for Music Educators*, edited by Gena R. Greher, and Suzanne L. Burton. New York: Oxford University Press. Oxford Scholarship Online. Accessed June 6, 2022, https://doi.org/10.1093/oso/9780190078119.003.0004.
Freire, Paolo. 1970 [2018]. *Pedagogy of the Oppressed: 50th Anniversary Edition.* Translated by Myra Ramos. Foreword by Donald Macedo (2018) and Afterword by Ira Shor. (2018). New York: Bloomsbury.
Greene, Maxine. 1988. *Dialectic of Freedom.* New York: Teachers College Press.
Lewis, Judy. 2020. "How Children Listen: Multimodality and its Implications for K-12 Music Education and Music Teacher Education." *Music Education Research* 22: 373–387. https://doi.org/10.1080/14613808.2020.1781804.
Maas, Andrea. 2021. "Facilitating Musical Expression in School Choirs: Honoring Individuality, Seeking Unity." *International Journal of Research in Choral Singing* 9: 116–142. Accessed June 6, 2022, https://acda.org/wp-content/uploads/2021/12/IJRCSVol9Maas.pdf.
Marte, Jonnelle, and Aleksandra Michalska. 2021. "Pushed by Pandemic, Women Struggle to Regain Footing in U.S. Job Market." Reuters. Accessed July 9, 2021, https://www.reuters.com/article/us-health-coronavirus-women-jobs/pushed-out-by-pandemic-women-struggle-to-regain-footing-in-u-s-job-market-idUSKBN2AW19Y.
National Core Arts Standards. 2015. Accessed September 9, 2021, https://www.nationalartsstandards.org/.
Noddings, Nel. 2012. "The Caring Relation in Teaching." *Oxford Review of Education* 38, (December): 771–781. Taylor & Francis. https://doi.org/10.1080/03054985.2012.745047.
Oliveros, Pauline. 1971. *Sonic Meditations.* Sharon, VT: Smith Publications.
Robinson, Nathalie G., Cindy L. Bell, and Lenore Pogonowski. 2011. "The Creative Music Strategy: A Seven-Step Instructional Model." *Music Educators Journal* 97: 50–55. http://www.jstor.org/stable/23012591.
Webster, Peter R. 2016. "Creative Thinking in Music, Twenty-Five Years On." *Music Educators Journal* 102, (March): 26–32. https://doi.org/10.1177/0027432115623841.
Webster, Peter R., and David Brian Williams. 2018. "Technology's Role for Achieving Creativity, Diversity and Integration in the American Undergraduate Music Curriculum: Some Theoretical, Historical and Practical Perspectives." *Journal of Music, Technology & Education* 11: 5–36. https://doi.org/10.1386/jmte.11.1.5_1.

Chapter 11

Curating Open Spaces

Digital Learning and Democratic Pedagogy

Judy Lewis

What would pedagogy look like if anything were possible?

The sudden lockdown in March 2020 forced all music educators online. Most, at the university level, were unprepared, having limited experience in teaching on digital platforms. As such, all of us were forced to either struggle to translate our familiar music teaching paradigms to an online space or to search for different approaches that would work in the new and unfamiliar digital environment. With the understanding that spending hours in online synchronous classes was not educationally productive, the question of how to sustain and enhance student engagement became a pressing issue.

This chapter is about how I re-envisioned one of my courses in response to this challenge. Put differently, it is about finding myself in the unique position of being free to imagine possibilities; to "look at things as if they could be otherwise" to quote Maxine Greene (1987, 3). It is about a decision to embrace the unique affordances of digital spaces rather than impose digitization on pre-existing content. It is about a course becoming a space for student-driven exploration, student-designed content, and collaborative meaning-making; a shared experience in emergent pedagogy fueled by students' assets, interests, and sense of shared purpose. It is about how through this *experiment in pedagogy* we all discovered our agency, our voice, and a unique form of community. Finally, it is about how this foray into a space of open possibilities gave me a new perspective on my role and purpose as a music teacher-educator that I carry with me back into the classroom with four walls.

Democratic Pedagogy

In fall of 2020, I started a new teaching job at a university in New York State. Beginnings are hard in normal circumstances. But, in August when we were told our fall classes would be online, I realized I would not have the opportunity to meet my students in person, something which is critical for all teachers and even more so for those beginning in a new setting. And so, because of pandemic restrictions I was challenged with not only constructing courses that would relay specific content online but doing so in a way that the students and myself (and the students and each other) would feel some sense of connectedness.

One of those courses was *Secondary General Music Practices*. The focus of this course is on ways of *doing music* with high school students who, for whatever reason, do not participate in traditional large ensemble offerings. As such, it can be a rich experience for preservice teachers who may be primarily focused on performance-based pedagogies. It serves as a forum in which to explore the many ways of being musical, the deep relationships adolescents have with music, and how we, as their teachers, might enhance and sustain those relationships. Historically, the course has highlighted popular and vernacular music and I was eager to keep this focus.

I have long been a proponent of democratic music education—spaces where all voices are impactful (Woodford 2005). I have, within the constraints of higher education, always had an eye for ways to make my courses more collaborative and open experiences; spaces where students' voices are as important (if not more important) than my own. I also consider myself a pedagogical disciple of Paolo Freire (1970) and his work with democratic pedagogy. I spent several years implementing a Freirean pedagogy in an elementary school setting in New York City, pedagogy grounded in the children's generative themes and with striking results (Lewis 2016). I now found myself excited about the possibilities of conceptualizing this course as just such an *open space* (Allsup 2016).

As I sat and thought about what *wouldn't* work in this newly imposed digital environment, I realized this might just be the chance I was waiting for to *blow open* the educational space in ways even I could not imagine. Many of the constraints of higher education had fallen to the wayside as administrations put more agency in the hands of individual professors. I, like many others, just wanted to find something that worked, and my sense was that all options were open.

I recalled bell hooks (1994, 20) warning that "my voice is not the only account of what happens in the classroom." My overriding sense at the time was that if we were going to succeed in creating a meaningful experience, my students and I needed to do it together; or, as Randall Allsup (2016) writes, we needed to "create participatory spaces" (15); "an ethos of co-authoring and facilitation" (34).

Yet I was concerned with how my students, for the most part educated in teacher-driven spaces since the age of six, would respond to my *blowing things open*. I wondered: *How does one curate open spaces for democracy to happen? How does one plan for openness?* In the pages that follow, I share my exploration of these questions and some answers I and my students found.

UNDERSTANDING THE DIGITAL SPACE

Since before the start of the pandemic, my scholarly research has focused on digital technology and media literacy and the implications of these fields for how we teach and learn music and train future music educators. I'll admit, when we went fully online in March of 2020, I was excited for the opportunity to translate key discoveries from my research into solutions for constructing my online courses.

I decided to go back to my discoveries about digital spaces and use them as a guide in navigating the disruptions and challenges I and my students were about to face.

From my research, I discovered that scholars in the field of media literacy recognize specific, unique qualities of interaction at the core of online engagements. The first quality is that of *choice*. In online engagements, the individual has a powerful opportunity for autonomous choice based on their personal interests and preferences. That is, I, as the digital *reader*, decide what content I engage with, how I engage with it and in what sequence of actions and activities the engagement unfolds. I *construct* my experience through my choices. Given the distinct meaning-making processes at work in digital engagements, Gunther Kress (2010, 54) argues the need for "a new social semiotic theory of contemporary communication," what he refers to as a "theory of multimodality." Put differently, the fluid, nonlinear and social qualities of online engagements represent a rupture to more traditional ways of understanding meaning-making and hence, teaching and learning (Kress 2010).

The second quality is *participation*. Henry Jenkins (2006) notes that the ubiquity of digital spaces has created what he calls a *participatory culture*. Potentially, anyone can make their creative voice heard, not only trained professionals. Kress (2003) suggests this has catalyzed not only a digital revolution but a social revolution, one that has changed how we understand the concepts of *authorship* and creative content. This quality of participation is strongly connected to notions of agency—the ability to recognize one's voice as a powerful and legitimate tool in one's own life and in the world at large (Adair 2014).

The third quality is *collaboration*. Digital spaces, particularly social media platforms, afford opportunities for collaboration in ways vastly different from in-person interactions. Take, for example, the online social media platforms of YouTube or TikTok. I can compose a song together with someone in the UK and that song can then be reimagined by a third person in India using a musical sample from a fourth person in Japan. This can then be shared and reviewed by someone in Australia and so on. Put differently, digital connectivity has the potential to break down barriers to inclusion in significant ways.

Last, is the quality of *design*. The New London Group (1996, 75) introduced the notion of *design* regarding specifically digital, multimodal experiences and defines the concept as "the process of shaping emergent meanings." Building on this, Kress (2003, 49) writes, "Design does not ask 'what was done before, how, for whom, with what?' Design asks, 'what is needed now, in this one situation, with this configuration of purposes, aims, audience, and *with these resources*, and given *my* interests in this situation?" When viewed in the context of education, design's focus on emergent meanings can engender a uniquely *bottom-up* approach to pedagogy, fueled by learners' context-specific interests, needs, and desires. That is, pedagogy grounded in the quality of design has the potential to move the learning community away from pre-constructed formulae and normative paradigms to imagining possibilities.

A COURSE REIMAGINED FOR PANDEMIC TIMES

With these understandings of the digital space in hand, I set about to design my *Secondary General Music Practices* course for the online context. My hope was that just as the qualities of digital engagements can enhance the voice and agency of independent users, embedding those qualities in my course may do the same for my students on a personal and collective level; that in this way, we might become a *community of inquirers*, not merely a professor and her individual students all struggling for some semblance of academic success in this difficult time.

I was reminded of Maxine Greene's (2000, 125) charge to teachers hoping to create democratic spaces, that they must "refuse to control what is discovered as meaningful." And so, I imagined four core activities for the course, each designed to move the *discovery of meaning* away from myself and into the hands of the students. These included: extended inquiry projects, student-led work groups, social annotation, and open-sourced homework submissions. I had no idea what new *meanings* we would discover together and, if I'm being honest, I found that tremendously exciting. In my perhaps naivety, I assumed my students would find taking ownership of the course exciting as well. And while many did embrace the opportunities presented for authorship and agency, others struggled with the responsibility demanded by this open paradigm (Allsup 2016), pushed back, or seemed unwilling (or unable) to imagine themselves as agents of change.

What follows are descriptions of each of the four core activities and how they played out in the course.

Extended Inquiry Projects

I designed the course to include two extended inquiry projects, one a collaborative endeavor and the other done individually.

Understanding SGM Students—A Collaborative Inquiry

Using the online platform *Miro*, I designed a *board* to serve as a communal inquiry space about adolescent music learners or *SGM students*. The title of the board was *Understanding Secondary General Music Students*. Miro is an online collaborative whiteboard platform that allows for creative graphic representation of information and ideas. Rather than positioning myself as the expert on adolescent music learners, my idea was to use this platform for us to explore together who our secondary general music students are, what we know about them and what we still would like to find out. On the first day of class, students reflected on their current understandings through three questions: Who are SGM students? What is music in their lives? What might they already know in music? In the second class we added a fourth question: What is our purpose here as SGM teachers? Each of these questions informed a distinct section of the board. The questions were presented as section headings and students shared their answers by pasting virtual *sticky notes* in the corresponding section. Inviting the students to grapple with these questions offered them an opportunity to reflect on pedagogy as a uniquely situated and social experience, not merely pre-determined content provided by myself as the instructor. Images of the Miro board can be viewed at rowman.com/ISBN/9781793654144.

Our engagement with the Miro board was ongoing. As such it served as both a continual synthesis of new understandings and as a springboard for new discussion topics. We revisited the board frequently as a group and students also visited the board on their own outside of class adding new ideas from projects they were working on or weekly readings. We also had a number of guest speakers in the course and asked each of them to view and add their ideas to our board as well. This allowed us to synthesize broader ideas into the course collage and to collaboratively include other people in our community. Toward the end of the course, one student took the initiative to add a fifth question to the board: What stereotypes accompany SGM students, that is, biases, myths or negative assumptions? The other students were quick to respond with their own ideas without any prompt from me.

Personal Inquiry Projects

The second extended inquiry project was a Personal Inquiry Project students worked on throughout the semester, centered around a topic of their choice. In what was, at the time, an expression of *putting my money where my mouth is*, I decided these personal inquiry projects would constitute the *Final* for the course. Each student's final grade would be to a large extent based on meeting the goals they set for themselves on a topic they chose to explore. This, I hoped, would go toward making the course a more personal journey and allow students to "design experiences that fund *their* needs and wishes" (Allsup 2016, *ix*).

The project was framed for the students with the following questions: What do you feel most comfortable with when you think about teaching music to SGM students? What is "out of your wheelhouse"? What would you like to know more about, or be able to do, that you believe will make you a more effective and engaging secondary general music teacher? Students began by reflecting on these questions and choosing a topic or pedagogical focus. Next, they formulated a *driving question* they wanted to answer, listed what they already knew or knew how to do and what they wanted to know more about. They constructed a few concrete goals they believed were attainable by the end of the semester. For the Final of the course, students would present their research to the group and design three consecutive lessons for a secondary general music classroom based on the topic of their Personal Inquiry Project.

The students engaged with the openness of this project to varying degrees. There were some students who remained firmly within the performance paradigm so prominent in our teacher-education programs. These students wanted to learn a musical performance skill they did not yet possess (playing guitar, ukulele, or bucket-drumming) often with the goal of using these performance options to teach more traditional elements of music like standard notation, theory, or standard repertoire. I found this a bit disappointing, though I did recognize that the performance skills these students were interested in were still, to some extent, outside the performance paradigm of band, orchestra, and choir.

Yet, many students chose to focus on aspects of music education pedagogy that are typically outside of our more normative practices. These students formulated driving questions such as: What is involved in the process of arranging music and how can I use arranging within the general music classroom? and What is music technology and how can I incorporate it into my classroom as a way to engage my students and increase learning? Two students were interested in exploring the art of sampling and posed the following questions: What are the practices of sampling and how can I integrate this into my work with secondary general music students? How do artists use sampling to create deeper meaning and intertextual connections?

Perhaps most surprising, several students chose distinctly theoretical or philosophical topics to explore in their personal projects. These students presented driving questions like: What are ways in which cultural competence can be more fully considered in music education classes; To what extent can cultural competence in music education be used to advocate for acceptance in cultural diversity? and How can I create safe environments to take creative risks? Why might students feel as if they can't create music; What structures stand in the way of developing student creativity? Through these questions, students tackled difficult, overarching topics and concerns related to music education and their role as future educators.

The resulting projects were inspiring, and students presented their research and ideas with personal passion. In addition, because of the deep engagement with their topics, students were able to imagine and design compelling lesson units to use in a future secondary general music setting.

Student-Led Collaborative Work Groups

Historically, this course meets three times a week for 50 minutes each time as a whole class. Doing so on Zoom did not seem the most effective learning strategy in the current situation. Student stress and *Zoom fatigue* were already well-documented effects of the extended pandemic restrictions. I decided that meeting once a week as a large group was the most that I could expect of the students and yet, I wanted to find ways for the group to have continuous interactions. And so, I decided to leave the space myself and put the students in charge. One meeting each week then became an opportunity for what I called *collaborative work groups*. Instead of meeting as a class, where I would inevitably be put in a position of authority, the students met on their own in small groups of three or four. The details of how to meet, how to structure the procedures, and the specific content of those meetings was left up to the students. My only involvement was to frame the session with an open-ended prompt as a starting point and to review weekly summary *talking points* students submitted to me after each meeting. The work done in these collaborative groups was not graded.

In these groups, students worked on multiple projects. For example, for several weeks of the course they met and helped each other learn to play ukulele, choosing, mastering, and arranging repertoire for future students. They also explored topics related to the week's class discussions. For example, in the second week each group constructed an interview protocol to use with a high school student of their choice. The protocol contained questions they felt essential to better understand secondary general music students and their role as their teacher.

Groups also worked on inquiry homework projects. For example, we discussed at length the contemporary musical engagements adolescents have daily in their out-of-school lives, and how we might incorporate and build on those engagements in our classroom. In line with these discussions, I designed a *Jingle Project* in which students researched contemporary jingles and then composed their own jingle to a product of their choice or that they invented. Finally, students created a lesson plan for a *Jingle Project* they could use as an introduction to composition in a secondary general music class.

The students completed the research portion of the project together in their work groups. They explored jingles online, grounding their inquiry in such questions as:

What is the purpose of a jingle? How long is an average jingle? What musical elements are central? How are they arranged? What makes a "successful" jingle melody? How does the music interact with (support) the text and imagery of the product? Having completed the initial inquiry as a group, students then worked individually on the subsequent parts of the project. Afterward, students commented that the opportunity to *jumpstart* their creative work with their peers went a long way in helping them to conceptualize their own creative ideas and their ideas for future pedagogy.

The collaborative work groups also provided a space for students to explore and discuss topics they were passionate about that related to the overarching aims of the course. Such student-chosen topics included (in the students' own words): "Ways to promote student autonomy and student choice," "exploring music videos in secondary music education," and "interdisciplinary lessons that combine art forms," to name a few.

While a majority of the students readily embraced the opportunity to take control of their learning, some students at first struggled with autonomy. There were students who, after the first few weeks, started frequently missing group meetings or contributed little. This could have been due to the overwhelming toll the anxiety of COVID-19 was having on student mental health or simply because they knew group work was not being graded. I have no way of knowing. Yet, as the semester proceeded, it appeared some of those who struggled or detached were brought back onboard with the help of their peers' enthusiasm.

Reading as a Social Activity

Academic readings are part and parcel of any undergraduate course. This is usually accompanied by a worksheet or *Think Sheet* that checks for student comprehension (and that they read the material). Out of my desire to enhance our sense of community and to create open spaces directed by the students, I sought a way to alleviate the isolation of reading texts. I decided to use the social annotation platform *Hypothesis* for all of our course readings. I uploaded articles to the platform with a link from our learning management system so that rather than reading and highlighting in isolation, students did the same on the communal documents. They highlighted sections of personal interest, made comments, and posed questions that peers could read and respond to. And so, reading became a communal conversation outside of our weekly class meetings. I was surprised when, a few weeks into the course, students began to make connections to external online materials by using hyperlinks in their comments. This student-initiated response expanded the breadth of the discussions and ultimately the scope of the course.

On each article's annotation page, I posted an initial, open-ended question related to the reading for all students to respond to and I encouraged them to read and comment on each other's posts. The students appeared to enjoy this interactive aspect of *reading together*. As a result, student-directed online conversations emerged out of my weekly prompt. Beyond this, the students conducted conversations among themselves in each week's annotations, catalyzed by highlighting or comments they made on the reading or questions they posed to the group. Student-initiated online conversation topics included: the challenges of using Hip Hop in K–12 music education, and the failings of higher music education to prepare future teachers for a contemporary learning environment, to name just a few. While I sometimes commented on a student-initiated topic, for the most part these discussions were conducted among the students themselves and represented a space for students to explore ideas and critical issues that were of particular interest to them as preservice teachers.

For the most part, this social digital space for dialogue among the students appeared to be a positive experience for them. As other chapters in this volume attest, students may be willing to share their ideas and opinions more readily in a chat-like forum than during in-person discussions. Yet, this freedom to express, along with my general refrain from these conversations, also created several moments of tension among the students as they were forced to navigate peer opinions drastically different than their own.

One student in the course seemed to hold more traditional opinions about music and music education. In one annotation, this student posted that in their opinion popular music lacked "beauty, depth and true aspirations" and should be avoided in school music class. Several students posted articulate arguments against this student's opinion. Unfortunately, the original student did not reply.

Several weeks later, in response to the article, "The Fifth Element? Using the Tradition of Knowledge and Education in Hip Hop to Transform Classroom Outcomes," by Meacham, Muhammad, and Mennenga (2018), this same student posted: "Diversity issues are overrated." I waited for a response from the other students, but none came. And then, a group of three students reached out to me with a request for a meeting. In that private meeting, the students articulated their outrage with what their fellow classmate had written. "We are feeling targeted and unsafe," one student commented. I was taken aback. I had not considered how this open space—albeit, at times confrontational—might trigger such feelings in my students. We proceeded to discuss how one can respond to opinions they find offensive, while avoiding condemning the speaker. We talked about the need to engage with the voices of all our peers, even when that is difficult. I shared with them my own shock at having read this comment and my strategy in such situations to ask further questions of the speaker in hopes of eliciting deeper reflection; questions that begin with *"What do you think about . . .* or *How would you address . . ."* rather than engage in a semantic battle. The students listened attentively to my suggestions, and I was happy to see that the next time this student posted an unpopular opinion, the other students responded with intelligent probing questions. Unfortunately, the original student never replied to these comments and continued to share their outlier opinions throughout the course.

I had not anticipated this challenge when I introduced social annotation into the course. I did not consider how the digital space may invite opinion-sharing in a more *honest* way than face-to-face discussions. Periodically, I interjected my own questions in response to this student's controversial posts, but again, never got a response. Perhaps this space was not as communal or *safe* as I imagined. Perhaps, because the course had a clear focus on popular genres and issues of diversity, equity, and inclusion, this student was reticent to speak out further, imagining it might put her in bad graces with me, the instructor. Or perhaps this student was simply not interested in a dialogue.

At the end of the day, I am happy this student felt free to share what she thought with the group and that my other students were beginning to develop constructive tools for engaging with opinions drastically different than their own. I wish this had blossomed into full-fledged dialogues (despite how hard that would have been). How to make that happen is an issue I need to explore in the future as I continue to use social annotation in my courses.

A more positive and unexpected outcome of using social annotation was that as I read through the students' conversations each week, I discovered student-generated critical topics and I used them to help me construct the following week's whole-class meeting, adding yet another layer to the democratic and collaborative quality the of the course.

Open-Sourced Homework Submissions

Typically, in a college course, students submit homework directly to the professor and she is the sole viewer and assessor of their work. This is something that has always bothered me. Surely, there is much to be gained by sharing ideas not only in class but through the work we do individually. As professors, we recognize such collaboration as highly valuable in multiple aspects of our career, whether designing curriculum, doing research, attending conferences, or brainstorming classroom projects and activities with our colleagues. Yet, when we turn our gaze toward our students, we tend to isolate them and their work.

It was my focus on connection and community in the online space that led me to recognize my own complicity in this issue. I too always assigned homework projects to be submitted to me. I too always followed the prescriptive format of being the sole arbiter and grader of student achievement. Like my students, I taught in the way I had been taught without considering the blatant question staring me in the face: Why?

And so, I decided to institute an open-sourced homework policy. Students now had the opportunity to view and comment on their peers' work in an ongoing fashion. I planned to use this strategy for a majority of the student work and so I created a Google folder with a specific Google doc for each assignment. The first submission was an original poem I asked students to compose in response to a poem by Amanda Gorman about finding agency in trying times. That first week, the students' interactions in the open-source homework space were inspiring.

As homework assignments came due, students posted their work to the appropriate Google doc, viewed, commented, and drew inspiration and new ideas from the work of their colleagues. Students uploaded videos of body percussion routines they designed for a song of their choice, ukulele tutorials they constructed and filmed, and multiple original lesson plans, to name a few.

Beyond informally getting ideas from their peers' work, I turned the students' homework, at times, into focus material for exploration. When the students composed original raps with original beats, they uploaded them to Google docs and viewed each other's songs. I decided to ask them to analyze their peers' compositions for rhyme schemes, lyrical symbolism, rhythm schemes and the way the beat interacted and supported the rap lyrics and to post their analysis in the Google doc. This led to some good conversations between the artists and their colleagues.

A few weeks into the course something unexpected happened. As the students got to know each other better, they asked me to add a Google doc titled *Hobbies/About Us* where they could share outside, personal interests with the group. Students posted about family bands, crafts they did (one student displayed homemade face masks he created), and links to musical works they had arranged. One student shared his pet project—turning his apartment into a home studio. Students took the opportunity to view and comment on each other's outside interests and to ask questions.

It is possible this use of Google docs for homework was successful primarily because it was included as part of each assignment. At those times when posting was not part of a grade, only some of the students engaged with the Google doc. Yet, I don't plan to change how I design this element of the course in the future. Community cannot be forced. Still, the fact that my students "are always thinking about grades" (as one student told me) is an endemic issue that, I suggest, needs to be addressed by our field in general.

Students Reflect on Their Experiences

I imagined that this course, as it played out during COVID-19, was unlike any the students had previously experienced. And so, I was curious to get students' impressions on what, in their minds, worked and didn't work and what they found particularly impactful as students and future educators. I designed an online *exit ticket* and asked the students to comment on the course and their experiences.

I was excited to read that the students, for the most part, found the structure and content of the course exhilarating and that it catalyzed for many a rethinking of how they see themselves as music educators. Students talked about how they appreciated the openness of the course space and the focus it put on creating a more communal, democratic, and student-centered ambiance.

Many students specifically pointed to personal inquiry projects and how refreshing it was to be offered the opportunity to "choose [their] own direction" in their learning. They commented on how the projects encouraged them to "get out of their comfort zone," how they "broadened [their] horizons of music teaching and learning" and allowed them to focus on "what really interested" them. One student wrote: "This is definitely a keeper for next time!"

Students also commented that the collaborative work groups were a big part of their sense of community in the online setting. One student wrote that the groups "gave me the opportunity to get to know my peers more as well as hear perspectives on music education that I would not have thought of". Another shared, "Group meetings were the biggest contribution to a sense of community in this course. Seeing faces, having discussions—such a big part of community!". Yet, one student noted that group work was at times difficult given the already high levels of student stress.

No students mentioned the open-sourced homework aspect of the course. This could have been because by mid-semester most of the students had stopped posting their work. This is something I definitely need to rethink moving forward.

The one aspect of the course that seemed to demand attention was socially annotated reading. While a few students commented that they enjoyed this activity, several mentioned "feeling uncomfortable seeing [their] peers argue" online. Others "missed more in-depth classroom discussions" of the readings. These are both issues I plan to address next time the course is offered.

LOOKING BACK—LOOKING FORWARD

What happens when student voice fuels an emergent pedagogy and content is reimagined as communal exploration and inquiry? My students and I were given a rare opportunity to search for answers to these questions as the pandemic hit and we were all tossed into the online space. Forced to acknowledge those aspects of my own pedagogy that I knew wouldn't work, my students and I created a "pedagogy of travel and surprise" (Allsup 2016, 43).

The results of this experiment in open pedagogy led to the most vibrant student engagement I witnessed in my many years as an educator. As students took control of both content and direction, they became deeply and personally invested in our shared mission—to explore the "what, why and how" of teaching secondary general music students. They stepped up with original ideas and expertise, argued, questioned and interrogated normative practices, biases and assumptions because that is where their self-designed journey took them; Which leaves me wondering whether we, as music teacher-educators, preclude this type of enthusiastic and personal investment on the part of our students by designing our courses as *closed forms* (Allsup 2016), as preconceived models of teaching and learning under teacher control? Do we, as Maxine Greene warned, "control what is discovered as meaningful"?

Challenges

Working in this way in the online space revealed unique challenges for the teacher-educator in an open pedagogy.

I wrote a question at the start of this chapter: *How does one plan for openness*? I've related the ways in which I engaged in such planning. Beyond that, however, was a demand to remain open as I proceeded through this experience with my students; to be hyper-attentive to their voices; to listen in a radically open fashion to their desires, interests, and emergent themes; to the journey they each chose as their own (Lewis 2016).

In his article, "A Deweyan Theory of Democratic Listening," Jim Garrison (1996, 433) explains the relationship between listening and democratic education. For Garrison, to truly listen means to embrace a stance of "remaining open" and, as he notes, this "involves risk and vulnerability"; To truly listen, he writes, we "must be willing to live with confusion and uncertainty." Garrison's description of listening is highly reminiscent of how this course played out. All those involved—my students and myself alike—sensed the vulnerability required of us, the necessity to embrace the uncertainty of where our ideas might take us, and the willingness to take risks in the name of new discoveries of who we are and what we do as educators in music.

As students brought ideas to the class based on their own expertise and passion there were times I knew close to nothing about the topics. At those moments the students became my teacher as well as their peers'. As they introduced critical questions and ideas, I was challenged to interrogate my own understandings and biases. In short, I was continually required to be vulnerable in the face of my students; to be willing to say "I don't know, let's figure it out together." Not a natural position for an educator of many years. And yes, an incredibly exhilarating one.

I recall Jacques Rancière (1991, 12–13) and his vision of the "emancipatory master" who by "leaving his intelligence out of the picture, allow[s] the intelligence of [his students] to grapple" with the pedagogical materials. For Rancière, the goal of such an educator is for the student to "see everything for himself, compare and compare, and always respond to a three-part question: what do you see? what do you think about it? what do you make of it? And so on to infinity. But that infinity is no longer the master's secret; it is the student's journey" (23). And so, in addition to my own *becoming a learner*, my role transformed into one of a critical observer, sprinkling questions designed to push students to interrogate their self-guided work as well as the values embedded in that work.

Community

And finally, what of community? Popular opinion touts the belief that the ever-increasing use of mobile phones and digital technology has dramatically contributed to social isolation among people of all ages. This was a major concern for teachers and students alike going into the last year and a half of online learning. Add to this the fact that we were all living, for much of the time, in a state of physical isolation from everyone but those in our immediate household due to pandemic restrictions. Creating a sense of community among learners and teachers appeared to be almost a nonstarter. And yet, I was surprised, looking back, that one of my biggest takeaways from experience was a new understanding of how I, as a teacher-educator, can design my courses to encourage the formation of a vibrant community of inquirers whether online or off.

Randall Allsup (2016, 97) writes that pedagogy "designed to promote mutuality—to connect self-interest to interest of others—lay[s] the groundwork for community from the first encounter." This forced foray into online teaching and learning revealed to me (and, I believe, my students as well) that community and a sense of belonging is not dependent on the location of the pedagogical space (online or in-person), but rather is intimately rooted in one's voice being heard, one's desires and passions being valued and sustained and the recognition that we each have agency (both individual and collective) to impact the content, processes, and purposes of our work together. By framing this course through the qualities of the online space—choice, collaboration, participation, and design—all of these characteristics of community came to the fore. Designing multiple aspects of the course as communal endeavors—from reading to homework submission—promoted a sense of shared responsibility. And finally, opening spaces for students' voices to take center stage launched us on a multiplicity of learning journeys, each personal and personally meaningful while at the same time a part of the shared collective journey of us all.

It is likely I could have opened the space even more than I did in this course, but I am, after all, a product of normative teacher-driven education and the pressures of the academy. Perhaps, as I implement these newly discovered openings in future iterations, I will find new openings I have yet to imagine.

FINAL THOUGHTS

What would pedagogy look like if anything were possible?

I opened this chapter with that question. It reflects the sense of open possibilities I felt at that time. Yet, I recognize that my ability to ask this question and to act upon it is a reflection of privilege—mine and my students. In many locations of education in the United States (and beyond) the overwhelming sense has not been one of possibility but impotence—in the face of sickness, loss, and hardship. Despite this glaring disparity, I hope the lessons I and my students learned through this experience—the critical centrality of student voice, collaboration, and community—can find expression, and perhaps be part of the healing process, in these and other communities ravaged by loss because of the pandemic.

As I compose the final paragraphs of this chapter, I embark on another iteration of this course, this time in person. I am excited to see where this digitally inspired pedagogy will take us. As I rework the course for an in-person setting, I find myself holding fast to the qualities of digital engagement that initially inspired me: choice, participation, collaboration, and design. As a result, the four core activities that shaped the course during online learning are again the cornerstones of our work together—some with the use of technology and some not. COVID-19 restrictions were the catalyst for this redesign, forcing all of us to confront learning with and through technology. Those restrictions are now lifted, the dust has settled, yet the powerful pedagogical outcomes remain ever-present in my mind.

My new students are beginning to work in their collaborative groups. They have started to post homework to Google docs and are reading online using social annotation. We just discussed their whole-term personal inquiry projects. This time they will share them face-to-face, not over Zoom. I am curious to see how being in person may impact their choice of topics to explore.

I'm encouraged that, thus far, the consensus is that socially annotated reading is an exciting new way to *read together*. A new class, a new group of students, a new perspective—the essence of democratic pedagogy. We have conducted a communal dialogue about how we want to engage in discussions in this online social setting. Hopefully, this will serve to open spaces for honest dialogue. We may revisit this issue throughout the course as moments appear.

It is too early to predict how group work will unfold. Yet, I am determined to create spaces where my students can take charge and drive their learning in personally meaningful directions. I continue to search for new openings I may have missed the first time around.

I carry with me profound lessons learned from the past year and a half of remote learning. The digital space, if we understand it, has much to teach us about transformative music teaching and learning in all settings—both online and face-to-face. Through this experience I recognized the myriad ways student voice might be celebrated in my classroom (choice); the extent to which students might be positioned as teachers and drivers of learning (participation), the power of shared purpose (collaboration), and the possibility for pedagogy to be emergent, fueled by student agency rather than reified practices (design). Together, my students and I discovered how vibrant community is created. How curiously wonderful that the digital space we all feared would stifle us has taught us such powerful lessons!

REFERENCES

Adair, Jennifer Keys. 2014. "Agency and Expanding Capabilities in Early Grade Classrooms: What it Could Mean For Young Children." *Harvard Educational Review* 84, no. 2: 217–241. https://doi.org/10.17763/haer.84.2.y46vh546h4l12144.

Allsup, Randall Everett. 2016. *Remixing the Classroom: Toward an Open Philosophy of Music Education*. Bloomington, IN: Indiana University Press.

Freire, Paulo. 1970. *Pedagogy of the Oppressed*. Translated by Myra Bergman Ramos. London: Penguin Books.

Greene, Maxine. 1988. *Dialectic of Freedom*. New York: Teachers College Press.

Greene, Maxine. 2000. *Releasing the Imagination: Essays on Education, the Arts, and Social Change*. New York: John Wiley & Sons.

hooks, bell. 1994. *Teaching to Transgress: Education as the Practice of Freedom*. London: Routledge.

Jenkins, Henry. 2006. "Confronting the Challenges of Participatory Culture: Media Education for the 21st Century: An Occasional Paper on Digital Media and Learning." *John D. and Catherine T. MacArthur Foundation*.

Meacham, S., Muhammad, L., & Mennenga, K. (2018). The fifth element?: Using the tradition of knowledge and education in hip hop to transform classroom outcomes. *Journal of Popular Music Education* 2(1–2), 133–148.

Kress, Gunter. 2003. *Literacy in the New Media Age*. East Sussex: Psychology Press.

Kress, Gunther. 2010. *Multimodality: A Social Semiotic Approach to Contemporary Communication*. New York: Routledge.

Lewis, Judith. 2016. "Musical Voices from the Margins: Popular Music as a Site of Critical Negotiation in an Urban Elementary Classroom." Doctoral Dissertation, Teachers College, Columbia University. ProQuest Dissertations Publishing, 2016. 10117074.

Rancière, Jacques. 1991. *The Ignorant Schoolmaster: Five Lessons in Intellectual Emancipation*. Stanford, CA: Stanford University Press.

The New London Group. 1996. "A Pedagogy of Multiliteracies: Designing Social Futures." *Harvard Educational Review* 66, no. 1: 60–92.

Woodford, Paul. 2005. *Democracy and Music Education: Liberalism, Ethics, and the Politics of Practice*. Bloomington, IN: Indiana University Press.

Chapter 12

Choir Disrupted

Nils Klykken

As I write this chapter, I am mindful of how much suffering this pandemic has wrought upon us. I am mindful of the lives lost and the family members, friends, and colleagues who have been left behind. I am mindful of the economic hardships many have faced; the juggling of parenting, working, and teaching day-in and day-out. I am mindful of how this pandemic has disproportionately affected marginalized populations.

I am but one voice in the fields of choral music and music education. Even though we have a shared pandemic experience, each of our individual experiences is unique. In this chapter, I will share some of the ways in which the three entangled pandemics of COVID-19, racism, and the further deterioration of democracy in the United States have affected my work as an assistant professor of choral music within a large music education program at a public university in upstate New York. I will share with you how I responded as an individual, and how these experiences helped to shape the curriculum of one choir I taught remotely during the 2020–2021 academic year. Finally, I will share with you what emerged from this experience and what potential long-term implications there may be within schools of music.

THE DISRUPTION BEGINS: THE ONSET OF A GLOBAL HEALTH PANDEMIC

> I recognized winter. I saw it coming (a mile off, since you ask), and I looked it in the eye. I greeted it and let it in. I asked myself: What is this winter all about? I asked myself: What change is coming? (May 2020, 238).

I first became aware of the new coronavirus in late December 2019. I didn't think much of it. "How significantly worse can this be than the flu?" I asked a colleague when she hosted my husband and me over for tacos. But by January, it seemed that the epidemic in China had worsened. There were headlines of super-spreading events. An entire city shut down. The virus appeared in Korea. News stories speculated that the virus may sweep the globe. What was happening?

The headlines only continued to worsen, and by late February, I became quite anxious. I was to give a presentation in just a week's time at the American Choral Directors Association conference in Rochester, NY. Was it safe to go? Should I cancel? How could I avoid virus-laden droplets and expelled air at a *choral* convention? "No," I thought: "this is too important for my career." And so, I made the four-hour trip to Rochester. I rented a car from Enterprise. I didn't trust who may have had the vehicle before me, so I sprayed the entirety of the interior with Lysol. My eyes burned the entire drive.

The coming pandemic loomed over the conference. Colleagues did not want to shake hands (those who did were quick to use hand sanitizer). I hugged friends I hadn't seen in years, and immediately questioned this decision each time. Thousands of us poured into Eastman's Kodak Theater for a concert by Bobby McFerrin. A little girl seated behind me coughed throughout. Was she infectious? Were we all going to get sick? Were we in a collective denial about what was occurring? How badly did we want to cling to this world as we knew it?

Between attending interest-sessions, presenting, listening to choirs, and seeing old friends, I spent time on my phone, furiously absorbing as much news as I could. This only fueled my sense of paranoia. I e-mailed my dean to tell him how uncomfortable I was leading choral rehearsals in tight spaces after spring break. He thanked me for my e-mail and assured me that serious conversations were now underway. I felt a bit less paranoid but had no answer for what we would do upon returning. I spent the remainder of the conference hiding in my hotel room already convinced that I must be sick. How could I not be?

Then everything shut down. Campus emptied. Ensembles stopped meeting. We had a week to put our classes online. Not wanting to abandon either of my choirs, I held optional classes that became a space for exploring interests and to meet the overwhelming need for connection and community. In one class, we held listening parties, where students shared music that was meaningful to them. My students expanded my soundscape, and despite only seeing them in small boxes on a screen, I grew to know them better. The days seemed long but the weeks blurred by, and the semester ended.

THE DISRUPTION INTENSIFIES: RACIAL AND CIVIL UNREST

> Efforts at good behavior and pursuit of good policies have proven to be no match for the deep embeddedness of what is the foundation of, and has been intricately woven throughout, every facet, institution, and relationship of the United States and the psyche of its inhabitants: the racialization of people and its underlying presupposition—the superiority of white-skinned peoples. (Williams 2016, xii)

After the semester ended, I found myself looking forward to the summer break. I would have time to plan for the fall. I was sure the end of the academic year would bring much-needed relief. I was wrong.

White police officer Derek Chauvin casually and brutally murdered George Floyd in broad daylight. People took to the streets to protest. The twin pandemics of systemic racism and COVID-19 further entangled themselves into one another, and the disruption intensified.

Like many White Americans following the murder of George Floyd, I asked myself, "How could I not have seen this before?" But this wasn't true, I had seen instances of anti-Blackness. I just hadn't allowed myself to truly notice, to fully absorb, and to ethically respond to it. I felt confused, disoriented, and an overwhelming sense of shame. How could I be so complicit? I felt an overwhelming sense of White guilt and panicked. I needed to understand. Like many, I protested. I read, talked, and listened. I gained a better understanding of slavery as it was practiced in the United States, Jim Crow, and mass incarceration. I learned how systemic racism is an outgrowth of our racial caste system. I came across terminology that was new to me, including BIPOC, anti-blackness, and antiracism. As a White American benefiting in this racial caste system, I had a greater awareness of my responsibility to be antiracist. As part of my journey to understand better what antiracism is, I visited the website for the National Museum of African American History and Culture that states:

> Being antiracist results from a conscious decision to make frequent, consistent, equitable choices daily. These choices require ongoing self-awareness and self-reflection as we move through life. In the absence of making antiracist choices, we (un)consciously uphold aspects of white supremacy, white-dominant culture, and unequal institutions and society. Being racist or antiracist is not about who you are; it is about what you do. (National Museum of African American History and Culture 2021)

With regard to my professional work, I wanted to better understand how I could make antiracist choices in ensemble environments. I interrogated my approach to making music and the structures in which I make music. What racist decisions was I unwittingly making regarding the music we experienced, how I taught the music, and how we performed it? What antiracist choices could I make to disrupt the White-dominant spaces in which I work? How could the already-present COVID-19 disruption afford space for these lines of inquiry?

As I was asking myself these questions, the United States was holding a presidential election. In his attempt to hold power, Trump continued to dangerously subvert democratic norms. I thought about what civic responsibilities we as individual citizens do (or do not) have. I thought about how much Americans may or may not value our civic responsibilities. I thought about my professional life and what responsibilities I may have for instilling democratic values in my classrooms.

I recognize that choral music is not inherently democratic, and thus, does not necessarily cultivate a greater sense of civic awareness. This artform emerged within monarchical systems of Medieval Europe (including both secular courts and the Roman Catholic Church), hundreds of years before the Enlightenment and birth of liberal democracy as a concept. When examining some of our standard practices, I am able to perceive authoritarian values: the leader is right, individuals follow orders, independent thought is devalued, and so on. If I must actively make antiracist decisions to disrupt racism, do I not also need to make antiauthoritarian decisions to disrupt authoritarianism?

I do not know if I always welcome these observations and the questions they raise. They challenge me. They make what I do more difficult. They can potentially marginalize me in a field that may or may not want to ask these same questions. Students may struggle with new practices. The stress of designing and performing concerts is already difficult. But I recognize, following inherited practices is not enough: I must evolve. Here again, the ongoing disruption afforded a space in which to inquire and experiment.

IMAGINING AND IMPLEMENTING A NEW CURRICULUM

The classroom remains the most radical space of possibility in the academy . . .

Urging all of us to open our minds and hearts so that we can know beyond the boundaries of what is acceptable, so that we can think and rethink, so that we can create new visions. (hooks 1994, 12)

The entangled pandemics consumed me as I stepped into the fall semester of 2020. I couldn't will away this new reality. I would be teaching remotely for the year: my approach to choral music broke. Without the ability to have a normal year, normal expectations and pressures abated, including concert cycles. Without the regular scrutiny of performing publicly, the curriculum could breathe.

As a field, our approaches to teaching choir in a virtual modality varied. Some conductor-teachers edited together asynchronous singing to create an end-product resembling a live choral performance—a virtual choir. Although I was aware of this curricular approach, I had no practical way to address the challenge of editing without paying for a professional or overburdening a singular student to mix over eighty students' recordings into a final product. I wondered if a virtual choir would be "too close" to the pre-disruption, yet different enough as to feel artificial. I wondered if it would further emphasize what we *could not do* instead of what *could be possible*. I wanted to create a curriculum where we could explore these possibilities, and I was curious to discover ways of music making that already thrived in asynchronous settings, such as popular music. What would it mean to record tracks individually and mix them into a single recording? What would it mean to make music that was intended for this digital space? I decided that we would spend the year experimenting online, a laboratory if you will. This lab of ours could become anything, including a space to explore what ensembles could be. Hopefully, this lab would become fertile ground for responding to the disruption so far.

My mind was consumed with questions. How could I share power with students in order to create a less authoritarian environment? How could I make antiracist decisions in which to center issues of Diversity, Equity, and Inclusion (DEI) to address systemic racism and anti-Blackness? How could I center students' curiosity and allow for much of the curricular design to be process-oriented? What structures would I need to put in place in fall 2020, so as to cultivate further independence in spring 2021?

And so, I designed a yearlong curriculum. This would be an open-music classroom situated in student interest. I would facilitate, and students would engage in, consensus-based, democratic practices to guide their experiences. This curricular framework played out in five distinct phases: Beginning in fall 2020, I would place students in small groups to explore the Digital Audio Workspace (DAW) SoundTrap so that students could learn to make music asynchronously with one another. Second, I planned to ask students to engage with Beyoncé's Peabody-Award-Winning album *Lemonade*, an unapologetically Black album in which race, gender, religion, age, and intersecting identities are centered. Third, I would have students study popular genres that thrived in recorded spaces. Fourth, I would ask students to create covers or original compositions in any genre well-suited to asynchronous music making. Lastly, in spring 2021, I would ask students to respond to their work from fall 2020: what happened, what did they notice, and what curiosities did those experiences cultivate? I would ask them to design a student-directed project within a curricular framework that I would establish.

For this curriculum to work, the students needed to become more comfortable working with one another remotely in a digital environment. This was a new experience for many of us, including me: I could not position myself as an expert, but I could create a space to facilitate and model learning alongside my students. And so, I didn't directly teach them how to use the DAW Soundtrap; instead, I had them experiment with an emphasis on process as they began to create their own covers of either "Are You Sleeping, Brother John?" or "Twinkle, Twinkle Little Star." The students remarked on how free they felt to just explore and experiment. In addition to learning from one another about the various ways in which DAWs can be used, they created arrangements inspired by heavy metal, easy-listening, R&B, chorales, lo-fi, bedroom bop, and others. My favorite arrangement featured Carl Sagan's voice with a Phrygian arrangement of "Twinkle, twinkle little star" written for electronic bass, piano, voice, and synthesized percussion.

The students went on to study *Lemonade*. To begin, students watched and listened to either "Hold Up" or "Formation." After watching the video of their choosing, they read scholarship regarding issues of Black Lives Matter, feminism, and Yoruba religion, then returned to the video for a more informed viewing. One student already knew the album well, having already researched it; some students recognized these songs as singles, but didn't know much beyond it; other students had no prior knowledge. The reactions upon watching the videos were mixed. Some students found it to be *a bop*—Generation-Z parlance for music they like. Some had trouble understanding why Beyoncé was swinging around a bat in "Hold Up." Others were offended by perceived indecency. One commented that the music video contained "offensive blasphemy." Some students commented that they were uncomfortable with anything they interpreted as remotely political, including imagery of Black Lives Matter. Even those who didn't care for the music video had richer responses after reading scholarly work and watching the music video a second time. The student who originally wrote off the work as blasphemous now demonstrated curiosity about Yoruba religion. They were learning that musical and non-musical contexts help to give musical works meaning regardless of genre and the culture(s) of origin.

Functionally, this project also prepared students for their next project, in which they would explore genres of their choosing. Just as with *Lemonade*, they would need to situate their chosen genre in sociopolitical contexts, performance practices, and other identifying features that allow a listener to know what genre they are hearing; for example, *what makes punk music punk*. They did research, compiled resource guides for their peers, and presented to the class in whatever format(s) they chose. Students studied 1970s British Punk, R&B, heavy metal, lo-fi, bedroom bop, the golden age of musicals, and other genres.

For their final synthesis project, students had one month to create covers or original compositions of their choosing from any genre. They created a recording using a DAW of their choice, which they then shared within class. They presented their processes and how they might approach this project differently if they could do it again. They shared musicological and sociopolitical contexts to their work. I was surprised and excited by what I heard. They covered artists such as Billie Eilish, Rex Orange County, and the band Evanescence, artists I never expected to explore in a choral environment, but here they were. I was learning alongside them. I was also becoming more aware of my own blind spots.

The end of fall 2020 finally arrived, and we took a collective breath. Hope and fear and relief and exhaustion remained driving forces in everyday life. The election was over. Trump had lost, but we now had the Big Lie to contend with. Good news regarding vaccines arrived, though cases were on the rise, and we had yet to experience the explosion of cases and death in the United States that deep winter would bring. I continued to watch the news and watched our democracy further atrophy. My sense of urgency heightened as I watched insurrectionists breach the Capitol Building. I texted a former work colleague and Trump supporter who tried to assure me that the insurrectionists were Antifa. What was happening?

I became more keenly aware that democracy doesn't *just happen*. It isn't some fixed state of being that once achieved becomes permanent. Rather than conceiving of it as a thing, a noun if you will, I found it more helpful to think of democracy as a verb in which we *do democracy*. Only when we practice these values that we must explicitly identify, adhere to, and renew can we call ourselves a democracy. If I was going to create a democratic classroom, I had a responsibility to name the insurrection as an attempted coup juxtapositionally opposed to democratic values. I would need to move beyond simply practicing democratic values. I would have to teach democracy and make it a cornerstone of the curriculum.

I began by assisting the students as they created their ground rules for communicating across differences, respecting colleagues, and honoring those in the minority. They reminded one another to argue ideas rather than argue people. They were responsible for both what they discussed and how they were discussing it. They examined the student learning outcomes and set off on the task of creating a project that could meet these goals. As the facilitator, I would insert myself to summarize what I was hearing, to ask questions that allowed for further interrogation, to reflect on the quality of discussion and to help them make connections to civic responsibilities an individual has in a healthy and thriving democracy.

In creating a safe space for students to speak more freely, I unintentionally created a safe space for them to publicly challenge me. I did not expect this. Many students specifically wanted to sing choral music and create virtual choirs. I was surprised (and dare I say, somewhat disappointed) that many students specifically wanted to study mainstream choral music. Why would they choose to study something that cannot be as authentically practiced in an asynchronous setting? A great amount of popular music is written with the idea of a recording first, followed by live performances—would that not lead to a more authentic and rewarding experience? I understood that they missed choral singing (I very much missed it too), but would it "feel real?" And then I realized that perhaps my trepidations didn't matter. Even though I wouldn't have intended for many of them to choose this route, I realized that they were choosing to experiment *how* they could create choral music remotely. They were problematizing. They were experimenting. They exposed yet another blind spot.

Students openly criticized how I formed groups in fall 2020. They spent three class periods responding and debating how they would like to form groups for their spring projects. Although I knew democracies are inherently less efficient forms of governing due to a diversity of life experiences, beliefs, and values, I did not expect the process to take so long. Yet, it was important to me that I follow their lead. So despite my frustration, I allowed their deliberation to play out slowly.

Eventually, the students decided to create a concert album to be streamed in April. They decided that both choral and nonchoral musics would be featured on this album. They found consensus on how to create groups for this project. Each group met with me once weekly and worked autonomously for the remainder of the week; meaning that I saw one-third of my students each class period. I was able to help my students identify problems and strategies to address these problems. I was able to listen and respond to what I was hearing musically and asked questions to help them to listen more critically. In April, we live-streamed their work on the school's YouTube channel. Students elected delegates, who would give each project a first listen in order to determine the concert order, meaning that the majority of students did not hear their colleagues' work until the night of the concert.

It wasn't perfect. Voices were not in complete alignment, the mix of voices was not always balanced, but for many students, audience-goers, and me, it seemed to be a success. Students encouraged one another in the chat as they listened to mashups of Michael Jackson and John Denver, Eric Whitacre, and Craig Hella Johnson. Their reactions to this project were overwhelmingly positive. One graduating senior commented that this was his favorite project throughout his undergraduate career (his group composed experimental electronic music). Another student shared that she had never enjoyed singing choral music before but did in this project (her group performed Thomas Morley's "April Is In My Mistress' Face").

Some students were less enthralled. One wrote on their course evaluation that "Democracy in the classroom is bullshit." While I cannot get inside the mind of this individual student, I would wager that their perspective likely emerges from the dissonance between their course expectation and the course experience, as has been suggested by scholars (Allsup 2016). This student also wrote about the lack of structure in the class, perhaps misperceiving ideas of a closed learning environment (in which specific content flows from the master teacher to the student) with a more open environment, in which content emerges organically from within the learning community. Despite these criticisms, I believe the semester was successful. The students met their course goals: they followed their own musical curiosities, further developed musical agency, negotiated conflict democratically, and created performances that were meaningful to most of them. Through this work, they grew as individuals, citizens, and musical artists—what more could I ask for? By this metric (and much to my surprise), Spring 2021 may have been the most successful semester of my career thus far.

RETURNING

The road was new to me, as roads always are, going back. (Jewett 1896)

After three semesters of working remotely, I returned to my office in a largely empty building. The only people present were my custodial colleagues. We chatted about the pandemic and how difficult the last year had been for their work: the building was in disarray as our facility underwent a major renovation project, but they continued to do their best to prepare for the semester ahead and the return of face-to-face teaching.

It struck me that my custodial colleagues and I had been doing the same work of uncovering, responding, and adapting to new situations. But as I began to prepare for in-person classes of fall 2021, I noticed that I was returning to old practices and old scripts that I know. I spent weeks searching for new music to perform, trying to put together the *perfect program* for our concert. A forgotten yet familiar stress returned. I felt as if I was returning to *what was*. Had I learned anything during my year of teaching remotely or was 2020–2021 a *lost year*?

I felt confused. I couldn't go back to standard-operating procedure. I couldn't erase the experiences I had now had. The disruption had unmasked much of what I previously took for granted. Just as when I looked up at the exposed ducts and wiring in the hallways outside my office, I could more clearly see the *nuts and bolts* of what makes choral singing and ensemble music making so special. The importance of being able to physically share a space, sing, and respond in real-time only became clearer. I made a mental note to conscientiously hold onto this realization.

As soon as I was back in the classroom, I found myself *rehearsing the choir*. I know how to rehearse—even when working with new repertoire and the unique challenges embedded within. I had lost the expansive feeling of opportunity that remote teaching offered and was once again trotting upon the now too familiar. I found I did not have the same passion for these practices that I once did. Since the disruption, this had become tedious and uninteresting work. And then it hit me—this disruption had broken me. Looking back now, I see that this frustration and boredom was a good sign—it was the red flag of treading too closely to the familiar. Upon returning, my teaching had become too closed and too conductor focused. I could feel the students relying on me for every step of their music making.

And so, midway through fall 2021, I flipped the classroom. The past year had already shown me that students can independently work together to prepare musical material—they do not need me to *teach them* the music. I assigned passages for the students to learn outside of our rehearsal setting. They practiced as individuals or in groups and uploaded performances of their work to our learning management system. They reflected on the process: How did they approach learning this music? What happened? How might this experience influence future processes for learning music?

Although we preserved my predetermined title and theme of the Fall Concert (Peace & Love), my choir deviated from what I initially intended. Over the summer, I had programmed three pieces out of the European tradition by Pärt, Sigurbjörnsson, and Tormis. I also programmed a Negro Spiritual by Undine Smith Moore and a yet-to-be-determined gospel piece that we would learn by rote. However, this is not how the semester unfolded.

After Dr. François Clemmons's residency in October 2021, we changed course. Dr. Clemmons is a culture-bearer for the Negro spiritual tradition. The students decided that our experience with him was too rich to not include his music in our concert, so we cut the compositions by Pärt and Sigurbjörnsson and instead sang his arrangement of "Steal Away." We added a third spiritual that the students learned aurally. They listened and responded to a 1939 recording of "Motherless Child" as performed by Julia Griffin, Johnny Mae Medlock, and Clifford Reed—three Black women and culture bearers of this tradition. In our attempt to learn the music as these three women may have learned it, the students created an improvisation without notation. Through experimentation, evaluation, and refinement, the students created their own version to sing in the concert. Even in concert the students were process oriented. I celebrate their bravery and musical curiosity, and perhaps most of all I celebrate the messiness they intentionally embraced for the sake of experimentation and expression, especially when performing before an audience.

THE WORK AHEAD

> Kintsukuroi (n.) (v. phr.) "to repair with gold"; the art of repairing pottery with gold or silver lacquer and understanding that the piece is more beautiful for having been broken. (Sen 2016, lines 36–37).

In his book "Wabi-Sabi for Artists, Designers, Poets & Philosophers," Leonard Koren explores the Japanese aesthetic of *wabi-sabi* (2008). He describes *wabi-sabi* as the following: "It is a beauty of things imperfect, impermanent, and incomplete. It is a beauty of things modest and humble. It is a beauty of things unconventional" (7). In comparing and contrasting the aesthetics of modernism and *wabi-sabi*, he writes: "[modernism is] absolute ... looks for universal and prototypical solutions ... [is] mass-produced and modular ... believes in the control of nature ... [values] geometric organization of form (sharp, precise, definite shapes and edges ... is intolerant of ambiguity and contradiction ... [and] perfect materiality is an ideal." Conversely, *wabi-sabi* is "relative ... looks for personal, idiosyncratic solutions ... [is] one-of-a-kind and variable ... believes in the fundamental uncontrollability of nature ... [values] organic organization of form (soft, vague shapes and edges ... is comfortable with ambiguity and contradiction ... [and] perfect immateriality is an ideal" (26–29).

I recognize the ideals of modernism in choral music as I understood it and my own motivation to strive for these ideals. The ideals of modernism present "a culture of closed forms ... one of perfection; not uncertainty; submission, not play; elitism, not access; merit, not democracy" (Allsup 2016, 55). I understand the prototypical process of programming music, rehearsing, and then performing. I understand the value of precision and definition: are we all releasing the final consonant at the same moment? I have experienced striving for technical, artistic, and personal perfection—at one time it felt normal to me. But this is not a model I can completely return to, even if I wish to do so. This model and my conception of myself within it are broken. I think about *kintsukuroi* and how I can mend myself with gold lacquer, and as Sen writes earlier in his poem, become "better than the perfection/of its prior shape" (Sen 2016, lines 29–30). I recognize that mending this way means allowing for what has happened and being changed because of it.

The last two years have taught me how to enter and embrace disruption and develop a more process-oriented pedagogy. When I stop to reflect on my work, it's clear that teaching, rehearsing, and performing are always processes, and that the unknown is an always present and necessary component. The unknown is fluid and gives space for organic processes to unfold. The known can too easily become static and fixed. The unknown exists in a space of greater potentiality. Perhaps *wabi-sabi* better reflects the world as it is, whereas modernism may try and control it, even while futile. Given what I have experienced, *wabi-sabi* feels as if it is better grounded in reality, whatever that may be.

My work is at an inflection point, and I know that I am not alone in this feeling. Our global disruptions have brought many issues facing our field (and our world) into clearer focus. I find myself asking what responsibilities we have as individuals and how institutions might respond to this deepened awareness. How can we center DEI as individuals, in our immediate work, and in the systems in which we find ourselves? What is our ethical responsibility to our students' (and our own) mental and physical health? How can curricular and structural reforms within classrooms, institutions, and the field address these needs? What's both difficult and promising is how entangled these issues are with one another. It is the work ahead.

I now have a greater awareness that DEI and health cannot be separated. I can more clearly see that racism, sexism, homophobia, transphobia, classism, and all the other "isms" are diseases of society. I have a better understanding of how I and others may be afflicted. I am interested in continuing to center DEI in my work, and yet I also recognize that this is not enough.

I am asking myself questions: If we have a concert featuring minoritized composers whose music is derivative of the Western classical tradition, are we not still prioritizing and privileging hegemonic practices? If music from non-Western cultures can only exist in ensembles with Western notation, are we not still privileging Western ways of learning and understanding to the exclusion of others? And how are we performing this music? Do we perform exclusively in formal concert halls wearing European evening wear to largely silent audiences?

Additionally, what ensembles do we offer, and from those offerings, which get to count as *major ensembles* and work toward degree requirements? Do these ensembles only reflect those centered in the European tradition? For many of us, that answer is yes. If our students need a greater variety of performative experiences, we cannot expect that to happen exclusively within Western ensembles. It's also unfair to ask these Western ensembles to be what they are not. For as inclusive as we can be, a choir will never be an orchestra, an orchestra will never be a mariachi band, and a mariachi band will never be a Javanese Gamelan ensemble. To expect an orchestra to be a mariachi band is problematic for both orchestras and mariachi bands.

I feel a pressing need for a greater number of ensembles that centers students and their curiosity—ensembles that allow for open approaches. The disruption to choral music has shown me that this is possible. My experiences from teaching remotely have shown me that this is possible. I believe that it is something that we both can and must do. When students' inquiry drives the music-making process, it is inherently more relevant. The ensemble becomes emergent or eclectic. After one year of remote teaching, a colleague (and co-conspirator) and I created such an eclectic ensemble on our campus. This is some of the work I am most excited about as it is structurally brimming with potential. I am very much looking forward to learning from my students and satiating some of my own musical curiosities, just as I was able to do during my year of remote teaching.

In fall 2021, my section of the eclectic ensemble had eight students, split into two groups. Five students explored Nordic and Celtic folk music traditions as they are performed today. They wrote poetry and created an original composition of praise to Odin and Jesus, in which they explored the similarities between these two figures. They changed their approach to singing in these styles, and they embraced more authentic performance practices. They drew on salient features from these traditions, including drones, percussion, improvisation, and ornamentation. The second group of three students created and performed an original composition in verse-chorus form. They wrote poetry, determined harmonic progressions, and played on popular instruments outside of their major concentrations. Because these two groups performed in November as part of the choral concert, the concert itself became eclectic with original compositions, popular music, improvised choral singing, pop-a cappella, and Western Art Music. These eclectic ensembles alleviate the need for choir (or band or orchestra) to be all things all the time.

To engage with any of this work is to embrace the unknown. To engage with this work is to embrace vulnerability and to be comforted by it. To engage with this work is to continuously seek disruption, even if these are disruptions that we must ourselves create. Perhaps this is the most important lesson I have learned from this pandemic: in embracing disruptions, we free ourselves from what was, so that we might explore what can be.

REFERENCES

Allsup, Randall. 2016. *Remixing the Classroom*. Bloominton, IN: Indiana University Press.

Glück, Louise. 2012. "The Wild Iris." In *Poems 1962–2012*, 245. New York: Farrar, Straus and Giroux.

hooks, bell. 1994. *Teaching to Transgress*. Oxfordshire: Routledge.

Jewett, Sarah Orne. 1896. *The Country of Pointed First*. Public Domain.

Koren, Leonard. 2008. *Wabi-Sabi for Artists, Designers, Poets & Philosophers*. Point Reyes, CA: Imperfect Publishing.

May, Katherine. 2020. *Wintering: The Power of Rest and Retreat in Difficult Times*. London: Riverhead Books.

National Museum of African American History and Culture. n.d. "Being Antiracist." Accessed July 1, 2021. https://nmaahc.si.edu/learn/talking-about-race/topics/being-antiracist.

Sen, Sudeep. Accessed January 18, 2022. "Kintsukuroi." *The London Magazine*. https://www.thelondonmagazine.org/article/kintsukuroi/.

Williams, Angel Kyodo, Rod Owens, and Jasmine Syedullah. 2016. *Radical Dharma: Talking Race, Love, and Liberation*. Berkeley, CA: North Atlantic Books.

Epilogue
Transformative Change and Music Teacher Education
Andrea Maas and Judy Lewis

> We may have reached a moment in our history when teaching and learning, if they are to happen meaningfully, must happen on the verge ... confronting the void, confronting nothingness ... (Greene 1988, 23)

Maxine Greene posits in her *Dialectic of Freedom* (1988) that disruption is an opportunity for change in education. She describes a process of confronting obstacles to change and then engaging in principled action informed by one's ideals, suggesting that through such work, teachers may find alternative paths forward, around, and through the very barriers that were holding them back.

In March 2020 a deadly virus swept across the globe and led to unimaginable obstacles in the form of physical isolation, mental health challenges, economic downturn, and social upheaval. Fear and uncertainty made it difficult to navigate the swift and seemingly relentless changes taking place all around us, impacting every facet of our lives. Music teacher-educators found themselves in the center of the greatest seismic shift our field had seen since Julia Crane founded the first music teacher preparation program in 1886.

At the onset of the pandemic, we witnessed debates regarding the extent to which music teacher-educators were willing to engage with whatever the new, pandemic version of music teaching and learning was going to be. Quite literally, some declared, "This is not what we do!". What "this" was, however, was yet to be seen. While some balked, others paused, considered their options, sought support, and became determined to take a risk and try something new. Others still ran full tilt into the fire, enthusiastically implementing new and creative ideas that they had been sitting on, waiting for an opportunity to incorporate into their classrooms. Regardless of how one met the pandemic, it catalyzed, for music faculty in higher education, a movement out of a place of comfort and toward interrogating philosophies and practices that had long gone unchallenged.

This story could have been one of ultimate scapegoating—blaming the pandemic for the dismantling of music education worldwide. But it doesn't seem to have turned out that way. When music teacher-educators were faced with the inability to make music in person, a loss of instructional time, limited financial and instructional resources, and declining enrollment—just to name just a few—many responded with innovative teaching approaches including shifts to humanize their pedagogical aims and make these new learning experiences more relevant for their students. The process of seeking openings for change allowed those educators to see and hear their pedagogy, curriculum, and students differently. Everyday practices appeared worn down, outdated, or dysfunctional. The process of considering *if, why,* and *how* they would continue to teach music under such extraordinary circumstances compelled many to challenge what they thought they knew about music teaching and learning and consider alternative paths toward meaningful learning experiences with their students. The COVID-19 pandemic had successfully propelled many music teacher-educators out of their *stuckness* and into a space of possibilities that required deep and intentional critique.

PEDAGOGIES FOR CHANGE

We recall our friends and colleagues describing the immediate weeks after lockdown as though they were "spinning out"; a "dark void." One likened their experience to a "bouncy fun house"! There seemed to be a common sense that core elements they had previously used to guide their teaching had disappeared, or were at the very least, unstable. The proverbial floor had fallen out beneath them, and they were reaching for solid ground in an attempt to regain their footing. Regardless of the specific ways they experienced this moment, each of them was in pursuit of sound and meaningful ways to interact with their students through curricular materials and activities. They were in essence, seeking out pedagogies for change.

In the chaos of disruption, the contributing authors in this book returned their gaze to their specific teaching contexts and the needs of their students, enacting what Paolo Freire might describe as "situated" pedagogy. (Freire 1970 [2018], 98). They acknowledged how they and their students were impacted by the abrupt move to digital environments, illuminating immense challenges as well as untapped potential for music teaching and learning. In many cases, students became the instructors, demonstrating not only their knowledge of specific tools but also, the multitude of ways they understood (or did not understand) technology for musical learning and creativity.

It became clear however, that the digital spaces they were inhabiting were only an entry point for how they would ultimately conceptualize and attend to these new teaching environments. The computer screen, video conferencing platform, or digital audio workstation served as a window for observing students' much more intimately in their homes, with family and caregivers, and through creative work. This new view shined a stark spotlight not only on the specific and tragic impacts of the ensuing public health crisis but also the systemic inequities and ongoing trauma experienced by vulnerable populations. Societal crises of racial and ethnic violence, poverty, dependent care, and overall economic upheaval continue to scream for attention as music teacher-educators desperately try to find meaning in their work.

Ira Shor, when reflecting on Freire's work fifty years later, writes of education as a, "critical pedagogy to question the status quo in the name of social justice" (Shor 2018, 186). The stories in this book illustrate movements toward humanity and care for one another, prioritizing student identity, calling out and naming injustices, and creating space for previously marginalized or silenced voices. From these stories we see that when students engage in critical pedagogies—analyzing and interrogating musical works as well as their own philosophies for music teaching and learning—they reveal to us opportunities for acting through music education toward social change.

Educational philosophers have long positioned education as a vehicle for individual and societal change (Dewey 1934; Freire 1970 [2018]; Greene 1978, 1998; hooks 1994; Ladson-Billings 1995). These scholars and others specifically look to the arts as a means of pursuing change through artistic expression (Benedict, Patrick, Spruce, and Woodford 2015; Greene 1995; Hess 2019; Talbot 2018). bell hooks urged teachers to recognize their role as those who enact curriculum, calling for "pedagogy in relation to the practice of freedom" (hooks 1994, 6). As noted in the Prologue, she encourages "teaching that enables transgressions—a movement against and beyond boundaries . . ." (12). Her use of the word "transgression" is a reminder that the pursuit of change in education often requires teachers to push back against, or reject normalized practices, expectations, and perhaps even formal policies. The stories in this book exemplify teaching practices as transgressions. What's more, they challenge us to remain unstuck and resist the urge to settle into a new cozy corner, no matter how inviting that might seem.

REACHING TOWARD WIDER SPACES IN MUSIC TEACHER EDUCATION

The COVID-19 pandemic posed a disruption of such magnitude that it propelled many of us, in music teacher education, out of our stuck-ness and into a trajectory of change. Yet, Peter Moss (2014) makes a distinction between momentary change and transformative change: "Transformative change is ... about opening up to a continuous state of movement, not just a short burst of movement whilst traversing from one static point to another" (9). As the dust of this particular moment begins to settle, there are some who may fall back into business as usual. Others, who embraced the moment and looked for innovative responses, may find comfort in defining their new ways of being and settle into a new holding pattern.

Maxine Greene would encourage us to stay *wide-awake*, to keep looking and listening for conditions with which we are dissatisfied, that might otherwise find their way into the fabric of everydayness; to keep peeking around the corner for new opportunities for change. She would remind us, as only she could, that "the very existence of obstacles depends on the desire to reach toward wider spaces for fulfillment, to expand options, to know alternatives" (Greene 1988, 4). When put that way, we begin to see obstacles to change as positive encounters, rather than big scary monsters that live under the bed. We wonder then, what would it mean to continue to "reach toward wider spaces" in music teacher education? To look beyond this moment, to resist complacency and a sense of *done-ness*. How might music teacher-educators remain unstuck?

The authors in this book placed their students at the center of their work, looking and listening carefully for how this period of intense disruption was impacting their lives, their learning, and the meanings they found in their work. Each story in this book reflects a practice of opening spaces for acknowledging and validating student experiences, exploration, imagination, and creativity. Through their stories, the authors demonstrate pushing through immediate obstacles to actively seek out ongoing opportunities for change; to resist stagnation, complacency, stuck-ness.

Scholars write about the notion of *open forms* (Allsup 2016; Greene 1995) and *open pedagogies* (Freire 1970 [2018]; hooks 1994) enacted by teachers and students. But what would it mean for music teacher preparation to be approached as an open form all its own– one that is malleable, shapeshifting, with no predetermined end—allowing space for preservice teachers to interrogate teaching contexts, identify obstacles, and locate new openings for musical meaning? How might we, as music teacher-educators, help our students embrace the discomfort of *not knowing,* and in so doing make intentional turns toward possibilities? It is difficult to imagine any progress that is not born out of a moment of not knowing; a moment that begs a question, an answer to pursue.

As we read in the stories in this book, teacher-educators have an opportunity to be sources of positive disruption for our students: nudging them into discomfort and challenging them to think otherwise; helping them imagine possibilities to avoid the complacent acceptance of the status quo, or be paralyzed by the challenges they will inevitably face; engaging their imaginations "not to resolve [but] to awaken, to disclose the ordinarily unseen, unheard, and unexperienced" (Greene 1995, 28). The authors in this book were not just interested in getting to the other side of the pandemic. Rather, finding themselves *on the verge*, they pursued alternative courses of action, presenting new ways of being and thinking that will ripple outward through their students. With each undulation, we imagine the spaces becoming wider, making room for the possibilities that will emerge as we all seek out new paths and write new stories for music education.

REFERENCES

Allsup, Randall. 2016. *Remixing the Classroom: Toward an Open Philosophy of Music Education*. Bloomington, IN: Indiana University Press.
Benedict, Cathy, Patrick Schmidt, Gary Spruce, and Paul Woodford. 2015. *The Oxford Handbook of Social Justice in Music Education*. New York: Oxford University Press.
Dewey, John. 1934. *Art as Experience*. New York: Pedigree Books.
Friere, Paolo. 1970 [2018]. *Pedagogy of the Oppressed: 50th Anniversary Edition*. Translated by Myra Ramos. Foreword by Donald Macedo (2018) and Afterword by Ira Shor. (2018). New York: Bloomsbury.
Greene, Maxine. 1978. *Landscapes of Learning*. New York: Teachers College Press.
Greene, Maxine. 1988. *The Dialectic of Freedom*. New York: Teachers College Press.
Greene, Maxine. 1995. *Releasing the Imagination: Essays on Education, the Arts, and Social Change*. San Francisco, CA: Jossey-Bass.
Hess, Juliet. 2019. *Music Education for Social Change: Constructing an Activist Music Education*. New York: Routledge.
hooks, bell. 1994. *Teaching to Transgress: Education as the Practice of Freedom*. New York: Routledge.
Ladson-Billings, Gloria. 1995. "Toward a Theory of Culturally Relevant Pedagogy." *American Educational Research Journal* 32, (September): 465–491. https://doi.org/10.3102/00028312032003465.
Moss, Peter. 2014. *Transformative Change and Real Utopias in Early Childhood Education: A Story of Democracy, Experimentation and Potentiality*. New York: Routledge.
Shor, Ira. 2018. *"A Luta Continua": Afterword to Pedagogy of the Oppressed*. In *Pedagogy of the Oppressed: 50th Anniversary Edition*. By Paolo Freire, translated by Myra Bergman Ramos, 1970 [2018]. 185–188. New York: Bloomsbury.
Talbot, Brent, C. 2018. *Marginalized Voices in Music Education*. New York: Routledge.

Appendix

Office of the Governor
225 W State Street
Trenton, NJ 08625

New Jersey Department of Education
PO Box 500
Trenton, NJ 08625

October 8, 2020

Dear Governor Murphy, Interim Commissioner of Education, Kevin Dehmer, and Content Coordinator of Visual and Performing arts for the New Jersey Department of Education, Dale Schmid,

On behalf of the faculty of music education degree programs in the State of New Jersey, we are writing to respectfully request a state sanctioned waiver of the edTPA requirement for music teacher certification for the 2020 - 2021 academic year.

The implementation of edTPA as a requirement for certification has been challenging for teacher candidates even prior to the global pandemic. Upon its implementation, many school districts refused to accept student teachers due to privacy concerns over the live video requirement of the assessment. The educational upheaval caused by COVID-19 has dramatically exacerbated this problem, particularly for music teacher candidates.

Given safety concerns regarding the spread of COVID-19 via aerosol droplets emitted when playing and singing, many school districts have restricted music teaching to asynchronous modes of instruction. Within this teaching modality, <u>students are unable to record the video material required for successful edTPA completion</u>. edTPA has provided inadequate guidance for this type of learning environment. For example, in the supplemental materials disseminated to teacher candidates for "Completing edTPA in a Virtual learning environment," edTPA states the following regarding asynchronous instruction: *"Asynchronous instruction learning environments do not allow the teacher candidate to capture evidence that meets the handbook or submission requirements for Task 2 Instruction."* Additionally, if the teacher candidate has no other option but asynchronous instruction, edTPA suggests the following: *"If the candidate is unable to capture synchronous instruction for Task 2, they should contact their educator preparation program or building level administrator for guidance on meeting state licensure requirements."* As faculty of the education preparation programs, we have received no information on how to provide guidance to our teacher candidates to meet state licensure requirements, nor have our building level administrator colleagues.

In addition, the financial cost of completing the edTPA is a significant challenge for many teacher candidates during a normal school year, but given the severe economic constraints placed upon many families due to the pandemic, several of our students have been forced to find additional part-time employment to support themselves, their families, and to pay college tuition. As teacher educators, we feel that it is unethical to require teacher candidates to complete the edTPA under these conditions.

Entering the classroom for the first time was challenging for pre-service teachers prior to COVID-19, but this cohort of teacher candidates have been additionally tasked with assisting their in-service colleagues in creating safe and productive learning environments under extremely difficult circumstances. Even veteran teachers are struggling to keep pace with the extraordinary demands placed upon them. This unprecedented level of confusion and turbulence during such a formative period of a novice teacher's career is overwhelming to begin with, but the added burden of completing edTPA under these circumstances is simply too overwhelming; especially given the lack of flexibility and guidance provided by edTPA.

While this is a challenging time for all educators, music education has been disproportionately, negatively impacted, with asynchronous instruction as the only option for many music teachers. Unless the edTPA requirement is waived, music education students who are paying full tuition for a student teaching experience where live instruction is <u>not possible</u> will be ineligible for music teacher certification in our state, through no fault of their own.

We respectfully implore you to issue a state sanctioned waiver of the edTPA requirement immediately so that we may focus our efforts on the needs of teacher candidates during these challenging times. This, in turn, will allow the teacher candidates to focus on the educational and developmental needs of the New Jersey K-12 students in their care. Thank you for your consideration and please do not hesitate to contact us if you require additional information.

Sincerely,

Dr. Nicholas McBride
Assistant Professor of Music Education
The College of New Jersey

Name hidden for privacy

Name hidden for privacy

Name hidden for privacy

Name hidden for privacy

Name hidden for privacy

Appendix

Name hidden for privacy

Name hidden for privacy

Name hidden for privacy

Name hidden for privacy

Name hidden for privacy

300 POMPTON ROAD • WAYNE, NEW JERSEY 07470-2103
WWW.WPUNJ.EDU

Name hidden for privacy

Index

Page references for figures are italicized.

Acellus online program, 97
"affinity space", 90
AIDS, ix
Alecrim Dourado Formação Musical, 145–48, *147*, 157
Allsup, Randall Everett, ix–x, xv, 139, 170, 184, 188–89, 191–92, 199, 201, 213, 215
"alone together", 82–84
American Choral Directors Association, 206
Arbery, Ahmaud, 82
assessment, 78, 91, 117, 119–22, 140, 197–98
Au, Wayne, 130

Bandura, Albert, 148
Bannerman, Julie K., 77
Barcellos, Luiz, 67–84
Bauer, William I., 6, 7, 11–12, 183
Baxter, Marsha, 87–93
Biggers, Carter, 118
Black Lives Matter, x, 82, 92, 207–10
Blackshaw, Jodie, 117–18
Bowe, Marie-Louise, 87–93
Bowman, Wayne, 19
Bradley, Deborah, 24–25

Brazilian music education, 143–59
Brittin, Ruth, 119
Broock-Schultz, Angelita Vander, 143–59, *150*
Brookfield, Stephen, 24, 26–28, 31
Brooks, Rayshard, 82
Bruff, Derek, 21, 32
Bruner, Jerome, xii

Camus, Albert, ix–x
CARE (community awareness, reflection, and empathic action) framework, 129–40
Chadwick, Sheelagh, 19–33
Chambers, Carol Brittin, 119
charter schools, 97–98, 100–106
chat (*Zoom*), 19–33, 70–71, 90; content-forward, 24–26; etymology of, 21; social-forward, 23–24
"checking-in", 73
choral curriculum, 100–106, 169–85, 208–17
Chrome Music Lab, 182
class portrait, 112–13
Clemmons, François, 214
cognitive presence, 22
Coleridge-Taylor, Samuel, 175, 178

Index

collaboration, 12, 29, 68, 77–83, 91, 165, 172, 177, 184, 190–98, 201–2; collaborative learning, 13, 72, 77, 80, 90, 151, 171–82, 187–97, 202; through group work, 7–8, 103–4. *See also kūpuna*, 175–80, 193–94; using social annotation, 32, 195–97
community building, 10, 16, 20, 22–23, 30–33, 58, 90, 97–98, 105, 109, 127–29, 133–37, 181, 187, 190, 195, 197–201, 206
composition lessons, 46–47, 64
computer music courses, 54, 64–65
"connected teaching", 172
"conscientization", 27
Crane, Julia, 219
Creative Music Strategies (CMS), 177–81
culturally responsive practices, 110–12, 115–24

Davis, Miles, 93
decolonial approach, 98–100
democracy, x, 31, 189, 205, 208, 211–12, 215
democratic practices, 24, 28, 31, 91, 134, 187–202, 208–11
Dewey, John, 134, 183, 200, 221
digital audio workstations (DAWs), 55–65, *56–59*, *61*, 209
"digital musicianship", 64, 91
diversity, 196, 209, 216–17. *See also* inclusiveness
Dorfman, Jay, 183
"Driving Questions", 10, 69, 192–93
drum machines, 56–57

Eclectic Ensemble, 183–85, 217–18
Ekmekci, Ozgur, 10–11
electronic music courses, 54, 64–65
emancipatory pedagogy, xv, 27, 184, 188, 200
empathy in music education, 127–40
Enwezor, Owui, 30
extended inquiry projects, 191–93

Faust, Drew Gilpin, 137–38

FCHC (Fostering Community & Human Connection in the Music Classroom), 133–37, 140
Fielding, Michael, 132–33
Fleming, Renée, 110
Flipgrid software, 10, 72, 77, 182
Floyd, George, x, 82, 92, 207
Fontana, Lucio, *xiv*, xv
Frankel, James, 183
Freer, Patrick K., 67–84
Freire, Paolo, xv, 27, 184, 188, 220–21

Garrison, D., 21
Garrison, Jim, 200
Gee, J. P., 90
Gilbert, Sophie, 137
Giroux, Henry A., 131
Gonzaga, Luiz, 149
Gorman, Amanda, 197
Gottschall, Jonathan, xii
Greene, Maxine, x–xi, 133–35, 172, 187, 199, 219, 221–23
Griffin, Julia, 214–15

Halprin, Daria, 90
Hansen, Bryce, 124
harmonic dictation, 60–62, *61*
Hendricks, Karin, 134, 136
Hendry, Petra Munro, xiv
hip-hop music, 195–96
historically underrepresented composers, 114–26, *123*
historic preservation, 102, 169–70, 185
homework, open-sourced, 197–99, 202
Hookpad, 47
hooks, bell (Gloria Watkins), xi, 92, 173, 188, 208, 221
Huebner, Dwayne, xv
hybrid learning, 53
hypothesis, 195

inclusiveness, 30–31, 162–65, 173, 190; diversity and, 196, 209, 216–17; multiculturalism and, 25

innovative approaches, xi–xii, 15, 91, 183, 220; to assessment, 71; improvisation, 43, 47, 164; to performance pedagogies, 68; problem-solving, 177; through technologies, 169
instrumental music teaching, 37–50
interdisciplinary lessons, 194

Jenkins, Henry, 189–90
Jenkins, Lynnel Joy, 134–36
Jersild, Arthur, 93
Jewett, Sarah Orne, 213
Jones, Rodney, 4

Kahaunaele, Kainani, 101–2
kāko'o (content area specialists), 104–6
kanikapila (storytelling through song), 100–6
Kaomea, Julie, 101
kauhale (village community), 105–6
King, Maxwell, 134, 136–39
King, Thomas, xiii
kintsukuroi (repair with gold), 215–16
Klykken, Nils, 205–17
Kong Drum Designer, 58
Koren, Leonard, 215
Kramer, Larry, ix
Kress, Gunther, 189–90
kūpuna wisdom (of elders), 103–6

Ladson-Billings, Gloria, 111, 114, 119, 221
Lake, William L., Jr., 161–66
Laptop Orchestra, 54, 64, 65
learning management system (LMS), 8–11, 15, 16
Lee, Albert R., 161–66
Levy, Dan, 7
Lewis, Judy, xi–xv, 179, 187–202, 219–23
Lewis, Patrick, xii
Lil'uokalani, Hawaiian queen, 106

Maas, Andrea, xi–xv, 169–85, 219–23
Macmurray, John, 129, 131–32, 136

Madalozzo, Tiago, 143–59, *147*
Madalozzo, Vivian Agnolo, 143–59
Martignetti, Frank, 89
May, Katherine, 205
McBride, Nicholas Ryan, 127–40
McCandless, Greg, 64
media literacy, 189
Medlock, Johnny Mae, 214–15
mele (song), 101–4, 106
melodic dictation, *58*, 58–59, *59*
Mercier–De Shon, Michelle, 67–84
meter detection exercises, 58
MIDI editor, 54–60, *56–59*
Millican, J. Si, 43
Miro, 177–79, 191–92
mo'olelo (storytelling), 100–6
Morley, Thomas, 213
Morrison, Toni, 92
Moss, Peter, xiii, 222
multiculturalism, 25. *See also* inclusiveness
MuseScore, 182
Musical Drive Thru, 145–46, *147*
musicalização, 143–47, 151–59
musictheory.net, 55
music theory textbooks, 64–65
Music with Family program, 146

National Core Arts Standards, 40, 171
National Museum of African American History and Culture, 207
neoliberalism, 130–31
New London Group, 190
Nishimura, Cait, 138–39
Nuño, Derrick, 123
Nussbaum, Martha C., 109, 140

O'Leary, Emmett James, 3–16
'ōlelo no'eau (proverbs), 99–103
Oliveros, Pauline, 181
Olujimi, Kambui, 92
O'Neill, Susan, 90
"openings", *also* "open spaces", xiv–xv, 173, 183–84, 187–89, 195, 199, 201–2, 220–22
open-sourced homework, 197–99, 202

participatory culture, 189–90
"pedagogical pivoting", 67–84
pedagogy, 5–6, 187, 199; for change, 220–21; democratic, 187–202; emancipatory, xv, 27, 184, 188, 200; integrity of, 79–82; open, 222
personal learning network (PLN), 7, 15, 16
Perusall, 31
The Playlist Project, 113–15, *114*, 122
popular music, 45, 188, 209–13
Princeton Girlchoir, 134
protest songs, 72
Pukui, Mary Kawena, 102–3
punk music, 210–11

quantization, 60

race, 138, 162–64; Black Lives Matter and, x, 82, 92, 207–10
Rancière, Jacques, xv, 200
reading, as social activity, 195–97, 202
Reaper, 176
Reason music editing software, 54–65, *56–59*, *61*
Reed, Clifford, 214–15
rehearsal configurations, 172
reorientations, 172–73
rhythmic dictation, 54–58, *56*, *57*
riffing, 22, 26–27
Rogers, Fred, 133, 134, 136–39

Sagan, Carl, 210
SAMR (substitution, augmentation, modification, and redefinition) model, 11–16
Saplan, Jace Kaholokula, 97–106
Sarmento, Manuel Jacinto, 144, 156–57
Schaller, Jonathan G., 37–50
Schotsko, Cesare, 20
screen-time, 154–55, 193
secondary general music students, 188, 191–93
Sen, Sudeep, 215–16
Shor, Ira, 221
Shulman, Lee, 5–6
Silverman, Marissa, 25

Slack, 32
social annotation, 32, 190, 195–97
social presence, 22
Sommerfeldt, Jerod, 53–65
Sonobus, 176
Sound Learning program, 67–84
SoundTrap, 43, 46, 182, 209
Spotify, 119
Spruce, Gary, 30
"standard" musical works, 113–14, *114*
storytelling: centrality in human experience, xii–xiv; in Hawaiian traditions, 100–6
student-directed projects, 210
student learning styles, 111–12, 115

Taylor, Breonna, 82, 92
Teaching Artist Journal, 75
Texas Music Educators Association, 118
Thies, Tamara T., 109–26
Thomas, Michelle Amosu, 67–84
TPACK (technological, pedagogical, and content knowledge) framework, 5–12, 15, 16
trainedear.net, 58
transformative change, 219–23

vernacular music. *See* popular music
VIGIL (video), 92, 195–96
virtual ensembles, 12–14

wabi-sabi (beauty of imperfect things), 215
Walker, Hezekiah, 165
Wardrobe, Katie, 13
Webster, Peter R, 183
Whitacre, Eric, 12
Wieseltier, Leon, 137–38
Wille, Regiana Blank, 143–59
Williams, Angel Kyodo, 207
Wurdeman-Thurston, Katherine, 101

Yob, Iris M., 136

"Zoom fatigue", 154–55, 193

About the Contributors

Randall Everett Allsup is professor of music and music education at Teachers College-Columbia University in the City of New York. Randall earned degrees in music performance and music education from Northwestern University and Columbia University. He is an awardee of a Fulbright grant that brought him to the Sibelius Academy, Helsinki, Finland, to teach and conduct research. He has taught courses at Xiamen University, China, and Toyo University, Tokyo, Japan. He is the proud recipient of the Outstanding Teaching Award at Teachers College. Randall is book series editor of Counterpoints in Music and Education, at Indiana University Press.

Luiz Barcellos is currently completing a PhD at Georgia State University, focusing on musical creativity, informal learning, and arts-based research. Barcellos is an MYP music teacher at Atlanta International School. Previously, he studied at Universidade Federal do Paraná, where he taught preservice teachers as part of a MA studentship funded by CAPES. He has taught primary music lessons at The British School and Escola Americana in Rio de Janeiro and received the Culture Brazil Connection award by the British Council and the Brazilian Ministry of Culture. Barcellos has traveled the world leading Brazilian music workshops and has facilitated innovative and interactive experiences for students. He has presented his research and shared his teaching practice at *NAfME, MISTEC, GMEA, Oxford Symposium, ANPPOM, ISME Latin American regional conference, and APME*.

Marsha Baxter teaches undergraduate and graduate music, theater, and dance education majors at New York University. She is the 2021 recipient of an ISME-Sempre Music Education Research Grant for *Hototo! (Song of the fearless spirit): A project of freedom and resistance, unity and hope*, a song project with teachers and students in the New York City DOE music programs and the LEAP Boundary Breakers in Chennai, India. She is also the recipient of the *SUNY President's Award for Excellence in Research and/or Teaching Relating to Cultural Diversity* and the *SUNY Chancellor's Award* for her design and implementation of the Spanish Immersion—Music Teaching Practicum in Puebla, Mexico. Her recent documentary, *For the Love of the Mambo*, chronicles the passage of the Afro-Cuban tradition as expressed by Tito Puente and his band members to future young musicians.

Marie-Louise Bowe is assistant professor of music education in the School of Arts Education and Movement, Institute of Education (Dublin City University) where she teaches undergraduate and graduate music education modules within the primary and secondary education degree programs. Having previously worked as a post-primary music and Irish teacher at Belvedere College, Dublin, she is a passionate advocate of the transformative effects of public schooling and arts education. As a Fulbright scholar (2010–2014), she earned her doctoral degree from Teachers College, Columbia University, NYC with her dissertation titled *Post-Primary Music Education in Ireland: Principals' Perspectives* investigating the extent to which music was implemented in second-level (secondary) schools across Ireland. She is a committee member of the Society for Music Education in Ireland and was a commissioner for the International Society for Music Education (Music in Schools and Teacher Education, MISTEC). Marie-Louise combines a life of teaching and research while also maintaining a busy schedule as a viola player and fiddle player.

Angelita Vander Broock is assistant professor of music at the Federal University of Minas Gerais (UFMG), director of the Centro de Musicalização Integrado (CMI) at UFMG and creator of the Bambulha Group: Music for Childhood. She holds a doctorate (2013) and a master's degree (2009) in music education from the Federal University of Bahia (UFBA). She is a researcher at the Research Group Music, Cognition and Human Development Research Group at UFMG. Angelita is a member of the Brazilian Music Education Association (ABEM), where she serves as Editor of the Revista Música na Educação Básica (Journal of Music on Basic Education)—MEB.

Sheelagh Chadwick is an associate professor of music education at Brandon University in Manitoba, Canada. She teaches courses in community music, high school general music, and foundations. She has taught music and music education on three continents and presented at conferences in Africa, China,

South America, and North America. Most recently she has been researching Manitoba music teachers' experiences of teaching during the pandemic.

Patrick K. Freer is professor of music at Georgia State University where he currently conducts the tenor-bass choir and directs the doctoral programs in music education. He is former visiting professor at the Universität Mozarteum Salzburg (Austria). His degrees are from Westminster Choir College and Teachers College-Columbia University. Dr. Freer has conducted or presented in forty states and twenty-nine countries, including recent guest conducting for multiple All-State and Division/Region ACDA Honor Choirs, and more than seventy-five professional and/or honor choirs in the USA and abroad. Dr. Freer is Editor of the *International Journal of Research in Choral Singing*, past editor of *Music Educators Journal* and member of the ACDA National Standing Committee for Research & Publications. He chaired the philosophy sub-group within the task force responding to COVID-19 concerns for the National Collegiate Choral Organization.

Nils Klykken is an assistant professor of choral music at SUNY-Potsdam. He holds degrees from the University of Michigan (BM in Music Education) and the Eastman School of Music (MM and DMA in Conducting). Dr. Klykken's conducting and creative work is centered around evolving choral music practices for the twenty-first century: He is interested in how historical performance practices in Western Art Music can serve as referents for twenty-first-century improvisation, the exploration of notationless music traditions in choral settings, and the intersections between music performance, music education, democratic processes, and social justice. Dr. Klykken has served as a guest conductor for Regional All-State Choirs in the State of New York and has presented at regional and national conferences, including conferences for the American Choral Directors Association, The Society for Music Teacher Education, and the New York State School Music Association.

William L. Lake Jr. is assistant professor of music and director of concert bands at George Mason University in Fairfax, Virginia. He is the founder of *I See You*, an organization aimed to affirm the representation of Black, Indigenous, People of Color in music. His current professional activity includes presentations on race and music education across the nation, championing the art of minoritized demographics in wind repertoire, and preparing music education students for field experiences. During the summer of 2020, Dr. Lake led a social media activism campaign titled *"When They See Us: Giving Voice to the Pain"* to over 10,000 viewers. He is the recipient of a doctor of music arts in instrumental conducting degree from The University of

North Carolina at Greensboro, a master of music in wind conducting degree from the University of Maryland—College Park, a master of music education degree from Boston University, and a bachelor of arts degree in jazz piano from the University of Maryland—College Park.

Albert R. Lee is the Yale School of Music's inaugural director of equity, belonging, and student life. His doctoral treatise at Florida State University explored "The Poetic Voice of Langston Hughes in American Art Song." In 2017, Dr. Lee gave a TEDx presentation accessed over 6,000 times called, "When I Sing the Anthem." With degrees from the University of Connecticut, The Juilliard School, and Florida State University, he has made a career as a classical vocalist in opera, oratorio, recital, and liturgical music. As a professional opera tenor, Dr. Lee blends his impeccable voice with relentless passion as a powerful beacon of change.

Judy Lewis is assistant professor of music education at the Crane School of Music, SUNY-Potsdam. She holds an EdD in Music & Music Education from Teachers College, Columbia University, and has been a postdoctoral research affiliate of the *Institute for Urban and Minority Education* (IUME) at Columbia University. Her research explores the intersection of urban minority music education, popular music, and social justice. She has presented widely at international conferences including giving the Keynote Address at the *Music Education and Social Justice* conference at Bowling Green State University, Ohio (2019) and the *Conference of the National Network for Music in Teacher Education*, Bode, Norway (2018). Her scholarly writings have appeared in *Music Educators' Journal, Music Education Research, International Journal of Community Music, Philosophy of Music Education Review, School Music News, Psychomusicology: Music, Mind, and Brain* and in the edited volume *Narratives and Reflections in Music Education: Listening to Voices Seldom Heard* (2019).

Andrea Maas is coordinator of music education and director of choirs at the University of Vermont. During the authorship of this book, she was assistant professor of music education at the Crane School of Music, SUNY Potsdam. She holds an EdD in music and music education from Teachers College, Columbia University. Her work is informed by broad experiences in PK–12 music education in general music, vocal and instrumental ensembles, musical theater, and music education technology. These experiences coupled with research interests in musical expression drive her to challenge students toward more meaningful musical encounters, prioritizing culturally sustaining teaching approaches and flexible musicianship. Additional research interests include the intersections of curriculum, policy, and accreditation as they pertain to breaking down barriers to music education. Maas' work has been presented at the International Symposium for Music Education, International Conference on Music and Emotion, National Symposium for Research in Music Education, Society for Music Teacher Education, and the National ACDA Research Symposium in Choral Singing.

Tiago Madalozzo is assistant professor of music education at the State University of Paraná (Unespar), where he teaches undergraduate courses in Music Education, Early Childhood and Teaching Preparation. He has taught and coordinated music courses for children 0–8 years at Alecrim Dourado, a music school in Curitiba. He holds a PhD in Music from the Federal University of Paraná (UFPR), where he currently develops a postdoctoral study on Education. He is a member of the Research Group Art, Education and Teacher Training—GAEFO (Unespar) and of the Research Group Childhood and Early Childhood Education—NEPIE (UFPR). Tiago is an active member of the Brazilian Music Education Association (ABEM), where he serves as a member of the Editorial Board of the Association's journals.

Vivian Agnolo Madalozzo is the founder and coordinator of music courses for children 0–6 years at the Alecrim Dourado music school. She is assistant professor of music education in the Department of Music at the Pontifical Catholic University of Paraná (PUCPR), where she teaches undergraduate courses in music education and early childhood. She is also a doctoral researcher in childhood studies at the University of Minho, Portugal. Vivian is a researcher at the Research Group Policies, Teacher Formation, Teaching and Social Representations (POFORS/PUCPR) that integrates the UNESCO Chair in Teaching Professionalization.

Nicholas Ryan McBride is associate professor and coordinator of music education at The College of New Jersey where he teaches various undergraduate courses in music education. In addition, he has advised master's theses and taught graduate history and philosophy of music education at Westminster Choir College, The University of Delaware, and Rutgers University. Dr. McBride's research interests include LGBTQ+ and gender issues in music education, music teacher education, and empathic learning processes in music education. His research appears in *The Bulletin of the Council for Research in Music Education, Music Education Research, Visions of Research in Music Education,* and the *Music Educators Journal,* and he serves on the editorial board of the *Journal of General Music Education.* He earned doctoral and master's degrees in music education from Teachers College-Columbia University, his dual master's in choral conducting and music education from Northwestern University, and a bachelor of music education from Westminster Choir College.

Michelle Mercier-De Shon is currently a full-time instructor in music education at Georgia State University. Her teaching experience is in elementary general/choral music, with certification in the Orff approach. She has taught a variety of undergraduate and graduate courses in music teacher education, including K–12 general music methods, introduction to music education, music curriculum and assessment, foundations of music education, and philosophy of music education. She has extensive experience with coordinating university-community music partnerships. Since 2001, she has been involved with *Sound Learning,* a collaborative community music and arts program in Atlanta-area public schools, both as a music specialist, a coordinator, and a supervisor. Her research interests focus on music teaching and learning, with emphasis on children's development of musical identity, informal music learning, and community arts partnerships. In addition to studying classical piano, she also enjoys playing drums and keyboards in rock bands.

Emmett James O'Leary is an assistant professor of music education in the School of Performing Arts at Virginia Tech. He previously served as associate professor of music education at the Crane School of Music, SUNY-Potsdam. Dr. O'Leary has led courses in instrumental music education, secondary general music, and music technology. Prior to his work in teacher education, he served as an assistant band director at the University of Notre Dame and held public-school music teaching positions in the Lake Havasu City (AZ) and Meridian (ID) school districts. His research interests include competition in music education, instrumental music pedagogy, popular music pedagogy, phenomenology, technology in music instruction, and creativity. His research has appeared in the *Bulletin of the Council for Research in Music Education, Journal of Music Teacher Education, Journal of Band Research,* and the *Journal of Popular Music Education.* He has presented at national music education conferences including the American Educational Research Association National Meeting, New Directions in Music
Education Conference, Desert Skies Symposium, and the Society for Music Teacher Education Symposium

Jace Kaholokula Saplan serves as the director of choral activities and associate professor of Choral Conducting & Music, Teaching, and Learning at Arizona State University where they teach courses in graduate choral conducting and choral literature, conducts the ASU Concert Choir, and oversees the graduate choral conducting program. Known for their work in celebrating Pasifika choral traditions, they are the artistic director of Nā Wai Chamber

Choir and Nā Mamo Vocal Ensemble, Hawai'i-based vocal ensembles dedicated to the preservation and propagation of Native choral performance. Their research focuses on decolonial approaches to the choral arts, queering choral conducting pedagogy, and trauma-informed rehearsal practices.

Jonathan G. Schaller is a visiting assistant professor at the Crane School of Music, State University of New York Potsdam where he teaches courses in wind band practices and general music. He earned his PhD in music education at the University of Illinois at Urbana-Champaign. He was a music educator for eight years in the Marion Center Area School District in western Pennsylvania where he taught middle and high school instrumental music and elementary chorus. His research interests and scholarship include place-based pedagogies, instrumental music education, popular/vernacular music, and LGBTQ intersections in music education.

Jerod Sommerfeldt is an associate professor at the Crane School of Music at the State University of New York at Potsdam. He teaches coursework in electronic music, composition, music theory, aural skills and directs the SUNY-Potsdam Electronic Music Studios (PoEMS) and the Crane Laptop Orchestra. In his work in and out of the classroom, he explores modular synthesizers, digital audio workstations, computer music programming, and collective improvisation. Dr. Sommerfeldt is a graduate of the University of Wisconsin—La Crosse, the Peck School of the Arts at the University of Wisconsin—Milwaukee, and the College-Conservatory of Music at the University of Cincinnati.

Tamara T. Thies is director of music education for the Bob Cole Conservatory of Music and coordinator of music education for the Single Subject Credential Program in the College of Education at California State University, Long Beach. Currently, she teaches undergraduate and graduate music education courses as well as guides post-baccalaureate students through the credential program. Her creative and research interests focus toward music education at the intersection of innovation, technology, and cultural relevance which open numerous possibilities for her to present professional workshops, sessions, and research through state, national, and international platforms. She earned a PhD in music education from The University of Iowa, bachelor of music education and master of arts degrees from the University of Northern Iowa, and a conducting diploma with honors from the Liszt Academy in Budapest, Hungary.

Michelle Amosu Thomas is the general music teacher at Robert J. Burch Elementary in Tyrone, Georgia and is currently pursuing her doctoral degree in music education at Georgia State University. Prior to her time in elementary general education, she spent seven years as an assistant band director at McIntosh High School in Georgia and another year at Litchfield Middle School in Alabama. She holds a master's and bachelor's degree in music education from Jacksonville State University. Born and raised in Georgia, Thomas enjoys being able to share her love of music and passion for education with the community that raised her. Although enjoying her time as a band director, she has found her home in elementary education. Her research focuses on preservice music teachers and their transition to independent teaching.

Regiana Blank Wille holds a PhD in education from the Federal University of Rio Grande do Sul (2013) and a master's degree in music education from the Federal University of Pelotas (2003). She is associate professor of music education at the Federal University of Pelotas (UFPEL). Regiana has experience in music with emphasis on music education, working mainly on the following topics: music education, teaching and learning music, teacher training and pedagogical practice, professional identity, music and childhood (babies), inclusive music education, and music on autistic spectrum disorder. She coordinates the Projeto Musicalização Infantil da UFPEL, as well as the Teaching Project GEEMIN (Study Group in Music Education and Inclusion) and is the leader of the Research Group Teacher Education and Music Education (UFPEL).

www.ingramcontent.com/pod-product-compliance
Lightning Source LLC
Chambersburg PA
CBHW020114010526
44115CB00008B/828